WOMEN AND EVIL

WOMEN AND EVIL

Nel Noddings

University of California Press

Berkeley · Los Angeles · London

University of California Press
Berkeley and Los Angeles, California

University of California Press, Ltd.
London, England

© 1989 by
The Regents of the University of California

Library of Congress Cataloging-in-Publication Data

Noddings, Nel.
  Women and evil   /   Nel Noddings.
    p.   cm.
  Bibliography: p.
  Includes index.
  ISBN 0-520-06570-0
  1. Good and evil.   2. Women.   3. Feminism.   I. Title.
BJ1401.N63   1989
170'.88042—dc19   88-8000
                                                          CIP

Printed in the United States of America

1   2   3   4   5   6   7   8   9

To my daughters—
Chris, Laurie, Nancy, Sharon, and Vicky—
whose love and companionship have
meant so much to me,
and to my sons—
Howard, Buzz, Bill, Ed, and Tim—
whose tenderness with children and
animals gives me hope for a better world.

Contents

Acknowledgments

Many people helped with this project. I would like to thank Joann Barbour, Andrea Boyea, Ron Glass, Patti Gumport, David Nyberg, Pam Tyson, and Byron Bland, who made useful suggestions on early drafts of the first chapters. Thanks go also to David Tyack and Elizabeth Hansot, whose ideas and comments were helpful.

I give special thanks to Hazel Barnes, who read every page of the penultimate draft and made suggestions that I have included in the final manuscript. Similarly, I thank Rosemary Radford Ruether and Daniel Maguire for their generous reviews and helpful suggestions. Their recommendations for further reading reduced my ignorance considerably.

People at the University of California Press have been wonderful to work with. Jack Miles (now with the *Los Angeles Times*) and Naomi Schneider encouraged the work from the outset. Sheila Levine guided the manuscript through the review process expeditiously and with no pain to the author. Amy Klatzkin did a thorough job in copyediting, and I appreciate her skill and patience.

My husband, Jim, too, deserves thanks. He has lived with *Women and Evil* for so long that he might be forgiven for suspecting that there really is an odd link between the two after all.

Several people provided regular encouragement even though they were unable to read drafts of the manuscript—among them Thomas F. Green, Madeleine Grumet, Sara Ruddick, Jean Watson, and Denis Phillips. I appreciate their support. My secretary, Jane Wassam, deserves very special thanks. Neither of us will forget the multiple revisions of chapter 1. Throughout the project she bore with my errors and changes of mind and not only did superb work herself but steadily encouraged me in mine.

Finally, I want to thank the many people whose work I have not been able to cite. Any study that uses huge topics as illustrative content—poverty, pain, and war, for example—inevitably omits work that is relevant and sometimes inadvertently leaves out work that has actually influenced the author. For such omissions, I apologize.

Introduction

Human beings love to fictionalize evil—to terrorize each other with stories of defilement, horror, excruciating pain, and divine retribution. Beneath the surface of bewitchment and half-sick amusement, however, lies the realization that evil is real and that people must find a way to face and overcome it. What we require, Carl Jung suggested, is a morality of evil—a carefully thought out plan by which to manage the evil in ourselves, in others, and in whatever deities we posit.[1] This book is not written from a Jungian perspective, but it is nonetheless an attempt to describe a morality of evil.

One suspects that descriptions of evil and the so-called problem of evil have been thoroughly suffused with male interests and conditioned by masculine experience. This result could hardly have been avoided in a sexist culture, and recognizing the truth of such a claim does not commit us to condemn every male philosopher and theologian who has written on the problem. It suggests, rather, that we may get a clearer view of evil if we take a different standpoint. The standpoint I take here will be that of women; that is, I will attempt to describe evil from the perspective of women's experience.

Two serious questions arise immediately. First, if our initial complaint is that moral philosophy has been written unconsciously from a male standpoint, should we now consciously write from a female standpoint? Isn't this a perverse repetition of error? Second, can there be such a thing as "women's experience"? Doesn't such an attempt risk reducing all women to some stereotypical Woman?

An answer to the first question is that a standpoint morality is not in and of itself an error. Indeed, we might defend the thesis that all actual epistemologies and moralities are created from and represent standpoints. Such an admission does not commit us to relativism, for one standpoint may be better than another,[2] and the recognition of standpoints allows us to consider moving about to get clearer views on all aspects of a problem. The notion that one standpoint may be better than another, however, implies some standard by which to judge. This is a thorny problem for standpoint epistemologies, particularly when they directly address science and science making, but it is less troublesome in moral theory. The test should be whether the theory uncovers something that will help human beings live less painfully and fearfully, whether it finds ways of life that will give us some relief from that which harms or threatens to harm us—from evil.

The second question cautions us to avoid the traditional error of supposing that all women are sufficiently alike that there can be a universally valid women's standpoint. It is probably true that women's experience reveals more commonalities than men's, because women have for centuries been confined to domestic life. Even so, the idea that only one moral perspective can grow out of this experience is clearly questionable. When I assume a woman's standpoint, I will take the perspective of one who has had responsibility for caring, maintaining, and nurturing, and I will try to work out the logic of a morality from such a perspective. It is clear, however, that my perspective is constrained not only because I identify with all women for whom domestic life has been at least a societal expectation, but also because I am white, an academic, not impoverished, happily married, and so on. If what I argue here can be as well or better argued from another standpoint, each such argument will move us toward a more genuinely constructed universal.

The book begins with a description of traditional views of evil. These, I will argue, are not only male but *masculine* in the sense that they maintain and even glorify traits and opinions that have been genderized in favor of males. It is impossible in a work aimed at developing a female morality of evil to describe fully every view of evil that has influenced our culture. I have chosen those that seem most prominent and familiar. A trained theologian would almost certainly go at the task somewhat differently and with considerably more sophistication, but it is not my purpose to repair faulty theology. Rather, I want to lay out the view that has contributed to continuing strife among human beings and, especially, to the devaluation and distrust of women.

To develop a woman's perspective, it is necessary to locate women's place in the old view. Therefore chapter 2 undertakes an account of women as evil. Surely creatures who have themselves been branded as evil or peculiarly susceptible to evil must develop a special perspective on evil, especially when they are also, and paradoxically, exalted as possessing a special and natural form of goodness. The paradox is resolved when we realize that the dichotomous view of woman as evil (because of her attraction to matters of the flesh) and good (because of her compassion and nurturing) served as a means of control. Women were taught to think of themselves as good when they lived lives of obedience and service. In chapter 3 I complete the setting for a woman's view by describing this "good" side of women—Coventry Patmore's *Angel in the House* and Hegel's Beautiful Soul.[3] Here we see another set of expectations that many women have internalized and that has affected all of us.

In chapter 4 I reverse the view. Instead of looking at evil through the lens of traditional pronouncements on the problem of evil, we take up the standpoint of women to look directly at evil itself and through what we see there at the old views. In this examination I use a modified phenomenological method. Through the use of examples I attempt to draw out the logic of situations in which we face evil and to probe for the underlying commonalities in our experience with evil. What we will find is a pervasive fear of pain, separation, and helplessness.

Having established a feeling for evil uncolored by theological or philosophical propositions (as nearly as one can consciously accomplish that task), I then examine significant forms of natural, cultural, and moral evil from this alternative perspective. It is impossible, of course, to investigate every candidate for evil in these huge categories, but in each category I choose an important example and attempt to apply the framework constructed from a woman's standpoint. The ultimate test of what we accomplish is whether we can avoid some forms of evil and whether the ways of relating described may lead us to live more serenely and supportively with the elements of evil that we cannot escape entirely.

In the examination of pain, poverty, war, and torture, I place great emphasis on the power and generality of the methods and concepts developed in chapter 4. I certainly do not claim to solve these enormous problems in the chapters devoted to them, but I do hope to argue persuasively for a clear approach to their solution. I also explore briefly the task of educating for a morality of evil. Finally, I consider the possibility of spirituality and what it might mean for men's and women's lives and for the development of a morality of evil.

I

Evil and Ethical Terror

People have always been fascinated by evil—by that which harms us or threatens to harm us. Primitive people sought to escape evil by magic, ritual, and appeasement. Philosophers have attempted to redeem evil by elaborate analyses designed to show that evil is somehow necessary, and theologians have produced a body of work on the "problem of evil." Women have until recently been relatively silent on evil, in part because they have been silent on most matters, but largely because they have themselves been closely identified with evil in the traditional view. Women who have attempted to speak on moral matters have often been effectively silenced by the accusation that speaking and thinking on such things automatically separates them from the feminine principle and thus from their only claim to goodness.

Today, of course, women have awakened to the injustice of this treatment, and feminist theologians are urging us to look with a new focus on what Mary Daly calls the "images and conceptualizations" of evil. Rosemary Radford Ruether says: "Feminism represents a fundamental shift in the valuations of good and evil. It makes a fundamental judgment upon some aspects of past descriptions of the nature and etiology of evil as themselves ratifications of evil." [1]

Further, the new look at evil will be phenomenological; it must look at evil from the viewpoint of experience. Ruether comments, however, "The uniqueness of feminist theology lies not in its use of the criterion of experience but rather in its use of *women's* experience, which has been almost entirely shut out of theological reflection in the past." [2] This is the task I will undertake in this book, but before starting it, I must clarify the view that feminists are rejecting.

There has always been general agreement that evil involves pain, suffering, terror, and destruction. Feminists do not disagree on this appraisal. It has also been customary to separate natural evil from moral evil. Suffering that occurs without the deliberate or negligent agency of human beings is construed as natural evil; violent storms, drought, disease, earthquakes, and natural death are all examples of natural evil and part of the world we inhabit. Difficulties arise with attempts to justify natural evil. If, for example, we can find a justification for God's allowing us to suffer (or even for his inflicting pain on us), moral evil cannot be entirely identified with our infliction of pain on one another, for we too might be justified. If the God so justified is all good and all powerful, then clearly we are at his mercy, and we need to pay more attention to him than to one another. If he demands our obedience and we fail to give it, we have fallen into evil from which we cannot rescue ourselves. Moral evil, in this view, becomes sin.

The problem (or miscasting of it) begins with the attempt to rescue God from collaboration in evil. When men posited a God supposed to be all-powerful, all-knowing, and all-good, the "problem of evil" emerged. How can there be evil in a world created by such a God? "The problem of evil," says John Hick, "concerns the contradiction, or apparent contradiction, between the reality of evil on the one hand, and religious beliefs in the goodness and power of God or of the Ultimate on the other."[3] This concern gives rise to *theodicy,* the philosophical attempt to reconcile the goodness of God with the existence of evil. Theodicy is not the only philosophical approach to evil, of course, but it has been the most influential one, and it is associated with the problem of evil by definition.

We might try to redeem evil by arguing philosophically for its necessity without reference to God. At least one of these views will prove interesting, and it will be necessary to examine it from a feminist perspective. I will look closely at Nietzsche's notion that evil is necessary for good, that pain is necessary for pleasure, and suffering for joy. But the view I ultimately embrace will be closer to Sartre's in spirit. Speaking of evil and the need for people to retain a sense of evil as *evil,* he says:

> We have been taught to take it seriously. It is neither our fault nor our merit if we lived in a time when torture was a daily fact. Châteaubriand, Oradour, the Rue des Saussaies, Tulle, Dachau, and Auschwitz have all demonstrated to us that Evil is not an appearance, that knowing its cause does not dispel it, that it is not opposed to Good as a confused idea is to a clear one, that (it) is not the effects of passions which might be cured, of a fear that might be overcome, of a passing aberration which might be excused, of an ignorance which might be enlightened, that it can in no way be diverted, brought back, reduced, and incorpo-

rated into idealistic humanism, like that shade of which Leibnitz has written that it is necessary for the glare of daylight.[4]

In this passage Sartre mentions all the prominent philosophical ploys to redeem evil; I will not discuss them individually except as they arise in connection with the standard treatment of evil or in the phenomenology of evil that I discuss later. He goes on to give experiential justification for dismissing all these arguments as failures:

> Perhaps a day will come when a happy age, looking back at the past, will see in this suffering and shame one of the paths which led to peace. But we were not on the side of history already made. We were, as I have said, *situated* in such a way that every lived minute seemed to us like something irreducible. Therefore, in spite of ourselves, we came to the conclusion, which will seem shocking to lofty souls: Evil cannot be redeemed.[5]

Sartre's position, although admirable in its courageous rejection of the idea that evil can be redeemed, does not shed much light on the ways philosophical and theological views have actually contributed to evil. As we examine how scholars and ordinary people have dealt with evil, we will see that they have made significant choices. Plato's description of evil, for example, arises from a god's-eye view. From this perspective a thoroughly good person (one who understands what goodness really is) is safe from evil; what happens to the body is unimportant so long as the soul is incorrupt. Not only is this an otherworldly view that denigrates the body and the things of this world—thus denying the possibility of an ethic that grows out of, say, motherly love—but it also suggests that goodness and the happiness associated with it are within the control of the human agents who pursue them wisely. Aristotle's view is far more realistic and attractive to most of us. Here we find acceptance of our human interdependence, acknowledgment that goodness and happiness depend to some degree on luck and felicitous associations, and acceptance of tragedy in the lives of people of good character.[6] From the perspective of women, Aristotle's ethic is a vast improvement over Plato's detached and perfect soul.

A new difficulty arises, however, when Aristotle makes emotion depend on belief. To suggest, for example, that pity depends on our belief that the one suffering does not deserve to suffer opens the door to ethical cruelty; as we will see, Christian theodicy has used the notion to justify natural evil. Further, acceptance of a tragic view can lead in at least two directions. It can lead—but has not yet done so— to a rejection of divinities and great principles that ask us to accept and even to inflict suffering, or it can lead to a glorification of the tragic condition. That is, the insights of tragedy can be used to heighten our admiration for tragic heroes and distract us from the task of building a world in which a bit less will depend on luck. The main job of this chapter is to examine the possible choices we have in facing up to evil.

EARLY VIEWS OF EVIL AND
THE POSSIBILITY OF AN EVIL GOD

The earliest views of evil are accessible to us only through the interpretation of artifacts and myths. Although it is not my purpose to provide a history of evil and our conceptions of it, we must explore the possibilities open to us. Which have led us astray and increased our pain? Which invite closer inspection? Because we depend on myth in this part of the investigation, it seems reasonable to begin with a discussion of myths and their role in increasing human understanding.

Paul Ricoeur tells us that the power of myths grows through a process of "demythologization"; that is, when a myth loses its early explanatory power, it takes on a new symbolic power. Deprived of its initial literal meaning, it opens up to manifold interpretations and thus contributes to knowledge of ourselves, the mythmakers. To label something a myth, then, does not destroy it—"only a myth" is an odd and contradictory juxtaposition of words—but rather enriches it by conferring on it the power of symbolism. In Ricoeur's terms, a myth grows more powerful as it loses it false logos.[7]

The earliest notions of evil described in myths were bound up with natural evil. Marie-Louise von Franz, a Jungian, comments: "The evil forces of nature . . . belong to the archetypal experience of evil: hunger, cold, fire, landslides and avalanches, snowstorms, drowning, storms at sea, being lost in the forest, the big enemy animals, the ice bear in the North, the lion or crocodile in Africa, etc."[8]

Jung and his followers construe the great natural evils as both concrete entities and archetypes—psychic realities that may present themselves symbolically and hence with a variety of meanings. The *sea*, for example, is a concrete cosmic entity; as archetype it represents not only a cosmic reality, but also a psychic reality with respect to which we are all somehow situated. Poetically it often stands as a sign of the feminine. Further, it can present itself in a variety of manifestations: in dreams of sailing, diving, drowning, walking on the shore, fishing, floating, being threatened by waves. Jungian analysis considers both archetypal and personal factors in interpretation. The presentation means something in itself (archetypally), but it also has special meaning arising from the particular personal unconscious. Similarly, a large enemy animal is a concrete reality and so a potential natural evil, but it may also be a monster in the psyche and poetically a metaphor for evil.

Views of evil almost always connect to the spiritual and often to the explicitly religious. A manifestation of evil strikes us with terror and a frantic desire to escape. In childhood it causes us to seek the security of a parent's loving arms; in its most elemental forms it continues to induce a similar urge. When the concrete parent is not present to protect us, we reach toward a spiritual parent or deity, and if this entity fails to aid us we often suppose that someone (we ourselves or some other) has done something to incur its righteous wrath. To avoid evil outcomes, then, we must avoid defilement—the contamination that is evil and leads to evil.

Here we see the beginnings of a great mistake that has followed us into the present century. Scholars have concentrated on the terror induced by disobeying a father, god, or authority and thereby incurring its wrath. They have paid relatively little attention to the desire for goodness that is aroused by loving relations with the mother. Freud, for example, almost ignores the pre-Oedipal child and locates the birth of the superego in the absolute terror of the Oedipal conflict.[9] This way of looking at things turns the protector into a source of new terror and constructs ethics on a foundation of fear.

Ricoeur describes a progression in the symbolism of evil from defilement to sin to guilt.[10] The symbolism of defilement springs from a primitive religious attitude, but the rituals connected to its removal are still embedded in contemporary religious practice. Even if Ricoeur is right in claiming that we can no longer coordinate ritual action with "any type of action for which we can construct a theory today," elaborate theorylike rationales are still created, promulgated, and believed. "What resists reflection," Ricoeur says, "is the idea of a quasi-material something that infects as a sort of filth, that harms by invisible properties, and that nevertheless works in the manner of a force in the field of our undividedly psychic and corporeal existence."[11] When he says that "we" can no longer understand such an orientation, he means, of course, that philosophy cannot make sense of such a position, not that there are no living persons who believe in forces of defilement. Later in this chapter we will see that belief in such forces is still active and is perhaps even growing. The history of the human psyche teems with devils, demons, and witches, and women have long been associated with evil in the form of defilement.

As we will see in chapter 2, women's bodies have been suspected of harboring evil, and menstrual taboos were established in congruence with this belief. The primitive notion that menstrual blood is a form of defilement has survived in contemporary Roman and Anglican church rituals that require the purification of women after child-birth.[12] Primitives considered not only menstrual blood but the men-struating woman herself to be a source of defilement. M. Esther Harding, a Jungian, comments:

> For it is believed that if a man "looks upon a menstruating woman his bones will soften, he will lose his manhood," will even die, while his weapons and implements will become useless, his nets will no longer catch fish, and his arrows will not kill deer. And, in addition, the power of the "war-bundle," which represents a warrior's commitment to the warlike undertaking and at the same time is a charm or amulet for its success, will be destroyed by such a contact, so fatal was the power of instinctive desire aroused by the woman's condition believed to be.[13]

Terror seems to be the basic affect of defilement. Ricoeur refers to "ethical terror," a fear of transgressing and thus calling forth harm, but surely pure uncritical terror historically and genetically precedes ethical terror. It will be necessary to explore the experiential roots of the turn from pure terror or dread to ethical terror. As I have noted, our childhood terrors are not first of this sort, and a loving parental embrace can banish them. Similarly, young children may comfort dolls or pets thought to be suffering terror. The young child in such situations may be showing the earliest signs of ethical concern—that is, concern to relieve the pain of an other. In our fear of defilement, however, we have passed from pure terror to an early stage of ethical terror. The turn to ethical terror rather than, say, ethical concern already posits a threatening parent or deity who may impose suffering for a mistake, transgression, or even a bit of misfortune. In contrast, ethical concern would be a move toward protecting loved others—a recognition that natural evil threatens all of us and that we should therefore band together lovingly to offer aid and comfort. A feminine phenomenology of evil will have to return to pure terror and see what next suggests itself to consciousness.

The move to ethical terror almost certainly represents an attempt to gain control through ritual and taboo, but taboo may also signify a dangerous decision to locate evil in the other—to project the perceived evil of instinctive desire onto the object of desire, for example, onto menstruating women. Because the desire was apparently overwhelming, the remedies had to be powerful. Not only must women be periodically isolated and purified, but men must adhere to a strong code of honor. Men must not allow themselves to be diverted from their perceived duties by the allure of females. Over time this insistence on maintaining control over instinctive desire led to the justification of deeds construed as honorable by men and evil by women, although most explications of evil have been masculine. Jungians go so far as to say that men and women are mirror opposites in their spiritual assessments. Harding, for example, declares, "That which to man is spiritual, good, to be sought after, is to woman daemonic, powerful, and destructive, and vice versa." [14]

But Harding fails to resolve the apparent contradiction, and she does not explore the full moral potential in the feminine view. She seems to accept the male code of honor and blames the woman who distracts her man from it: "The typical story is that he must join his regiment. When he goes to say goodby to her she coaxes him to remain or is so alluring that he forgets his obligation, and the army entrains without him." [15]

When we look at evil from the standpoint of women's experience, we will question the whole tradition of honor that has grown up around war and violence. This will not be simple work, for it is not merely a matter of rejecting war and supposing that men enjoy killing one another; we cannot easily brush aside considerations of principles and fidelity to companions. Yet this way of thinking started somewhere in a way of life and mode of experience alien to women, and women have, in spite of their insights and sound intuitions, inexplicably agreed that they are somehow deeply wrong to tempt men toward what might be argued as *good.* Harding continues by evaluating the story of the regiment: "All true women blame the woman who acts in this way, rather than the man. They know that such an action takes an unfair advantage of the man's vulnerability." [16]

Jungians thus acknowledge a tremendous feminine power that is neither reasoned nor moral, but instinctive, unconscious, mysterious. Men striving for rationality would have to fear such a power and set up a countervailing force that could, by creating even greater terror, offset it. Hidden entirely in this account is the great protective love of the mother for her infant and the first stirrings of other-feeling in the young child who wants to please this loving parent and *give* love in return.[17]

Ethical terror, the fear of transgressing against gods, may have been in part a move to rescue men from both the moral and the biological power of women. If the deity so conceived was in their own image and all-good, so much the better, for it would become easier to draw the lines between good and evil. But primitive people did not draw that line so cleanly. Their gods were neither all-powerful nor all-good. Primitive gods were responsible for both creation and destruction, and primitive people made no attempt to justify destruction as ultimately good. Rather, they instituted elaborate rituals to turn away or mollify the destructive rage of the gods. The earliest gods seem to have been as capricious and whimsical as the forces of nature must have seemed to our predecessors.

Not only were good and evil mixed in individual deities, but, as differentiation occurred, good and evil deities competed for power. Hence even if the move to ethical terror were accepted as necessary, there are still alternatives fanning out from this unfortunate decision point. Why select and argue for an all-powerful god? Why posit one who is all-good? Ricoeur points out that the possibility of an evil god leads to a tragic sense of life; as we shall see next, there is something deeply rational and attractive in that view. Primitive views of evil often located good and evil in the same divinity, and the Greeks brought this view to its greatest sophistication in their tragedies. Ricoeur notes that the theme of divine wickedness is "expressed with surprising force and constancy" in Homer's *Iliad;* again and again the gods take possession of men and their acts. "This darkening, this leading astray, this seizure," says Ricoeur, "is not punishment for some fault; it is the fault itself, the origin of the fault."[18] He remarks, however, that although the theme is replayed in spectacle (drama), it resists expression in speculation (theory). We cannot, he says, conceptualize an evil god. Although Ricoeur's claim is questionable, most of us find the worship of an evil god (Satanism, for example) pathological. The great strength in a position that postulates an evil god in addition to a good one is that we need not try to justify evil as the work of the good god we worship. But, of course, we must give up the insistence on that god's omnipotence.

Resistance to the concept of an evil god can take several forms. The most dangerous may be exactly the one taken by the mainstream theologies that ordinary persons believe and use to guide their lives. They insist that the words and acts recorded of a god, say, Yahweh, would indeed be evil if spoken or performed by men, but that coming from the god they must somehow be justified. It is hard to deny the wickedness of Yahweh as he is portrayed in the Old Testament. In story after story Yahweh reveals himself as jealous, vengeful, and small-minded. The book of Numbers catalogs the destruction that Yahweh did directly and that the Israelites accomplished at his direction. In surveying that chapter Martin Gardner remarks, "Numbers 31 is not only the most infamous chapter of the Bible; it is hard to find its equal in any other sacred book." The biblical account of the destruction Yahweh ordered is consistent with an evil god: his killings of Nadab and Abihu for a mistake in the mixing of incense, the stoning of a young man for blasphemy, the swallowing up of rebels against Moses and Aaron, the plague that murdered 14,700 people because some complained about their god's cruelty, the fiery serpents sent to bite and kill when people objected to the taste of manna.[19]

From a feminist perspective the killing of women and children is especially interesting, if deplorable. The Midianite women were almost certainly seen as a threat to the sovereignty of Yahweh, and the great campaigns of Joshua and Moses can be interpreted as violent moves to gain political and religious domination over an area in which the goddess was still worshiped. Merlin Stone, in her description of the cruelty of this campaign, comments on the irony of traditional interpretations: "At the risk of being repetitive, I cannot help thinking of Professor Albright's comment that the 'orgiastic nature worship' of Canaan 'was replaced by Israel with its pastoral simplicity and purity of life, its lofty monotheism and its severe code of ethics.'"[20]

Stone may or may not be right to interpret the slaughter of nonvirgin Midianite females as an attempt to stamp out female religion. Slaughters took place in those days—as in these—for a variety of reasons. In a feminine phenomenology of evil we will identify violence directly with evil through pain and terror, and we might well wonder why pain and violence came unstuck, as it were, from evil. We know in a sketchy way *how* it happened—through the move to ethical terror—but we still need to speculate on *why* it happened. From the perspective of persons whose experience centers on bearing and raising children, maintaining a secure and restful home, preparing food, making clothing, and nursing the ill, the separation of violence from evil seems inexplicable. One way of proceeding is, of course, the way suggested in the lines from Professor Albright: one simply brushes aside the actual violence, terror, and evil and concentrates on the progress of abstract thought. This way seems merely irrational—and perhaps blindly optimistic—but the way actually chosen, to justify violence and terror in the name of ultimate good, is far more frightening.

Even though we are clearly on the road to theodicy in our historical account, I must note that opportunities arise again and again for the notion of an evil or partly evil god to intrude itself. Indeed, a correlation between killing and godlike power has long held. As Marie-Louise von Franz notes, "The primitive idea that somebody who commits a murder or an outstanding crime is really not himself but performs something which only a God could do, expresses the situation very well." [21]

There is always the temptation, then, to equate the exercise of power with gods and with godlike behavior. Yet there remains a reluctance bordering on paranoic aversion to the association of the true God with evil. Indeed, historical accounts may be unable to catch the turning point, because they seem to involve notions of confession and repentance as far back as written records can take us. Confession and repentance, with which Ricoeur starts his discussion of evil, already contain the seeds of contradiction. Repentance makes it easy to recognize our own evil but to see it as temporary, inevitable, and redeemable; at the same time it tempts us to project true (unrepentant) evil outward onto others. Thus in our own time an American president called Russia "the Evil Empire," and many label the killing of children "terrorism" when done by other groups and "self-defense" when done by their own. Clearly the quest to establish a god who does all sorts of terrible things in the name of righteousness has a political as well as a spiritual basis. Von Franz notes that Christianity complicates the search for personal honesty in locating evil in ourselves, because at bottom only the unredeemed are permanently evil and therefore condemned. Further, we cannot find goodness by ourselves in Christianity but must be saved. Hence the things we do to one another are not nearly as important in our spiritual lives as our attitude and relation to God. Some, argue, of course, that a right relation to God will inevitably bring forth a right relation to people, but this claim is one for which we cannot produce much empirical evidence.

Echoes of an evil god come down to us from the Greeks. Poets working in the Greek spirit have been bold enough to recognize the evil god:

> Who shapes the soul, and makes her a barren wife
>> To the earthly body and grievous growth of clay;
> Who turns the large limbs to a little flame,
>> And binds the great sea with a little sand;
> Who makes desire, and slays desire with shame;
>> Who shakes the heaven as ashes in his hand;
> Who, seeing the light and shadow for the same,
>> Bids day waste night as fire devours a brand,
> Smites without sword, and scourges without rod—
>> The supreme evil, God.

In affirmation of this bold realization, Swinburne has the chorus continue:

> That these things are not otherwise, but thus;
>> That each man in his heart sigheth, and saith,
>> That all men even as I,
> All we are against thee, against thee,
>> O God most high.[22]

Swinburne's chorus sings a classic refrain on the evil god. No sooner are the recognition and bold renunciation announced than a retraction issues forth. It is agreed that silence is good, that reverence and fear make men whole, and that "silence is most noble till the end." [23] The injunction to be silent echoes in von Franz's comments on a story we will discuss later, that of Wassilissa and Baba-Yaga.[24] Human beings have always felt that it is unwise to point the finger at evil, especially at omnipotent evil, and so the fear of omnipotence has subdued the courage to construct a genuine ethicality. In the story of Job we also see fear overcome Job's sense of his own faultlessness. According to the story Job *is* faultless by his own assessment and even by God's, and so he appears to have a right to question God's goodness. But then he comes up flat against God's omnipotence: "Shall he that contendeth with the Almighty instruct *him?* he that reproveth God, let him answer it. Then Job answered the Lord, and said, Behold, I am vile; what shall I answer thee? I will lay mine hand upon my mouth" (Job 40:2–4).

This is exactly Wassilissa's response to Baba-Yaga; it is best to be silent about evil in the presence of the evil one, particularly if there is a good side to which one might appeal. "This motif," says von Franz, "is widespread in folklore stories." It reveals the essence of the mixed god. "We can conclude from this story that the Baba-Yaga is not totally evil; she is ambiguous, she is light and dark, good and evil, though here the evil aspect is stressed."[25]

People have long recognized the possibility of divinities split between good and evil. Indeed, the recognition holds within itself the potential for coming to grips with the shadow side of ourselves. If the gods are part good and part evil but value their good side more, would it not be possible for us too to promote our good side while remaining warily alert for the appearance of our own evil? This is what Jung urges in his discussion of good and evil in the emerging biblical God. According to Jung, Job taught God an ethical lesson, and God responded by becoming man to redeem humankind from the evil into which he had led us.[26] Such thinking is, of course, anathema to many religious thinkers, and to others it leads merely to logical and epistemological problems. Gardner mentions his teacher, Charles Hartshorne, who held this sort of position on God. God was for Hartshorne "finite," located in time, struggling and learning much as we are.[27] Gardner objects to Hartshorne's arguments because they depend so heavily on the concept of time. For Gardner, time is a bigger mystery than God, and he prefers one great postulate to several. Hence Gardner, like so many other intelligent beings, turns—albeit reluctantly—down the road toward theodicy.

As we begin the examination of theodicy—which of necessity will be brief—it is important to keep in mind where we are headed. Three questions guide us: Is a religious view necessary to define and minimize evil? What harm have the dominant views on evil done to us? What are the alternatives? We will return again to the notion of an evil god as we examine views on the devil, on instinctive violence, and on destroying evil. More important, we will return to the notion of a god struggling toward goodness as we consider the possibility of spirituality in a feminist view of evil. In that discussion we will find that a notion of human love and compassionate living can guide the search for a god we can live with.[28]

THEODICY AND HUMAN SUFFERING

If we believe that God is all-good and all-powerful, and if at the same time we see that there really is evil in the world, we find it difficult to understand God as both giver of ethics and creator. "The clearer God becomes as legislator," Ricoeur says, "the more obscure he becomes as creator," and vice versa. We are inclined to blame God for a lack of ethicality. As we have seen, however, the blame is usually resisted. The idea of God as evil is close to unthinkable and, once thought, is hard to sustain. Only a minor god can be evil—surely not the one we worship. People long after a good god as children long after a good parent. As Ricoeur points out, "There begins the foolish business of trying to justify God: theodicy is born." [29]

The Augustinian tradition provided the main line of thinking on theodicy, but the Greek Epicureans had already posed the problem as a trilemma in response to Stoic attempts at theodicy: if God could have prevented evil and did not, he is malevolent; if God would have prevented evil but could not, he is impotent; if God could not and would not, why call him God?[30] The answer might be political. An all-good, all-powerful authority was thought to have considerably more clout than a loving, fallible parent-figure. Augustine followed the path of the Stoics. Since it is not my purpose to write an entire volume on theodicy, I will look at the central questions Saint Augustine and his followers raised and answered, and I will note missed alternatives as we move along. In the "lofty monotheism" of Augustine we have to deal with a deity who is all-knowing, all-powerful, and all-good. Further, all being emanating from his creative hand is also held to be good. Creation is itself, then, good.

How could evil enter into the all-good creation of an all-powerful God? Augustinians answer this question in two main ways, both of which lay the blame on human beings. First, human beings, as God's creation, must be perfect. But because we are endowed with free will, we may turn from the greatest good, God, toward a lesser good. This turning—perhaps inevitable for a creature born free and curious—is itself evil. It is not that we turn *toward* evil, for in Augustinian terms there is no evil-as-entity toward which to turn. The turning itself is the source of evil.

The Augustinian notion of hierarchically arranged goods begins the attempt to save God from complicity in evil by putting God at the top—the supreme good. (Recall Swinburne's chorus singing the alternative—God as supreme evil.) The angels risk evil when they look toward lower creations such as man, and man runs a similar risk when he looks with undue interest below him. Man runs a special risk when he looks toward the creature next below him in the hierarchy, woman. Thus in Augustine we find a reintroduction and interpretation of Plato's divided line: Man and things of the spirit are above the line—lower than God but on the "right" side of the line. Woman and material things are on the "wrong," or corporeal, side and hence represent a dreadful temptation that man must fear and avoid.

The attempt to rescue God from accusations of creating evil locates evil instead in the willful turning of men and angels from God to lower entities, even though these entities are themselves good—as is everything God created. But this account does not explain why God should allow creatures with this weakness for turning to exist. Here Augustine introduces an aesthetic argument, relying heavily on the principle of plenitude rooted in the work of Plotinus. John Hick explains:

> Plotinus saw the ultimate reality as so superabundantly full that it 'gives off' being as the sun radiates light. The divine plenitude overflows, pouring itself outwards and downwards in a teeming cascade of ever-new forms of life until all the possibilities of existence have been actualized and the shores are reached of the unlimited ocean of non-being.[31]

God did not create the various forms as equal because there would then have been no reason to create such a multitude; indeed, there would have been a deprivation of being and, synonymously, of good. The resulting hierarchy of being actualizes the possibilities and maximizes *being*. Even the great philosopher Leibniz followed this line of thinking. He did not accept the Greek notion of *emanation* by which entities are created unconsciously—"as the sun radiates light"—but rather held that God in his omniscience considered all the logical possibilities for world building and from the vast array chose to actualize this best of all possible worlds.[32] Some theologians object to Leibniz's account on the grounds that it describes God as constrained by logic rather than as its master and thus threatens his omnipotence. Such an objection illustrates the tangle of knots created by the insistence that God must be all-knowing, all-powerful, and all-good.

Having attributed to plenitude the creation of entities likely to fall or turn, both Augustine and Leibniz insist that human sin was not *caused.* God foresaw the fall but did not ordain it; things could have been otherwise. For both thinkers evil in the world results from contingent acts of human beings. The aesthetic argument continues by describing God's role in the suffering we associate with evil. Here Augustine introduces the principle of harmony. First, he denies that suffering from natural evil is evil at all. Only because we cannot see the larger picture as God sees it do we call such suffering "evil." In the long run—God's run—all things work together for good. Second, suffering is required to balance moral evil. Since God has allowed human choice and that choice has produced moral evil, God must exact retribution to maintain harmony or balance. For Augustine hell is a necessary part of a perfect universe, even if the vast majority of humankind has to be consigned to it to keep the balance. Leibniz too accepts the wisdom of God's decision to allow most human souls to suffer eternal damnation.[33]

John Hick observes that the notion of God's bringing good out of evil, that he "indeed brings an eternal and therefore infinite good out of a temporal and therefore finite evil, is a thought of great promise for Christian theodicy."[34] Hick assesses the Augustinian project as fatally flawed, however, because *eternal* damnation contradicts an eventual and infinite good. But if we hold that those so damned are of little or no consequence and that they have earned their own condemnation, their eternal suffering can be part of the picture of eternal happiness for those who have done right or who have been chosen. (We need not feel pity, as Aristotle said, for those who deserve to suffer.) Indeed, for Augustine the contrast between the comfort of the saved and the misery of sinners might augment the happiness of some souls in heaven. Hick is less cruel—and perhaps less astute on human nature—than Augustine.

When we look at evil from the perspective of women's experience—through the eyes of people who bear and raise children, try to maintain a comfortable and stable home, feed and nurture the hungry and developing—we find much more wrong with the Augustinian theodicy. First, it requires something like the Adamic myth, some account of the first sin, to hold it up. When the Adamic myth combines with

Augustine's pronouncements on original sin, the burden on women becomes enormous, as we will see. But not only women have suffered. Ricoeur says: "The harm that has been done to souls, during the centuries of Christianity, first by literal interpretation of the story of Adam, and then by confusion of this myth, treated as history, with later speculations, principally Augustinian, about original sin, will never be adequately told."[35]

Second, it is not just eternal damnation that raises questions about the goodness of the God who decrees it. The problem of suffering is by no means adequately treated, and I will turn to that discussion shortly. Third, the explanation of suffering as retribution for sin sets the investigation of evil on the wrong track. This is a large part of the perversion Mary Daly, Rosemary Ruether, and other feminists condemn. The raw terror of natural evil is turned prematurely and arbitrarily into *ethical* terror, the fear of incurring the father-God's wrath. Our thinking, then, is distracted from the loving parent's attitude that would relieve and eliminate suffering to a long and perhaps hopeless quest to be justified in God's sight. In accepting this quest, we too often do harm to one another. It is odd that Freud, who looked on religion as something that should be outgrown, should suggest a mechanism—the Oedipal conflict—that leaves the basic evils of terror and righteous punishment intact.

Fourth, the image of God created in this long chain of arguments in theodicy has greatly favored his omnipotence and omniscience. Hence the religious tradition has blinded us ethically. Since God, who clearly has the knowledge and power to do otherwise, inflicts or allows the greatest of suffering, the infliction of pain cannot be a *primary* ethical abuse. Since God hides himself from us, the neglect of a loving personal relation cannot be a primary evil, and the responsibility for remaining in contact falls to the weak and dependent. Since God presents the world to us in impenetrable mystery, there is precedent for mystification, and the dependent and powerless must learn to trust authority. These will be the great themes of evil from the perspective of women's experience.

There are clearly many alternatives to the Augustinian God. Indeed, many theologians consider the Augustinian program to be intellectually weak and, in contemporary thought, almost a caricature of the Christian position. But this assessment, which sophisticated thinkers make so easily, is misleading. Not only do many laypersons still accept the elements of this tradition (a recent poll revealed that 53 percent of Americans still believe in hell, for example),[36] but the notion that the tradition is no longer worthy of our intellectual attention forecloses the possibility of a full discussion of the political programs that accompanied Augustinian theology. Mary Midgley is mistaken, then, when she supposes that we can ignore the Augustinian tradition in any thorough discussion of evil. I agree with her that simply getting rid of religion will not solve the problem either. She says of the idea of getting rid of religion, "Whatever may have been its plausibility in the eighteenth century, when it first took the centre of the stage, it is surely just a distraction today."[37] We cannot ignore either side of this long argument, because each accuses the other of a fundamental complicity in evil. Feminist theologians, as I noted, accuse the theological traditionalists of having "ratified" certain evils in their definition of evil; in contrast, fundamentalists see "secular humanism" as a radical evil. Reasonable thinkers like Midgley would understandably like to be rid of both extremes, but that banishment is not so easy. From a caring perspective, dialogue between these two groups is essential because, after all, both share some basic values that could be enhanced by their cooperation. Finally, the enormous influence of Augustinian theodicy on our political and social structures makes it imperative that all educated persons be familiar with its main points and effects.

Influential alternative theodicies exist, and although in my view none of these has been successful, I must consider at least one. The Irenaean type of theodicy (named for Irenaeus, ca. A.D. 120–202) views Adam not as a perfect creation who irrationally turns to evil but as a developing being—one who must seek knowledge and ethical understanding to achieve the capacity to communicate with God. From this perspective the Fall does not represent the loss of an original paradise but the beginning of a long quest for knowledge and goodness. Since the childlike weakness of Adam came to light in his Fall, the Fall itself turns out to be a blessing in disguise because it necessitates redemption. Adam's sin becomes a *necessarium peccatum* and a *felix culpa*—a necessary sin and a happy fault.

Although the Irenaean view is gentler in its assessment of human responsibility for evil and more generous in its emphasis on redemption, it too fails in its account of suffering. It leaves the problem not only in mystery (thus resigning its solution to faith), but in a state of contradiction as well. Accepting such a view, John Hick says:

We thus have to say, on the basis of our present experience, that evil is really evil, really malevolent and deadly and also, on the basis of faith, that it will in the end be defeated and made to serve God's good purposes. From the point of view of that future completion it will not have been merely evil, for it will have been used in the creation of infinite good.[38]

This view does not deny evil as merely an appearance that we misinterpret. Evil is real but somehow useful. No longer the great aesthetician, God becomes the foremost Utilitarian. How strange that even Immanuel Kant seems to have accepted a version of this doctrine in his account of the Fall and its role in soul making.[39] In Kantian ethics principles are absolute, and morality lies in the acts and their connection to principle—not in the effective production of some valued nonmoral good. The only way to avoid the awful contradiction of God's turning out to be a Utilitarian in a Kantian scheme is to fasten onto a grim and absolute conception of justice in which the infliction of suffering can be justified as obedience to a supreme law. This kind of thinking, transposed to the domain of human interaction, leads to the untold suffering of many people at the hands of righteous others.

The problem of suffering is central to theodicy and, as we have seen, the solutions often seem to ratify evil rather than to redeem it. Augustine tried to solve the problem through balance and harmony:

> If there were misery before there were sins, then it might be right to say that the order and government of the universe were at fault. Again, if there were sins and no consequent misery, that order is equally dishonored by lack of equity. But since there is happiness for those who do not sin, the universe is perfect; and it is no less perfect because there is misery for sinners.[40]

This solution is clearly unsatisfactory on several counts. First, even Augustine did not mean that all individual suffering was the direct penalty for individual sin; rather suffering is generally available in amounts to balance the sin that occurs. His is a long-run account; eventually the good will know happiness, and evildoers will reap misery. But all of us merit some suffering because we share in original sin. The doctrine of original sin—absent from older Hebraic versions of the Adamic myth—was invoked in part to explain the suffering of innocents. In this view there are no real innocents; all share in the guilt of original sin. In a later chapter we will see how human beings

have adapted this teaching to their own justification of killing innocents in warfare. When some questioned the bombing of German civilian populations in World War II, for example, part of the response
included a description of German civilians—"innocents" by the usual
rules of warfare—as *not* innocent by virtue of their Nazi contamination. This pernicious doctrine has penetrated our political and social
life; it has not been confined to esoteric theologies.

Second, Augustine's harmony and balance cannot adequately explain suffering inflicted on the just, and we will see how weak his
account is when we analyze the story of Job a bit later.

Third, his account does not in any way explain animal suffering.
As Hick points out, Augustine seems to have been little moved by the
pain of animals.[41] On the one hand, Augustine says that animal suffering helps human beings understand something called the "desire for
bodily unity"; on the other, he finds something aesthetically pleasing
in the transformation of one animal body into food for other animals.
Nowhere does he consider prolonged agony, the starvation of young
deprived of their mothers, or the terror of being constantly preyed
on.[42] He does not ask what sort of god would deliberately create a
world in which his creatures must eat one another to live.

The problem of animal pain provides another opportunity to consider a different, more fallible, sort of God or to adopt a tragic sense
of life. Considering the problem of animal suffering, Schopenhauer
says: "Brahma is said to have produced the world by a kind of fall or
mistake; and in order to atone for his folly, he is bound to remain in
it himself until he works out his redemption. As an account of the
origin of things, that is admirable!"[43] Indeed, it is admirable, and it
puts us into sympathy with both the erring god and our fallible human
companions. There is a lofty arrogance in the strict monotheism that
insists on the all-goodness of an all-powerful God who allows and
uses such suffering for his own purposes, and this sort of thinking has
maintained and promoted a social order in which disobedience or distrust of the patriarch (as church, state, or father) is the greatest sin.
What could be greater in such a system? For God himself commits all
the crimes we might, from a natural perspective, label evil.

Since the major project in this work is to redefine and describe evil
from women's perspective, we must return to Augustine's account of
human suffering. It is clear, however, that the existence of unjustified
animal suffering is enough to discredit the notion of an all-good and

all-powerful deity. Which characteristic should be sacrificed? When we discuss Satan we will see that it is tempting to give up God's alleged omnipotence; when we discuss Job it will be equally tempting to give up the claim of God's all-goodness.

The most prominent, but deeply flawed, solution to the problem of suffering lies in the concept of soul making. This idea, central to the Irenaean theodicy, echoes in Kant and in modern writers like C. S. Lewis. Ricoeur says of Kant that he understood "the fall, free and fated, of man as the painful road of all ethical life that is of an adult character and on an adult level." [44] This view helps explain why Kant felt that it was not our duty to contribute to another's moral perfection:

> It is contradictory to say that I make another person's *perfection* my end and consider myself obliged to promote this. For the *perfection* of another man, as a person, consists precisely of *his own* power to adopt his end in accordance with his own concept of duty; and it is self-contradictory to demand that I do (make it my duty to do) what only the other person himself can do. [45]

In the coming analysis of evil I will contest this way of looking at perfection and, in general, at moral life and action. But here we see that Kant's ethical perspective is consistent with his religious (or metaphysical) perspective. God leaves us free to choose our moral course, and we in turn have no obligation to promote the moral perfection of our fellows. Life is a painful and lonely struggle designed to "make souls." In the Christian design faith may lighten the struggle, but the suffering is no less real. Instead of concentrating on the alleviation and possible elimination of suffering, Christians are urged to find meaning in it. C. S. Lewis, for example, said of his wife's relentless pain from cancer: "But is it credible that such extremities of torture should be necessary for us? Well, take your choice. The tortures occur. If they are unnecessary, then there is no God or a bad one. If there is a good God, then these tortures are necessary. For no even moderately good Being could possibly inflict or permit them if they weren't." [46]

Completely immersed in a strict monotheism, Lewis fails to appreciate the possibilities in a fallible god—one who controls just so much and is perhaps still struggling toward an ethical vision. This sort of god—lovable and understandable to women—may be unattractive to many men because he cannot make absolute claims on us for worship, obedience, and authority, or if he makes such claims, we might be justified in challenging him and even charging the claim to his wicked or unfinished side. A fallible god shakes the entire hierarchy and endangers men in their relations to women, children, animals, and the whole living environment. Whether Lewis saw any of this is doubtful. He adhered to the Augustinian line, affirming with St. Paul "that the sufferings of this present time are not worthy to be compared with the glory that shall be revealed in us."[47] Justice will triumph.

In the story of Job we encounter another way to reconceptualize God. The doctrine of original sin was designed in part to explain why innocents must suffer. But why should the *just* suffer?

"There was a man in the land of Uz, whose name was Job; and that man was perfect and upright, and one that feared God, and eschewed evil" (Job 1:1). In this biblical beginning we have something like a philosophical fiction—an ideal case to test. How might we explain the suffering of a *perfectly just* man? Despite Job's perfection, God allowed Satan to put him to terrible tests of his faithfulness. Previously rich and well blessed in family life, Job was undeservedly deprived of everything: his servants were killed, his herds stolen, his seven sons slain by the wind, and, at last, his body afflicted from head to food with "sore boils." On top of all this physical and emotional pain he suffered the deepest of all pains, psychic or soul pain, as his friends suggested that he must have done something to deserve the evil that was visited on him and as he struggled to maintain a belief in the goodness of a God who willfully permitted him to suffer so. How could God be all-good and at the same time allow Satan to inflict deliberate pain on a just man? Why would an omniscient deity thunder on for seventy-one verses bragging about his omnipotence to a lowly servant long since convinced?[48]

Here again we might decide not simplistically and childishly that God is bad, but that God is fallible and himself subject to error and temptation. Jung, in his fascinating *Answer to Job,* asks us to consider a developing God (one Hartshorne mentioned and Gardner rejected, as I discussed earlier).[49] This God, says Jung, may have learned a moral lesson from Job, a mere man, and then was constrained to "answer Job" by becoming man himself, thus sharing the pain, ambiguity, and finiteness of the beings he had created.

This account reminds us of Schopenhauer's description of Brahma and his atonement for the mistakes of creation. But the story that follows in the New Testament is a strange mixture of loving redemption and savage destruction. In the final agonies of Revelation, the new God seems very like Yahweh, exacting terrible and irrevocable vengeance. Indeed, we human beings are sometimes exhorted to return good for evil not out of love for our erring fellows but in the full realization that by so doing we "heap coals of fire upon their heads." Further, the program of redemption involves two things that should be anathema to women: a disregard of human intimacy and a perpetuation of the ancient ritual of sacrificing the son.

Jung interprets this story as a signal that the growing God needs to be rejoined to Sophia, the feminine deity-companion, who will bring wisdom, compassion, and completion to divinity.[50] In this thinking Jung has made a bold choice. He accepts God as omnipotent and omniscient but not yet all-good. He sees God as striving to manage his omniscience, and the call for Sophia is a move to enhance this project. I will return to this theme in later chapters, but clearly Jung's thinking has had little influence on patriarchal Christianity.

The foolishness of theodicy has led us to search for the meaning of suffering. We have supposed, as a result of this long search, that suffering may be justified for retributive, therapeutic, pedagogical, or redemptive reasons.[51] Because God visits suffering on us for these reasons, we have inferred that we may cause one another to suffer for the same reasons. I will call all this into question in the later phenomenological investigation of evil. But before turning to that project (in which we encounter suffering *as* suffering without justification), we must ask about alternatives not yet considered. Suppose God is all-good but not all-powerful? Suppose God is at war with an equally powerful evil force?

DEVILS

One way to explain evil in the world is to posit an evil entity of great power who acts directly to bring about evil. This is a view several Eastern religions put forward, and it is the Manichaean dualist solution. According to the Manichaeans two great powers, light and darkness, are locked in battle for control of the world. Augustine accepted this view for some time, but then he rejected it, recognizing that it entailed a god who was not all-powerful. Hick says of Augustine's critical rejection of Manichaeanism: "It pictured the God whom men

worship as less than absolute, and as but one of two co-ordinate powers warring against each other." [52]

Such a view is, of course, incompatible with a strict monotheism.
It saves God from complicity in evil but sacrifices his omnipotence.
Further, a complex mythology grew up around the forces of good and
evil, making the position both confusing and unpalatable to the growing scientific orientation. (Not only is there a hierarchy of angels as in
Augustine, for example, but now there are devils, demons, and archons to arrange as well.) But this view reinforced and accentuated a
tendency already present in the Christian church to devalue the body
and associate it with materiality. Jeffrey Burton Russell comments:
"The presence of such dualism at the edge of the tradition sharpened
the tension between soul and body and enhanced the view of the Devil
as lord of matter, using the human body as the vehicle for his temptations." [53]

Manichaean dualism sees the body as a prison—a situation in
which the exiled soul must strive to find redemption. Describing this
view, Russell says of Jesus' message:

> Jesus goes to Adam and tells him the truth: that his body is an evil
> imposture invented by demons, and that he must try to rescue his soul
> for the world of light. Thus the function of men and women in the
> world is to grasp the saving gnosis, the message of Jesus, and to work
> at freeing the soul from the body. [54]

In spite of the rejection of Manichaeanism, its denunciation of the
body had tremendous influence on Christianity. In chapter 2 we will
hear Pearl Buck describe her mother as continually torn between her
love of earthly existence and matters of the soul. The title of Buck's
biography, *The Exile,* takes on new significance when we realize that
the duality of good and evil, light and darkness, comes to us from the
Orphic myth, described as the "myth of the exiled soul." [55] Although
Augustine had to brand as heresy any view of the body as evil in itself,
the weakness of bodies and the evils of "fleshiness" came to be major
themes in Christianity.

The dualism of the Manichaeans is not entirely absent from contemporary Christianity. M. Scott Peck, a Christian psychiatrist, takes
just such a view. Adopting what he frankly calls a "Christian model,"
he says: "According to this model, humanity (and perhaps the entire
universe) is locked in a titanic struggle between the forces of good and

evil, between God and the devil. The battleground of this struggle is the individual human soul. The only question of ultimate significance is whether the individual soul will be won to God or won to the devil." Peck then refers to a particular case in his practice:

> By establishing through his pact a relationship with the devil, George had placed his soul in the greatest jeopardy known to man. It was clearly the critical point of his life. And possibly even the fate of all humanity turned upon his decision. Choirs of angels and armies of demons were watching him, hanging on his every thought, praying continually for one outcome or the other. In the end, by renouncing his past and the relationship, George rescued himself from hell and to the glory of God and for the hope for mankind.[56]

Peck takes a "multifaceted" approach in his work that includes both a medical model and the Christian model described above, but he clearly accepts the notion of two warring powers. Another contemporary writer who believes in the reality of Satan, viewing Satan as "god of this world," is Hal Lindsey. He too believes in possession: "I believe that people are being given superhuman powers from Satan in order that they may promote his work on earth." And he believes in the host of demons and worker devils:

> How many believe they are making contact with a powerful, incredibly intelligent spiritual being who heads a vast, highly organized army of spiritual beings like himself? This host is dedicated to blinding men's minds to the gift of forgiveness and love which God offered through Jesus Christ and to destroying or neutralizing those who have already believed in Him.[57]

One possible advantage of dualistic systems (beyond their simple preservation of God's goodness) is their location of the source of evil in gods rather than human beings. From this perspective evil is not a mere privation or turning from the good; rather it is part chosen and part inherited. Ricoeur says "Evil does not begin because it is always already there in some fashion; it is choice *and* heritage."[58]

Again the opportunity for a tragic sense of life arises, but Christianity rejects it. Although it acknowledges the power of evil forces, those not rescued from possession are damned. Further, those who *choose* to align themselves with evil are often held to be irredeemable. Satan and his host of devils and demons are therefore doomed forever. "Once having sinned," Russell says in explaining Augustine's position, "the Devil and the other fallen angels are bound forever to the shadows and can never more do good." [59] This view has done enormous mischief. Far from relieving human beings from complete blame for the introduction of evil, Augustine's view combines original sin and diabology. Just as the fallen angels cannot be saved, so some people cannot be saved. But how can we tell which persons fall into this category? The dilemma caused real problems not only in technical analyses of predestination but also in such practical matters as, for example, judging witches. Those who had sealed pacts with the devil had to be destroyed; others, who had merely flirted, so to speak, with evil, were punished less severely.

A tremendous body of lore has grown up around the devil, and the concept has been and remains important in Christianity. Russell goes so far as to say:

> To deny the existence and central importance of the Devil in Christianity is to run counter to apostolic teaching and to the historical development of Christian doctrine. Since defining Christianity in terms other than these is literally meaningless, it is intellectually incoherent to argue for a Christianity that excludes the Devil. If the Devil does not exist, then Christianity has been dead wrong on a central point right from the beginning. [60]

Christian thinkers can sharply dispute this point. In one sense, of course, Russell is right: the devil is there historically. In another he is clearly wrong, for Christianity is not a static body of lore and dogma. It can be redefined without the devil as a central character. The most important point, however, is similar to the one Elisabeth Schüssler Fiorenza made with respect to women and scripture. [61] She argues that scripture should not be discarded on feminist grounds; rather it should be read and critiqued as a way of remembering what our foremothers suffered. It is part of our heritage as women. Similarly, we must remember the devil if we are to develop a morality of evil. We must try to understand why our predecessors needed such an entity and why some people still need devils on which to project their own evil.

Russell contends that the devil finds a role in every viewpoint that can logically be taken with respect to religion and evil. [62] First, when evil is construed as privation or nonbeing, as in Augustine, the devil (a fallen angel, created good) becomes *princeps mundi,* prince of this world—ruling the earth not as a competing deity but with God's tolerance and for eventual purposes of good. The view persists even though there is something incoherent in insisting that the devil is real, evil, and irredeemable while at the same time defining evil as nonbeing. Second, if evil is defined as the purpose and reality of a deity warring with God, the devil has his most powerful role, and human beings then have a duty to help the good God establish his final rule. This position has long been branded a heresy, but, as we have seen, it continues to spring up in Christianity and other religions. Third—and this view was foreshadowed in the discussion of Jung and Job—the devil is sometimes seen as part of God himself.[63] I will return to this view in later chapters where I will show it as one religious view compatible with a feminine phenomenology of evil. Fourth and finally, the devil even plays a role in atheistic views of evil. The role is metaphorical, of course, but its continual recurrence testifies to the power and romance of the idea.

In the last view, the devil is an entity to be courted and then subdued by those who desire power. Both Goethe's *Faust* and Nietzsche's *Zarathustra* illustrate this theme. William Barrett remarks that "both attempt to elaborate in symbols the process by which the superior individual—whole, intact, and healthy—is to be formed; and both are identically 'immoral' in their content, if morality is measured in its usual conventional terms." [64]

Barrett points out that Gounod's *Faust* is a moralized (or Christianized) version of the story. Unlike Gounod's hero, Goethe's is not destroyed by Gretchen's tragic death but begins a process of self-development:

> The strong man survives such disasters and becomes harder. The Devil, with whom Faust has made a pact, becomes in a real sense his servitor and subordinate, just as our devil, if joined to ourselves, may become a fruitful and positive force; like Blake before him Goethe knew full well the ambiguous power contained in the traditional symbol of the Devil.[65]

Nietzsche too advises us to incorporate our devils and become stronger. Nietzsche strongly attacked Christian debasement of the body; that which was evil in Christian terms became good in Nietzsche's. He chided Christianity for standing proper values "on their head." The spiritual men of Christianity, he said,

> smash the strong, contaminate great hopes, cast suspicion on joy in beauty, break down everything autocratic, manly, conquering, tyrannical, all the instincts proper to the highest and most successful of the type 'man,' into uncertainty, remorse of conscience, self-destruction, in-

deed reverse the whole love of the earthly and of dominion over the earth into hatred of the earth and the earthly.[66]

From a different perspective we would have to say that Nietzsche's great insights into the harm done by Christian abhorrence of the body and earthly life oddly intermixed with a profound misunderstanding of the church. When he referred to churchmen breaking down the "autocratic, manly, conquering, tyrannical," he spoke only of the church's gentle message—not of its actions or real intentions. Between the Christian moralist and the Nietzschean immoralist, we—both men and women—have little to choose if we seek a way of life free from domination, the deliberate infliction of suffering, and the unbridled power of a male hierarchy.

The notion of a Faustian science to combat evil is still popular. Ernest Becker in his analysis of evil claims that such a science must do three things:

It will have to explain evil credibly, and offer a way to overcome it;

It would have to define the True, the Good, and the Beautiful;

And it would have to re-establish the unity of man and nature, the sense of intimacy with the cosmic process.

Becker sees all this as a necessary move from the old theodicies (which he, like other writers, wrongly claims are dead) to a new theodicy—one that he calls an "anthropodicy." This anthropodicy would "settle for a new *limited* explanation [of evil and] . . . cover only *those evils that allow for human remedy*."[67] As Becker admits, this was the project of the Enlightenment. (We recall here the error Midgley warns against.) We transfer our faith from God to science. Instead of asking how we can best live in the inevitably tragic situation presented to us at birth, Becker finds reasons for optimism in the social utopia of Marx and the "understanding of man" provided by Freud. But Freud, as we know, left the basic evil of ethical terror firmly in place.

There is much in Becker's work with which we might sympathize—his call for community, his attack on agonism (the ancient Greek notion of life as a contest).[68] But he moves in the traditional pattern to global and sweeping solutions. Is it really necessary (or even possible) to define "the True, the Good, and the Beautiful," or might this very project maintain some forms of evil? Do we require a sense "of intimacy with the cosmic process"? Or do we need to recognize that our recourse stands beside us in the form of other human beings through whom we really do live and define our being? As we will see in chapter 4, women are in a peculiarly advantaged position historically to analyze a way of life that has necessitated living with and loving powerful human beings, men, who might properly be described as part-god, part-devil.

Finally, Becker wants a way to overcome evil. In a later work he writes of an escape from evil and describes human beings as longing to overcome evil.[69] But this longing, activated by fear, translates into action that sustains and renews evil through ignorance. We project the devil onto enemies, and we slay our enemies in the hope of overcoming evil. We also intend to incorporate the strength of our slain enemies and achieve a temporary victory over death. Primitive man and Nietzsche have much in common. The urge is always toward power, control, autonomy, and standardization—an odd assortment of objectives.

Becker, for all his insights and valuable suggestions, forgets that theodicy was an attempt to *justify* God in the face of evil and that anthropodicy might well lead in a similar direction. The present work looks evil in the face as in a mirror and sees that the face hardens and softens, that it is capable of smiling—of turning away from evil with a firm "This I will not do" and of living patiently with the evil in ourselves and others.

SUMMARY

The basic question of this chapter has been, Can evil be redeemed? At the outset I confessed some agreement with Sartre on the matter: evil cannot be redeemed. But I do not mean that persons who commit evil are irredeemable; and, of course, Sartre was not speaking the language of religion. He meant that no philosophical or theological attempt to justify evil or to show its nonexistence could succeed, and in this I agree with him.

In this brief look at views on evil we have seen that the earliest recognized evil in the cosmos and tried to ward it off by rites and rituals. Human beings were afflicted and sometimes even directed into evil by gods; they were not thought to be the originators of evil through sin. The gods themselves were thought to incorporate both good and evil; one begged the good side for protection against the evil side. Although there is clearly something psychologically healthy in this early view, there is also a moral dullness in it. If one man killed another, for example, it was clear that evil had befallen the one killed, but the killer was not necessarily judged to have committed evil. Interestingly, this view persists in some cultures where Christianity and paganism have blended. A contemporary Masai, for example, answered a visitor's question whether it was "all right" to kill a man by saying: "It is not so bad to kill a man. If you do it and are successful, it is not so bad, because God allowed the man to die. God agreed, and so it happened."[70]

Properly developed, the early views might have led to a tragic view of life in which people banded together against cosmic evil, and we will explore this possibility later. Where a tragic view did develop, however, it more often emphasized the tragic necessity of *doing* evil and accepting evil rather than a sustained commitment to stand against it.

The idea of gods in whom good and evil are undifferentiated leads to the notion of an evil god. This idea has arisen again and again. Even in early Christian sects the notion of an evil deity in combat with the God of light was prominent. It is perhaps more logical—and certainly simpler—than the concept of an all-good, all-powerful god who must somehow be responsible for the evil that we see and suffer in the world. But we saw that the idea is not easy to sustain; the longing for goodness—particularly with respect to omnipotence—is too great. A few bold and imaginative thinkers have suggested alliances with the devil or devils in order to grow stronger and more powerful, but even these writers were not in search of something they truly believed to be *evil*. They were reacting against a notion of evil that robbed life of its passion and people of their autonomy and courage.

The idea of an evil being appears even in strictly monotheistic views. The devil might be regarded as a projection of evil. Evil, then, is the other, right from God on down the hierarchy: evil is not in God but in Satan, who is irredeemable; evil is in the archons or demons, not in the angels; evil is in those who do not believe what authority dictates, not in the select; and evil is far more congenial to women (whose bodies make them especially susceptible) than to men. Russell surmises that this projection—the devil (although he does not label the devil a projection)—will persist:

> The concept of the Devil is very much alive today, in spite of opposition from many theologians as well as from those hostile to all metaphysics. Indeed, the idea is more alive now than it has been for many decades,

because we are again aware of the ineradicable nature of perversity in our own behavior, a perversity that has perhaps been more evident in the twentieth century than ever before. . . . We have direct perception of evil, of deliberate malice and desire to hurt, constantly manifesting itself in governments, in mobs, in criminals, and in our own petty vices. . . . This is the Devil.[71]

But unless we see these faults in our own governments and selves as well as in others, we are guilty of *projection,* an exteriorization of evil that leaves us blameless as we try to destroy it. An alternative, suggested in one form or another by Jung, Sontag, and James, is the integration of good and evil in both deity and humans. From this viewpoint God is still learning to control the evil within him and is good to the degree that he does so. So must we learn to recognize, control, and convert the evil within us. This is what Jung has in mind when he says that we need a morality of evil.[72]

The view that did perhaps the greatest harm in its definition of evil is the one described in the discussion of theodicy and suffering. Here we find human beings blamed for the introduction of evil into an originally good world, the identification of evil with the material and bodily world, a hierarchy of being that has been used to dominate women and exploit the animal world, and at bottom a thorough mystification of the problem of evil. This view justifies the infliction of suffering, and we lose the opportunity to investigate evil at its phenomenal roots. From the perspective that will guide the rest of this study, that long tradition has *ratified* evil in some of its most basic forms.

2

The Devil's Gateway

If all the harm that women have done
Were put in a bundle and rolled into one,
Earth would not hold it
The sky could not enfold it,
It could not be lighted nor warmed by the sun.
Such masses of evil
Would puzzle the devil
And keep him in fuel while Time's wheels run.
But if all the harm that's been done by men
Were doubled and doubled and doubled again,
And melted and fused into vapour and then
Were squared and raised to the power of ten,
There wouldn't be nearly enough, not near
To keep a small girl for the tenth of a year.
                    —J. K. Stephen, "A Thought"

In the first chapter we saw that man's desire to overcome evil often results in perpetuating and renewing it. In this chapter we will see that man often projects evil on woman, as in the bit of doggerel above.[1] Centuries of living with this projection has given women something like a privileged position (in a theoretical, not political, sense of the expression) from which to study evil, and so it is essential to understand what this projection has meant for women's experience.

Woman has been regarded, in Tertullian's words, as the "devil's gateway." We could hardly expect persons so labeled to be invited to speak on matters of good and evil. Indeed, those acts and relations that women regard as loving and good have often been considered dangerous to the moral development of men and boys and thus in need of careful supervision and constraint. The result has been a false and violently damaging description of evil. As Mary Daly points out: "The myth [of Eve and the Fall] takes on cosmic proportions since the male's viewpoint is metamorphosed into God's viewpoint. It amounts to a cosmic false naming. It misnames the mystery of evil, casting it

35

into the distorted mold of the myth of feminine evil. In this way images and conceptualizations about evil are thrown out of focus and its deepest dimensions are not really confronted." [2]

In this chapter we will look at three facets of the long association of the female with evil: the denigration of the body and its functions, the notion that demonic forces work through the feminine unconscious, and the pernicious scapegoating of women in myths of the Fall. In each of these sections I will try to foreshadow themes in the later investigation of evil from a feminine standpoint.

WOMAN = BODY

The feminine has a long association with matter and nature. From the days of Aristotle nature and body have been demeaned in favor of spirit and mind. The Judeo-Christian tradition has not only maintained this order of values but hardened it by accepting Aristotle's most damaging charge against female nature—a fundamental weakness in morality. In this tradition it is not just a lack of logicality that bars women from ethical debate, nor is it simply that woman's goodness is innate and unconscious so that it need not be articulated and might even be endangered by strenuous attempts at articulation, as Kant apparently thought. Although both views persist, the view that has done the greatest mischief was adopted readily by institutional religion. A mere lack of logic might, after all, be remedied in time by persistent efforts at education. Further, if it were truly believed that women possessed an unconscious goodness of the sort I will discuss in chapter 3, it would be reasonable to follow their lead in moral matters and even attempt an induction of feminine qualities in males. But if women are fundamentally deprived of moral sense, giving them more knowledge and power could only lead to depravity. What little goodness they possess must be confined to the realm in which it occurs naturally—that of home and children. In this setting the "law of kindness" can safely be allowed to function. Outside of this setting conscious logical thought by properly endowed moral (male) agents must settle moral matters.

What really bars women from ethical debate in this long tradition is not their minds but their bodies. The fear of women as physical bodies is older than the Judeo-Christian tradition. I noted in the first chapter that menstruation was associated with defilement and therefore came under the first known taboo. The menstruating woman was thought to be infected with an evil spirit or to be paying the price for an essential evil that is part of her nature (later menstruation would be known as "the curse"). Under either belief, associating with her is likely to induce evil effects. After noting how widespread the association of menstruation with evil has been, Harding says, "The question we must ask, however, is what is this 'evil' which has entered into the woman and how does it work?" She goes on to argue that primitive people were at one time almost certainly subject to the same instinctive mating habits as animals, and thus the menstruating female represented an enormous danger to emerging rationality.

> For the men of the tribe might dance all night to concentrate their attention on the coming hunt but if the party met a menstruating woman as they started out, weapons and determination would be thrown aside together. Anything which could so arouse their untamed desire must be considered an "evil". The men of the tribe would be compelled to protect themselves by segregating the dangerous female, and in this way protect themselves also from the devastating effect of their own sexuality.[3]

There are, to be sure, alternative accounts of women's periodic isolation, and some of these reveal a collective female sigh of relief to be free, at least cyclically, from male demands. But in Harding's account (the standard thesis) women serve as scapegoats for the evil men fear in themselves. Understandably, precautions would have to be taken against that evil (and women) at a time when human understanding was primitive. The scapegoat syndrome appears again and again and is certainly seen in the myth of Eve and Adam. Mary Daly refers to Erich Neumann's discussion of the scapegoat phenomenon:

> For "mass man," as for primitives, evil cannot be acknowledged as one's own evil, since consciousness is too weakly developed to deal with such an internal conflict. Therefore, evil is experienced as something alien. The outcast role of the alien is important as an object for the projection of the "shadow" (our own unconscious counterpersonality), so that this can be exteriorized and destroyed.[4]

Given superior size, strength, and mobility, men found it relatively easy to project much of their weakness onto women as evil. Besides the monumental injustice to women, this projection has led to a prolonged misunderstanding of evil and, as Daly points out, a misplaced emphasis in its discussion and treatment. Daly also says, "Repudiation of the scapegoat role and the myth of the Fall by the primordial scapegoats may be the dawn of real confrontation with the mystery of evil." [5] Overcoming the temptation to project evil onto others will be an important theme as we attempt an alternative description of evil.

The primitive fear of menstruating women infected both Judaic and Christian thought. The Old Testament contains many references to "uncleanness," a continuation of the mythic notion of defilement that Ricoeur discusses, and the Christian church extended the concept to include sexual intercourse and birth. The old fears, beliefs, and taboos were institutionalized in practices with only slightly different rationales. Superstition and ritual sustained each other. Eleanor Mc-Laughlin refers to the resulting "demonization of sex,"

> the common beliefs that no Christian should receive the eucharist the morning after he or she had sexual relations, or that a menstruating woman should not receive communion, or even enter a church. Menstrual blood was thought to be attractive to devils and unclean spirits, and a menstruating woman would by her presence sour milk and kill the grass she walked upon. . . . Similar views on the uncleanness and spiritual danger of the natural sexual functions of the female are implied in the service of the "Churching of Women" that followed childbirth. [6]

Clearly the new religion had difficulty moving away from its primitive beliefs and rites. It is important to understand, however, that the evil associated with menstruation in primitive times was not a direct accusation of women as evil. Menstruation was not something visited on women *because* they were basically evil, but rather a manifestation of evil in the universe. As such, enormous power was inherent in menstruation. Harding writes of the "magic power of menstrual blood":

> There are many records of its being used as a potent healing charm resorted to in extreme illness. In other cases the destructive effect of the menstruating woman may be used in a positive way, as, for instance, when a girl in that condition is made to run naked around a harvest field infested with caterpillars. . . . In these cases the destructive power is turned against the evil, while the crops are protected from harm. [7]

We see here again both the enormous power attributed to the feminine in primitive thought and the psychologically healthy acceptance of evil as part of the prelapsarian condition. Even goddesses were thought to menstruate (the early female deities were not all spirit!), and the full moon was thought to be the time of menstruation for

Ishtar, moon goddess of Babylon. Interestingly, this day was called "sabbatu," or evil day, and is the forerunner of the Sabbath. Thus initially the Sabbath was not merely a day of well-deserved rest and worship, but one on which all projects were prohibited because they were thought to be foredoomed by evil.[8] Biblical accounts attest to the perceived power of the great goddesses (although they are often masculinized), and it seems likely that many of the slaughters Yahweh ordered were violent attempts to overthrow feminine deities and to subjugate women.[9]

It is interesting to note, and we will see the theme repeated, that Hebrew thought often proceeded along the lines of polarities and reversals. Not only did the evil day become a sacred one, but also the ancient sign of immortality and wisdom—the serpent—became a symbol of evil and destruction. Woman (Eve) was born of man (Adam), the mystery of menstruation became a curse, and the tree of life and wisdom now tempted humankind to the destructive knowledge of good and evil.

Fear and denigration of the female body and its functions persist today. In chapter 3 we will hear Harding speak of the "primordial slime" of female beginnings. Margery Collins and Christine Pierce accuse Sartre too of identifying the female with holes and slime.[10] Sartre finds female sexuality obscene and the sex act itself the "castration of the man."[11] This attitude is clearly reminiscent of the ancient fear of momentary irrationality accompanying sexual ecstasy. So strong is the traditional fear that Sartre forgets his own major thesis. As Pierce comments, "A philosopher well known for denying the existence of an a priori human nature maintains that women possess a fixed nature [the In-itself], determined by their unfortunate sexual anatomy, which limits them to roles approximating the nonconscious, unliberated Being-in-itself." Pierce notes, further, that Sartre identified the human body, male or female, as "one of the strongest sources of nausea" because it is subject to contingencies of all sorts and is laid waste by time—in contrast with clean, sharp consciousness and perpetual logic. Still, observes Pierce, Sartre expressed exceptional disgust with *female* anatomy. He wrote on the obscenity of holes, not on "the obscenity of dangling."[12]

I should mention that this last comment represents a temptation for women scholars, who have, naturally, an inclination to strike back, to match obscenity with obscenity, to replace masculine deities with feminine, to interchange master and slave. But such responses would be a terrible mistake and could not possibly lead to a redefinition of evil and beyond that to a transformed moral world. Not only must we deny the obscenity of female bodies, but we must also deny the obscenity of physical bodies entirely. Perhaps at some far future stage of evolution we will become disembodied consciousnesses or consciousnesses with renewable bodies, but until that happens (if it ever does) we must love our bodies as integral parts of ourselves. Indeed, as we will see in a moment, a great strength of women has been that they have consistently cared for the physical bodies of their loved ones.

In sharp contrast to the usual feminine acceptance of physicality, saints of the church often hated and humiliated physical bodies—particularly their own. The body was thought to be the home of evil, the prison of the soul, needing continual castigation for the benefit of the spirit. Mary Daly quotes Simone de Beauvoir on the masochistic tendencies of female saints:

> St. Angela of Foligno tells us that she drank with delight the water in which she had just washed lepers' hands and feet. . . . We know that Marie Alacoque cleaned up vomit of a patient with her tongue; and in her biography she described the joy she felt when she filled her mouth with the excrement of a man sick with diarrhea; Jesus rewarded her when she held her lips pressed against his Sacred Heart for three hours.[13]

Clearly these disgusting acts were not meant to glorify the body, nor could they have brought much comfort to those in need of care and nursing. They were totally self-serving exercises meant to win the greatest possible rewards for the saintly soul at the most obvious expense of the earthly body. Even the other as one cared for was reduced to the status of instrument for the glorification of the tender nurse's soul. In acts of this sort both women and men contributed to the ratification of evil.

Although a distrust of the body is pervasive in Catholic tradition, a contradictory veneration of the body can also be found. Human personality and identity have been associated with both body and soul, and the feared corruption of the body has been accepted as the just desert of all descendants of Adam. The greatest reward of Jesus and Mary was the assumption of their whole beings—bodies and souls—into heaven, although Jesus "ascended" on his own power and

Mary had to be "assumed." For ordinary beings putrefaction is the natural course of events, and anyone seeking to avoid it by cremation or other means is thought to be guilty of defying God's sentence on Adam, "To dust you will return."[14] Further, wholeness of the body—virginity—has been greatly extolled as a means to purity of soul.

The Protestant Reformation brought some (temporary) alleviation of the spiritual illness of despising the body. Marriage and sexual union became respectable.[15] But even in this tradition virginity continued to be associated with the highest calling for men, and spirit was clearly more precious than body. Also for women the new celebration of marriage meant a renewed emphasis on motherhood as a vocation. The insistence on motherhood as woman's "glory" led eventually to the Victorian myth that I will discuss in the next chapter. The new era brought special pains to intelligent women who could not help seeing that their "glory" was very much a second-class achievement, however flowery the language describing it. Biography and fiction are replete with examples.

Pearl S. Buck, in the Nobel Prize–winning biographies of her parents, reveals the pain and confusion that persisted well into this century. Her father, a Presbyterian minister, valued soul and spirit above all else; her mother ministered to the bodies and earthly minds of her children and parishioners. (Indeed, Buck said she had intended to call the double volume "The Spirit and the Flesh.") All of life's events affected Buck's parents differently, but the deaths of children brought forth their greatest conflict. Her father, called Andrew in the biographies, was firm in saying, "Doubtless it was the Lord's will and the child is safe in heaven." His wife, Carie, in sympathetic agony for the mother, answered, "Oh, and do you think this fills the mother's heart and arms?" Then she immediately apologized—so confused was she about her moral status in a body-hating society and church. Her daughter wrote: "Once I heard someone say of another's dead child, 'The body is nothing now, when the soul is gone.' But Carie said simply, 'Is the body nothing? I loved my children's bodies. I could never bear to see them laid into earth. I made their bodies and cared for them and washed them and clothed them and tended them. They were precious bodies.' "[16]

This earthy, heroic woman, who lost four of her seven children in a foreign land (China) while her husband sought to save souls, never entirely lost her love of the physical world. Indeed, in her dying days she seemed almost sure that she had been right all along and her husband wrong. Watching her nurse perform a fox-trot (which she had never seen and therefore playfully requested in her liberated status as one dying), she said: "Well that's a pretty thing—so graceful and light. I should not be surprised if Andrew is all wrong about God. I believe one ought to choose the happy, bright things of life, like dancing and laughter and beauty. I think if I had it to do over again I would choose these instead of thinking them sinful. Who knows?—God might like them?" [17]

This woman, like most we will encounter, cared for particular others in their particular situations. As we will see, the Catholic church has considered affection for particular others—encouraging "particular friendships"—an impediment to the proper devotion of clerics and other religious to God. Although Protestant denominations have taken a somewhat different stand on particular others, both her church and her husband induced in Carie continual feelings of guilt for her appreciation and love of earthly companions. Unlike her husband, she was primarily concerned not with principles, but with persons. When a man and his two wives wanted to join the church, Carie sympathized with the second wife. But Andrew insisted that Mr. Ling would have to send his concubine away if he wanted to join the church. Carie protested, "But the poor woman has nowhere to go— it's not *her* fault!" [18] Andrew, of course, did not relent. Principles came first in his life.

Caring for the physical and emotional welfare of others has been basic to the feminine experience. It is important to affirm that this caring has not developed solely from a "slave mentality"—even though that interpretation is possible and probably deserves a thorough exploration in its own right. [19] Rather, it has been closely tied to the instinctive protection of offspring and, as part of that natural project, to the care of men. Judith Hauptman notes that caring for a man's welfare seems to be the primary mission of women in biblical and Talmudic accounts:

> Supporting these contentions, the Talmud cites many references to woman's solicitous care of man. Rabbi Eleazar's wife cooked him sixty different kinds of food to help him repair his health. . . . When Mar Ukba and his wife sought a hiding place and found it in a hot oven, he burned his legs on the embers, and she suggested that he rest his feet on hers to alleviate his suffering. This devoted care is also seen in the ways that rabbis' wives devised to serve their husbands food and pour their

wine during the wives' menstrual periods, when contact between husband and wife was forbidden.[20]

We see here clear examples of what we must change in our perspective on evil. Woman—the seductress, the illogical, the unconscious, the amoral—has often seen human suffering and misery as states to alleviate. To aggravate them is, for her, to commit evil. When principles encourage the infliction or maintenance of pain, she must reject them in favor of persons and their needs. We will see examples of this rejection over and over again, but in almost all cases the women who are heroic enough to perform the deeds of rejection still suffer pangs of guilt induced by the patristic system of morality. In William Faulkner's *The Unvanquished,* for example, Granny engages in a regular business of stealing mules from the Yankee army and selling them back. Apologizing to God, she points out that she did not sin for gain or greed. Rather, she sinned first for justice (a traditional and perhaps even masculine justification) and, after that, out of compassion—to feed and clothe God's creatures. Staunchly she admits that she held back some of the booty to care for her own dependents. Granny too exhibits a painful combination of loving independence and guilty doubt.[21]

In Carie and Granny we see the seeds of a truly feminine ethic—one that moves boldly beyond justice to the alleviation of human suffering. But sadly the seeds spring up dwarfed and warped, contaminated by the traditional overdose of fertilizer—sin and guilt.

At this point I mean only to foreshadow the discussion on principles and the redefinition of evil. I have aimed in this section to describe the age-old hatred of body and physical functions that has pervaded moral-religious thought. Woman as body, as vessel, has been worshiped, coveted, feared, and hated. The sexual passion of man has been explained by the seductive and insatiable desires of woman, and thus everything naturally related to woman has been morally suspect. Not only have we lost the eloquent feminine voice in moral matters, but by establishing half the human race as scapegoat we have failed to come to grips with the problem of evil.

WITCHES

In chapter 3 we will look at the long history of association between the feminine and the unconscious and at how Jung and his disciples maintained and enhanced that association into this century. Not only has female goodness been thought of as largely unconscious, but female evil too has often been construed this way. On first glance such an approach might appear to liberate women from the sort of moral responsibility demanded of men. But this bright side is sorely deceiving. A genuine moral agent, after all, may respond to reason and be rehabilitated; a physical body invaded by devils and demons must be exorcised or destroyed.

Some writers now claim that it is historically plausible to say that as many as nine million women may have been destroyed as witches during the European witch craze (from the late fifteenth to the mid-eighteenth centuries),[22] but this figure is far greater than historical studies have been able to document. Joseph Klaits notes that "over ten thousand cases have been verified," but he also remarks that responsible estimates range much higher.[23] Barbara Ehrenreich and Deirdre English agree with Daly that estimates run into the millions, but they do not cite sources.[24] Whatever the actual figures, many thousands were certainly accused, tortured, and executed, and there is agreement that 80 to 90 percent of the victims were women.

The witch craze, which reached its height in the sixteenth and seventeenth centuries, revived and exaggerated earlier associations of women and evil. McLaughlin notes that as early as the thirteenth century even the prince of this world, Mundus, was transformed from his original masculine form into Frau Welt, a creature

> with the same courtly aristocratic beckoning smile and hand seen from the front, and a behind eaten through by the creatures of hell and the grave. She is often accompanied by the iconographical symbol of fleshly lust, the goat, and sometimes appears as a fanciful creature, half human, half animal, the demonic devil's wife, who, just like the beauteous courtly lady, leads men to their destruction through preying on the lusts of the flesh.

McLaughlin speculates about the sources of this transformation, noting—I think significantly—that it occurred at a time "when the developing cult of the Virgin and the love ethic of the Goliards were supposed to have injected some positive notes into the medieval picture of the female sex." She writes:

> Whatever further research concludes with respect to this interesting problem, *Frau Welt* remains a public symbol of the high medieval Chris-

tian association of the feminine with the evils of sensuality and self-indulgence, for in *Frau Welt* the woman personifies worldly evil, that "materiality" and "fleshiness" which the theological tradition has identified with womanhood.[25]

Frau Welt, of course, dates from well before the witch craze. Witch hunting arose out of a new and complex combination of religious, social, and political changes. Were it not for the overwhelming proportion of females accused of witchcraft, we might even assume that the witch craze was a gender-neutral preoccupation of religious fanatics with supernatural evil. Indeed, even the persecutors felt the need to explain the imbalance. Once again the old arguments about female intellectual inferiority surfaced. But the persecutors also held that women were more sensitive to the supernatural; this sensitivity, coupled with materiality and sensuality, made it likely that more women than men would receive and entertain devils and demons. More than one hypothesis is required here, for obviously if women were more sensitive to the supernatural and were also *good,* the powers that spoke to them could have been authorized by God, as Joan of Arc claimed. Therefore it was imperative to believe that women lacked a fundamental moral sense and so would be quite as receptive to evil voices as to good ones—indeed more so to evil ones, since women's bodies propelled them to an interest in the sensual.

Mary Daly suggests another side of the story. The women accused of witchcraft may have threatened the power of the patriarchy. Many of these women were midwives and healers; in an age of growing male interest in medicine, they presented an actual threat to male credibility. Ehrenreich and English also suggest a medical conspiracy as part of the motivation for witch hunting. Their theory sounds plausible, but it seems even more likely that the craze served to remind women of their need for the protection of a strong male. Most of the women accused and convicted had, significantly, no such protection. Daly also suggests that the movement was a final—and terrifyingly successful—attempt to stamp out the last vestiges of a pagan (female) religion.[26]

The reasons that Daly, Ehrenreich, English, and other feminists put forward are credible given the social changes and misogyny of early modern times. Klaits remarks: "The witch craze often has been described as one of the most terrible instances of man's inhumanity to man. But more accurate is the formulation by gender, not genus: witch trials exemplify men's inhumanity to women. The sexually powerful and menacing witch figure was nearly always portrayed as a female." [27]

But misogyny cannot have been the whole cause of witch hunting. Other forces were also at work. As Klaits explains, elite members of society promoted the association of magic and witchcraft with heresy. A physical separation was growing between wealthy and poor members of society, and whereas both believed in magic and spirits, the poor were more likely to be accused of using such powers. The elites, perhaps seeking ways to consolidate their own political and economic power, sought to stamp out "superstition" in the masses. Cooperating with church reformers in Catholic and Protestant churches, educated elites, perhaps only semiconsciously, found a way to control women, dissenters, and the poor. The drive to control medicine may well have been part of such a program. To subdue folk healers would certainly have required powerful methods, and associating witchcraft with heresy—with serving the devil—made it a far greater crime than the ordinary malefice with which it had been linked in medieval times.

Another factor contributing to the witch craze was the widespread guilt provoked by religious reformation. Everywhere preachers bombarded people with fiery sermons about their sinfulness. The devil was ubiquitous and unflagging in his attempts to capture souls. Even priests, who had indulged without great penalties in pleasures of the flesh during the Middle Ages, were now threatened with eternal damnation for yielding to carnal temptations. In an age stricken with guilt, the most guilty and powerful find ways to project their guilt onto the less powerful. Klaits's comments on this feature of the witch craze are important in the context of our examination of evil:

> The rise and decline of witch trials can also illuminate other matters that remain tragically current. Plainly, we are not dealing with obsolete issues when we consider such problems as the sorts of intolerance, manifestations of prejudice against women and minorities, the use of torture by authoritarian rulers, and attempts by religious or political ideologues to impose their values on society. This is why the term "early modern" is an appropriate one for the era of the witch craze. The sixteenth and seventeenth centuries were "early" in the long-term development of today's historical patterns, but the continuation of such patterns shows that these centuries were "modern," too.[28]

Another aspect of early modern life pertinent to this discussion is the rise of individualism. This ideology was clearly masculine in that women were still thought to be pretty much interchangeable. Woman became a creature even more separate from man, and as liberal individualism developed, woman-hating became deeply entrenched in Western culture. Indeed, we may consider the explicit and implicit misogyny of fin de siècle culture as Bram Dijkstra recently described it a logical culmination of the steady rise of ethical and political individualism.[29]

Individualism brought an increased fear of death, and the renewed fear of judgment encouraged the repression of sexual impulses. The combination of these and other factors led to a new association of death with violence and sexuality. Philippe Ariès writes:

> Death is no longer a peaceful event. As we have seen, only three out of all the deaths in Camus [the reference is to Bishop Camus] were from natural causes. Nor is death any longer a moment of moral and psychological concentration, as it was in the *artes moriendi*. Death has become inseparable from violence and pain. It is no longer *finis vitae*, but, in Rousset's words, "a rending away from life, a long gasping cry, an agony hacked into many fragments." These violent scenes excited spectators and aroused primitive forces whose sexual nature seems obvious today.[30]

Fear, guilt, and violence were all mixed up with sexuality. Male prosecutors of witches often supervised the undressing of accused women and watched closely as the women's genitals were carefully examined for the confirmatory witches' mark. Torture was regularly used to obtain confessions and indeed was rationalized as a means of asking God to intervene for the innocent under trial.[31] One of the most dreadful legacies of theodicy is operating here: God the just would visit intolerable pain only on those who deserve it, and if God condemns unrepentant sinners to eternal suffering, then righteous men are certainly justified in inflicting pain to destroy evil and save souls. Some of the witch prosecutors really did seem to care deeply about the salvation of their victims. Again, the deep denial of interest in the body and material things led to terrible eruptions of distorted sexuality in the form of violence.

Although the centuries of witch hunting were a terrible time for women, they were the last age in which the ancient power of women—real or imagined—received explicit recognition. By the time we get to the Jungians, the classical feminine powers are relegated to antiquity. Indeed, modern women are castigated for losing touch with the feminine principle and thus with their greatest power. But we have largely forgotten—or at least greatly de-emphasized—that this enormous feminine power involved both creation and destruction. Harding reminds us that "the Moon Goddess is, in literal fact, the mother of all living things and yet, strange though it may seem, not only is she the life-giver but also the destroyer. She creates all life on earth, and then comes the flood, which overwhelms it. And this flood is her doing." [32]

Modern women are not only stripped of this divine power, but they are simultaneously accused of a new evil—losing their essential femininity in vain attempts to emulate masculine ways of being in the world. Indeed, this orientation guides even Harding's work.[33] In the next section, we see how the feminine unconscious can combat evil.

DEMONS, DÜMMLINGS, AND FAIR MAIDENS

In fairy tales and legends we find the themes of feminine unconscious victory over evil and masculine conscious heroism. The association between the fair maiden and the innocent youngest brother—or "dümmling"—manifests this theme. Both women and men are often favored with miraculous interventions as long as they are innocent, stupid, and friendly. Indeed, animals, another clearly unconscious group, frequently effect such interventions. It is as though the writers of these stories longed for effortless security and perhaps even envied the abiding human love females evince for their children. How lovely it would be, these stories suggest, if something in the supernatural had the same concern for innocent welfare that mothers have for their offspring! But consciousnesses as yet poorly developed could hardly acknowledge the loving wisdom of the mother. Men longed to be better but could not acknowledge actual moral behavior in any but the most consciously and physically powerful. Marie-Louise von Franz, a Jungian, sees fairy tales in part as attempts to compensate for the overemphasis on masculine prowess in the real world. Commenting on the need for a favored character to be "feminine," she says:

> Right from the beginning the disease has been the overemphasis on masculinity, so we see why being a hero would be wrong [for the favored youngest brother]: it would be again on the line of the old ruling attitude, stressing masculinity against instinct and love and the feminine principle. The youngest has a better chance by having such a shabby

horse, which deprives him of the possibility of a masculine heroic attitude.[34]

Examining the same story, we see that the dümmling-hero also shows kindness to a raven, a salmon, and a wolf. Indeed, in the last case he allows a starving wolf to eat his good horse. We might interpret this action as a complete sacrifice of masculinity to the unconscious good of the feminine. But von Franz notes that in this and other stories fear of the wolf pulls things in another direction. A different sort of feminine relation to the wolf appears, says von Franz, in the "strange devouring attitude women can have when possessed by the animus." We note here a fundamental disservice that Jungian analysis has done to women, an issue we will look at in greater depth in chapter 3. Act unconsciously, goes the message to women, and all will be well; begin to think, lay your own plans, conquer your own realms, and evil has taken possession of you. The wolf-woman, then, "wants really to eat the whole world." [35]

In addition to themes of unconscious evil and the unconscious triumph of good over evil is a theme of semiconscious adaptation to—or coping with—the powers of evil. This adaptation often involves the recognition of a mixture of good and evil in deities and other powerful figures. The Russian fairy tale "The Beautiful Wassilissa" powerfully exemplifies this theme, and, as we noted in chapter 1, so does the story of Job. Von Franz analyzes the Wassilissa story in great detail. Wassilissa's wicked stepmother and stepsisters force the young woman to encounter the dreaded Baba-Yaga, a great witch who regularly gobbles up human beings who cross her path. Wassilissa is terrified, of course, but she is not entirely unprepared. She takes with her the blessing of her deceased mother and a magic doll that was part of her legacy. Here we see a combination of wisdom and simplicity. Wassilissa has sense enough to know that she cannot survive an encounter with Baba-Yaga alone. She must have help, and the help comes through the powerful "good aspect" of the feminine embodied in the magic doll. A contest ensues between the forces of good and the forces of evil, and the good win, but in part their victory is due to something good in Baba-Yaga herself. She is not totally evil.

In addition to the theme of the mixed deity, we find in the Wassilissa story another important example of the power of silence in the presence of ambiguous evil. Wassilissa is careful not to ask questions that might awaken the evil side of Baba-Yaga. Like Job, Wassilissa puts a hand over her own mouth. Baba-Yaga has just enough good in her to be somewhat ashamed of her evil deeds, and she does not want to be reminded of them.

Sometimes, as we have seen, women or dümmlings win out because of innocence, silence, and miraculous intervention. But more often women need the help of a male hero. They cannot always turn evil aside by ignoring it. In the story of Snow White and Rose Red, their charity toward the wicked dwarf brings them repeated grief. But von Franz does not credit them with feminine charity; rather she says they are "silly sentimentalists," and so they must be rescued by a male hero who slays the dwarf.[36] From a Jungian view we might conclude that fighting evil requires a fine balance of the feminine and the masculine, and such interpretations of fairy tales and legends illustrate this balance nicely.

What is entirely missing from these accounts is the possibility of genuine feminine *consciousness* at work in response to evil. Another way of looking at the Baba-Yaga story is to credit Wassilissa with attributing the best possible motive to Baba-Yaga, responding to something not-evil that resided in her along with the more dominant propensities for horrible destruction. That conscious response can bring out the best in someone, if only temporarily, is a promising interpretation from the standpoint of women.[37] To develop this idea fully is an important task for a morality of evil. It involves a recognition that good and evil are mixed in humans and deities alike, that it is rational and courageous to accept both dependency and initiative in our approach to life's problems, and that it takes great conscious effort to subdue evil by living with it rather than stirring it up in misguided attempts to overcome it once and for all. Stories like the Wassilissa tale can help build new feminist interpretations of good and evil.

Similarly, female story writers might turn Snow White and Rose Red into heroes by complicating the story somewhat. The typically masculine tradition in myth, religion, and science gives us dichotomies and hierarchies. In the battle against evil the Christian tradition vacillates wildly between masculine authoritarian toughness ("Praise the Lord and pass the ammunition") and a gentle "feminine" turning of the other cheek that can either be admired as too idealistic or scorned as part of a slave mentality. But a truly feminine stance rejects both poles of the dichotomy: it would seek to prevent a second blow without striking back in violence. Snow White and Rose Red might have rescued the dwarf but kept him immobilized or under guard, or they might have exacted a magical self-destruct promise from him so that, in essence, he would destroy himself if he betrayed them again. They might even have rehabilitated him by persistent and firm efforts to bring out the best in him.

An attempt to describe real evil and real good might, by traditional literary standards, be either boring or a stinging challenge to standard morality. Simone Weil notes, for example, that "imaginary evil is romantic and varied; real evil is gloomy, monotonous, barren, boring. Imaginary good is boring; real good is always new, marvelous, intoxicating. Therefore 'imaginative literature' is either boring or immoral." [38] But we have not explored feminine versions of myth and legend to their full extent. The possibilities are unlimited once we have broken through the masculine mentality we have inherited, and the eventual reward might be a fuller description of human consciousness.

In closing this brief discussion of women in fairy tales, we note that it has added something to our previous discussion of women and evil. The account of witchcraft described women as both unconsciously evil (receptive as bodies) and consciously evil (receptive in mind). "When a woman thinks alone, she thinks evil," said the authors of the notorious *Malleus Maleficarum*.[39] In fairy tales the fair maiden often does not think at all. Instead she follows an unconscious path of goodness that helps her overcome evil. That evil is often at the same time personified as a wicked witch illustrates men's deep-seated belief in the magical connection of women to evil powers that can be used, paradoxically, for either good or evil.

THE FALL

Now we come to the unkindest cut of all—the pernicious notion that woman, through a grievous lack of moral sensitivity or will, caused the Fall of Man by accepting the serpent's enticement and tempting Adam to eat the forbidden fruit. Although parts of the "loss-of-paradise" myth almost certainly derived from earlier cultures, the Judaic versions single out woman as peculiarly culpable, and, of course, Christian writers have embraced these versions as well. The early African church father Tertullian (ca. A.D. 160–220) made it clear how the early church regarded females in a well-known admonition to women:

> Do you not know that each of you is Eve? The sentence of God on this sex of yours lives in this age: the guilt must of necessity live too. *You* are the Devil's gateway. *You* are the unsealer of that forbidden tree. *You* are the first deserter of the divine Law. *You* are she who persuaded him whom the Devil was not valiant enough to attack. *You* destroyed so easily God's image man. On account of your desert, that is death, even the Son of God had to die.[40]

To some people—even to some feminists—time and space given to an ancient and discredited myth could be better devoted to current problems such as job discrimination, poverty, and abortion. In view of the history we have been considering, this dismissal seems wrong, and those who make such statements overlook the enormous influence of the myth. According to Mary Daly, whom I quoted at the beginning of this chapter in connection with the myth and its resultant misnaming of evil: "The myth has in fact affected doctrines and laws that concern women's status in society and it has contributed to the mindset of those who continue to grind out biased, male-centered ethical theories. . . . The myth undergirds destructive patterns in the fabric of our culture."[41]

Because it has contributed to a mind-set and to patterns in our culture, it should be the focus of intensive educational criticism. It has played an enormous role in the subordination of women and thus in shaping the present status of women; yet our schools give little or no attention to this vital bit of female history. Why not? Would free and critical discussion of this damaging myth be a violation of our constitutional insistence on the separation of church and state? Consider what an affirmative answer to this question means! If critical discussion of the myth in school would constitute such a violation, then we must acknowledge that the "myth" is still an accepted religious doctrine. If our answer is no, then clearly we must have other reasons for neglecting the topic. I will elaborate on this and other suppressed conflicts in chapter 9.

We have at least two good reasons for studying and analyzing the myth of Eve and the Fall: its continuing effects on present patterns of thought and social structure and its influence on traditional conceptions of evil. These two reasons are interrelated. Part of our contemporary mind-set includes conceptions of evil that unfailingly depend on scapegoats—on conceptions of evil residing in the other and on notions that the other is a more likely agent of evil than oneself.

How did the myth arise, and what should women know about it? Merlin Stone gives a fascinating account of the likely political and social setting in which the myth played an instrumental role.[42] The ancient tribes of Israel competed for land and resources with people who worshiped "pagan idols,"—actually the Great Goddess known by such names as Ashtoreth, Inanna, Asherah, Ishtar, and Hathor. From surviving idols, reliefs, and other artifacts we know that the goddess was associated with sexual pleasure, reproduction, prophecy, serpents, and fig trees. From this list alone we obtain a glimpse of the characters and the scenario that would compose the myth.

In casting the serpent as evildoer, Judaic writers overturned a powerful earlier tradition that associated snakes with " 'wisdom' (magic), immortality, and fertility. As such they were the special companions of women, and often guarded earthly or celestial gardens of delight." [43]

Clearly the ancient goddess religions were earthy in the sense that they recognized sexuality in both humans and deities. Many "pagan" idols, for example, have well-developed breasts and sometimes bellies swollen with pregnancy. A religion that recognized the creative powers of female sexuality was likely to attract both women and men, albeit for different reasons. Therefore this religion had to be stamped out, and all its accomplishments and manifestations had to be tabooed or forbidden under sacred law. John Anthony Phillips discusses the centrality of sexual concerns in the story of Eve:

> Eve's sexuality is of special concern in the Western tradition. The Fall is regarded (whether literally or metaphorically) as a sexual event. Eve is guilty of wishing to be in control of her own sexual life. Some very deep, partially unarticulated fears are behind the male insistence that she be denied the freedom to make her own decisions about her bodily life. The notion of sexual renunciation, which is thrown into high relief by the Roman Catholic ideal of celibacy, is central to Christianity. As the Mother of All the Living, Eve has the power to deny life, and she must be convinced by religious and civil law that she cannot use this power. Therefore in Roman Catholicism the image of the obedient and dutiful Second Eve, the Virgin Mary, is held up to her, and in Protestantism the ideal of the Christian Mother is urged upon her.[44]

Even the suggestion of feminine deity severely threatens patriarchal tribes. Not only must they destroy the (pagan) deity, but they must also eliminate any illusion that woman could survive without the protection of some man—who would own her and thus care for her as his special property. How better to do this than to convince women that they need salvation—first by a human male who would shelter them, and second by a god-man who would die for their sins?

Because the serpent figured prominently in the goddess religions, it too had to be destroyed. Stone writes: "It seems that in some lands all existence began with a serpent. Despite the insistent, perhaps hopeful, assumption that the serpent must have been regarded as a phallic symbol, it appears to have been primarily revered as a female in the Near and Middle East and generally linked to wisdom and prophetic counsel rather than fertility and growth as is so often suggested." Statues and reliefs of the ancient goddesses often display serpents in the background or entwined about the goddesses themselves. Further, Stone suggests as a real possibility that the living snakes priestesses kept in their temples contributed through their bites to the hallucinogenic states in which priestesses prophesied "out of their own heads." [45] Perhaps, then, the writers of the myth were reacting to historical conditions when they wrote of the serpent speaking to Eve.

Further, the serpent has a long association with the Moon Goddess and thus with renewal. Both the moon through its cycles and the snake through its shedding become periodically new and whole. Harding notes, "Primitive and ancient myths also relate that the gift of immortality was brought to men sometimes by the moon and sometimes by a serpent, in other cases the serpent reveals to men the virtue that is concealed in the fruit of the moon tree or in the soma drink which can be brewed from it." [46]

Not surprisingly, the patriarchs tried to alienate snakes and women. The myth has God saying directly to the snake, "I will put enmity between you and the woman and between your seed and her seed." [47] Yet the association of woman, serpent, and demonic power persists in contemporary literature. Nina Auerbach finds it a central theme in the Victorian imagination:

> The mermaids, serpent-women, and lamias who proliferate in the Victorian imagination suggest a triumph larger than themselves, whose roots lie in the antiquity so dear to nineteenth-century classicists. These creatures' iconographic invasion may typify the restoration of an earlier serpent woman, the Greek Medusa. In Hesiod's account, the paralyzing Medusa was decapitated by Perseus, who became a hero when he refused to look her in the face. Burne-Jones and his Victorian associates force us to look into the serpent-woman's face and to feel the mystery

of a power, endlessly mutilated and restored, of a woman with a demon's gifts.[48]

Although the power of women and serpents collaborating is still felt in literature, it is considered an evil power, one that all right-thinking men and women should avoid. Mary Daly quotes Marina Warner on the encounter of the snake with the Virgin Mary, who crushes it beneath her foot:

> In Christianity, the serpent has lost its primary character as a source of wisdom and eternity. It is above all the principal Christian symbol of evil, and when it sprawls under the Virgin's foot, it is not her direct attribute, representing her knowledge and power as it does in the snake-brandishing statue of the goddess of Minoan Crete, but illustrates her victory over evil.

When we consider the ancient relation between woman and snake, between moon periodicity, snake renewal, and menstruation, between snake and bodily wisdom, it is, as Daly comments, "horrifyingly significant" that the "Immaculately Conceived Virgin" is portrayed crushing the snake.[49] The image seems to call on Christian women to repudiate their earlier powers and to demean their own physical functions.

The precise role of snakes in the goddess religion lies shrouded in antiquity, and present interpretations must work through layer on layer of legend. What is clear to us today is that the Yahwist's choice of creation story (Eve created from Adam's rib rather than a simultaneous creation of man and woman) and its enthusiastic adoption by Jewish and Christian patriarchs led the way to a severely misogynist tradition. As Phillips comments, "It is indeed remarkable that it is Eve's creation, rather than her actions in the Garden, that are the occasion of this misogyny, and that this misogyny so often takes the form of relating the newly created woman to the serpent." Phillips next discusses a batch of legends that ignore both biblical accounts of creation and connect Eve directly to the serpent. In various legends Eve is created from Adam's tail, the devil's tail, or a dog's tail; in another she is created from the serpent's feet—neatly explaining why snakes have no feet. Phillips comments: "Certainly these writings must be regarded as heterodox or, at the least, typical of neither Judaism nor Christianity. But we cannot really understand the imaginations of more orthodox writers without establishing the "demon-Eve" tradition, and considering how tenaciously it gripped the imaginations of the shapers of Eve." [50]

The tree of knowledge, from which Eve dared to eat, bears a fruit that contains sexual knowledge. Why should it be so bad for human beings to have this sort of knowledge? Stone tells us that the sycamore fig, which is probably the tree of knowledge, was an important live symbol at the shrines of Astoreth. These trees represented the knowledge of life and the creative power of the goddess: "The sacred branch being passed around in the temple, as described by Ezekiel, may have been the manner in which the fruit was taken as 'communion.' According to Egyptian texts, to eat of this fruit was to eat of the flesh and the fluid of the Goddess, the patroness of sexual pleasure and reproduction." [51]

The ritual endured, Stone suggests, but its original meanings were destroyed. The myth of the Fall effectively estranges woman from her early power and symbols. It turns her great natural gifts into mortal evils and justifies her subordination to man: "Thy desire shall be to thy husband, and he shall rule over thee." (Genesis 3:16). Judaism and Christianity have both used it to keep women silent on moral matters and to place undue emphasis on sexuality in moral discussion. For example, throughout most of history it has been considered evil for a woman to commit adultery (an evil so great that at times it even merited death), but until comparatively recent times it has not been thought evil for a husband to beat his wife. Even now, I must note, the former transgression is more often associated with the word *immoral* than the latter. [52]

The aspect of the Fall story that attributes the introduction of evil into the world to woman resounds in the myths of many cultures. The story of Pandora, often recounted innocuously in school texts as "Pandora's Box," is an early example. Eva Cantarella describes the "ambiguous evil" that is woman according to Hesiod. In this account Zeus sent woman as a punishment to man. Zeus was angry because Prometheus had stolen fire from the gods and given it to man. We see here the theme of a god in whom both good and evil exist. Hesiod describes the result of Pandora's arrival: "The other thousand miseries fly among men. The earth is full of evils, and the sea is full of them. Diseases come to men in the day, and at night uninvited, bringing evils for mortals in silence, since Deviser Zeus took away their voices. So there is no way to escape the mind of Zeus." [53]

Pandora, as Hesiod describes her, is an ambiguous evil—beautiful, crafty, potentially useful, and seductive. In the Greek story Pandora is Zeus's instrument of punishment. She visits evil on men for the transgression of Prometheus, and Zeus is the giver of evil. The story does not attempt to describe the deity as all-good or without a part in natural evil. In contrast to woman's initial condition of goodness in the Fall story, the first woman in the Greek myth is created evil; that is, her fundamental purpose is to harm man. The same theme emerges in many of the heterodox stories Phillips recounts, and the pervasiveness of these stories must have colored the more generous biblical accounts and the traditions that grew up around them. Thus Christian writers well into the Middle Ages felt the need to explain why females were created.

The effort to control female sexuality appears in other religious traditions as well, although sexual pleasure is not always considered evil in itself. Muslims differ from Christians in their assessment of sexual pleasure as good—but they react in a similarly controlling fashion when it comes to allowing women to determine their own sexual lives. From the Muslim perspective, however, men should not avoid women as temptations to carnal activity, but rather should use them and satisfy them appropriately so that women will not indulge their illicit desires.[54] Thus the Koran counsels men to flee to their wives when sexual passions are aroused, and the lives of women are carefully managed so that the precious commodity of sex will be legally distributed.

As we saw earlier, the Adamic myth and the later idea of Original Sin inflicted great harm on women and men alike, although women have suffered most obviously and directly. In particular we might argue that these myths and the structures that grew up around them suppressed the moral development of men. The continual charge of generic and personal sin coupled with the righteous desire to overcome evil has surely played a role in the violence men have directed against those they considered evil. Having engaged in violence, men then have to rationalize it, and so the cycle continues and the violence escalates.

SUMMARY

I have described above the long association of women with the material and thus with evil. I have also discussed woman as an "ambiguous evil" and outlined the violent struggle to control women's sexuality. It is not surprising that women, considered inherently inferior in morality, have not been heard in moral philosophy. Traditional thought has linked women with that which harms or threatens us—that is, with evil—and the "us" so universally threatened is not humankind but literally mankind.

Modern women have only recently begun to challenge this ancient story, and the challenge gives birth to a new examination of evil. What discourages women from pursuing the challenge? As we will see next, the view of woman as evil counterbalances one of woman as naturally good, gentle, loving, and selfless. Further, there have been rewards for women who accept the latter description.

3

The Angel in the House

Woman has been associated in a stereotypical way with both good and evil. As an "angel in the house," woman has been credited with natural goodness, an innate allegiance to "a law of kindness." But this same description extols her as infantile, weak, and mindless—a creature in constant need of male supervision and protection. Undertones of sadism run throughout Coventry Patmore's hymn to the angel who is in reality a prisoner in the house she graces.[1] The alleged angel was an image that all Victorian women were supposed to internalize. Virginia Woolf described her struggle with the angel in unforgettable words:

> It was she who used to come between me and my paper when I was writing reviews. It was she who bothered me and wasted my time and so tormented me that at last I killed her. You who come of a younger and happier generation may not have heard of her—you may not know what I mean by The Angel in the House. . . . She was intensely sympathetic. She was immensely charming. She was utterly unselfish. She excelled in the difficult arts of family life. She sacrificed daily. If there was chicken, she took the leg; if there was a draught she sat in it—in short she was so constituted that she never had a mind or wish of her own, but preferred to sympathize always with the minds and wishes of others. Above all . . . she was pure.[2]

I need hardly say that such an angel would make critical reviewing—or any professional undertaking—a tough task. But if a woman accepts her role as angel gracefully, the myth goes, she can inspire men to all good things, even to the divine. Thus in recent centuries women have even been entrusted with the moral education of children, community charity, and the fundamental support of places of worship. Natural goodness notwithstanding, women's voices have seldom resounded in the public realm of moral debate. Women have spoken out on moral matters, as we will see, but they have often suffered ridicule for doing so, and men have frequently co-opted their most promising programs. Women have not made a dent in formal moral philosophy.

Confined to the home and subject to men's rule, the obedient woman has been an angel in the house; loose in the world or rebellious toward male domination, she becomes "the devil's gateway," an ambiguous evil indeed.

This chapter will examine the good side of women according to the men who have created the ideals of womanhood. This examination is important for several related reasons. Many women, perhaps most, have internalized the expectations described in these ideals and have come to depend on the rewards associated with meeting them. Other women—many contemporary feminists, for example—reject everything that goes with these male formulations because they see them as limiting women's autonomy and serving primarily to maintain patriarchal structures. But perhaps many of the qualities developed in a subordinate state are nonetheless worth cultivating, and so we must question how women can nurture such desirable qualities as they lead more autonomous lives. What Paulo Freire calls the strength that grows out of weakness is worth analyzing.[3] In particular, people who have been long subordinated may develop dependable and resilient forms of moral agency, and the view of evil from this perspective may be especially enlightening.

CLASSICAL AND JUNGIAN VIEWS OF THE FEMININE

Both Plato and Aristotle had something to say about women, but neither of them made any attempt to study women or women's nature seriously. For Plato woman was potentially equal to man, although weaker physically—a creature who possessed basic human attributes but to a lesser degree of perfection than her male counterpart. Women in Plato's *Republic* might become guardians, and as such they would receive the same education as future male guardians.[4] Only their physical weakness was to be taken into account, and somewhat less difficult tasks would therefore be assigned to them.

For all the appearance of equality between the sexes in the *Republic,* Plato's writing clearly reveals its androcentric origins. In recommending communal marriages, for example, Plato advises that "wives" be held in common by all the men; he does not speak of "spouses" held in common. Many such slips make it clear that he has a male world in mind; he speaks, for example, of "guardians' wives," even though some guardians would be women. Further, he uses masculine experience as the norm to which capable women must aspire if they would join the upper ranks, and in several of his other works—for example, *Laws* and *Timaeus*—he accepts the supremacy of men.

His plan for begetting and rearing children foreshadows an important contemporary argument among feminists. In insisting that fathers and even nursing mothers should be parents to all the children born of a particular marriage festival and that none should know their own children, he anticipates by centuries the kind of argument embraced by the feminists known as "women's libbers"—although Plato's was considerably more radical. Alison Jaggar refers to many radical feminists who might accept Plato's communal childbearing. She quotes Shulamith Firestone, for example, as recommending *"the freeing of women from the tyranny of their reproductive biology by every means available, and the diffusion of the childbearing and childrearing role to the society as a whole, men as well as women."* [5]

Other radical feminists glorify motherhood and would surely reject a Platonic communal arrangement if it sacrificed the great strengths and beauties of personal motherhood. Jane Alpert comments:

> Feminist culture is based on what is best and strongest in women, and as we begin to define ourselves as women, the qualities coming to the fore are the same ones a mother projects in the best kind of nurturing relationship to a child: empathy, intuitiveness, adaptability, awareness of growth as a process rather than as goal-ended, inventiveness, protective feeling toward others, and a capacity to respond emotionally as well as rationally.[6]

In these two statements we see clearly some elements of the conflict that modern women face in reflecting on their experience. Women generally seem to have closer and more intimate relationships with their children than men do and are more likely than men to define themselves in great part through parenting.[7] Whatever the reason for women's greater attachment and concern for children—whether the reason be biological, psychological, cultural, or a combination of these—it seems right to say that a policy separating mothers from their children does not arise out of the usual female experience. The policy maker, whether male or female, is clearly not speaking from experience in a community of female thinkers. He or she is instead condemning that experience as inimical to full personhood.

As we trace the development of Platonic thought into medieval Christianity, we find women frankly and firmly associated with nature and the material, and men associated with the mind and the spirit.[8] Plato's hierarchy of values branded the feminine (as nature and matter) inherently inferior to the masculine. Still, we find in Augustine, as in Plato, ambivalence in the judgment of women and a frequent insistence that men and women should be judged equally on such qualities as obedience and chastity and that both are the "children of God." The combination of equality of souls and devaluation of the body led to a debilitating emphasis on virginity for both men and women. We find a judgment in favor of virginity over marriage in Christian writings from the earliest times through the present.[9]

Aristotle dramatically underscores the association of woman with matter and man with soul. For him the male is clearly better, and women are deformed or incomplete males.[10] The male is active and causal in the world; the female's essence is a lack or inability. It is natural and proper, then, that the man should rule over his wife. Aristotle also foreshadows a position that has plagued women for centuries—women's moral inferiority to men. To be sure, Aristotle assigns different sorts of goodness to men and to women (and we must keep in mind that our modern notion of virtue did not yet exist), but the virtues he assigns to women are those of underlings and subjects, not those of rulers and leaders.[11] The subordinate status of women persists in religious investigations such as that of Thomas Aquinas, who draws directly on Aristotle when he asks whether woman—the misbegotten male—should even have been created.[12] But as I mentioned at the outset, neither Plato nor Aristotle studied the feminine itself. Both considered women because they exist as natural relatives of men, and one must look at them if one is to deliberate on the best life for men.

Views of the feminine as a distinct and positive essence come to us mainly through Carl Jung and his pupils. These views are important in two ways. First, Jung and his followers provide a vivid description of much that has been expected of and internalized by women. Second, Jung uses the feminine in outlining a morality of evil, and I will draw on this usage in later arguments. The Jungians describe a cluster of attributes that are identified as the essence of the feminine. Some of the attributes are negative and some of dubious status, and I will discuss these later. But many are admirable. These generally include the positive qualities of compassion, maternal caring or nurturance, receptivity, responsiveness, relatedness (human understanding), patience (especially with human frailty), and an appreciation for renewal and repetition. Although these qualities have been named over and over again for centuries as the positive essence of the feminine—and hence as the qualities best cultivated in women—we must remember that they have been analyzed and written about largely by men. Even if we accept these attributes as the "essence" of femininity (and we are tempted to do so gratefully—since at least they are positive), even if we feel that we have lived with their manifestation, we still need to examine closely how they have been described, valued, and employed to shape the lives of men and women. A question arises whether this distinct, positive, and complementary feminine essence is or is not a great improvement over Plato's sexless guardian or Aristotle's "misbegotten male."

Harding, for example, speaks as a disciple of Jung when she describes the "feminine principle" as "an essence, or inner law, not as a law that is imposed by a legal authority but rather using the term as it is used in science, where we speak of the law of gravity, the laws of mathematics, or the law of evolution." Even though masculine and feminine principles are held to be laws of nature, Harding says they can be violated. She explains:

> In the Western world this is so in regard to the essence or principle of masculine and feminine. Not infrequently we hear it affirmed that there is no essential difference between men and women, except the biological one. Many women have accepted this standpoint and have themselves done much to foster it. They have been content to be men in petticoats and so have lost touch with the feminine principle within themselves. This is perhaps the main cause of the unhappiness and emotional instability of today. For if woman is out of touch with the feminine principle, which dictates the laws of relatedness, she cannot take the lead in what is after all the feminine realm, that of human relationships.[13]

Here we find a theme perilously close to that of the scapegoat. That women should not be "men in petticoats"—an image reminiscent of Plato's female guardians exercising equal rights in a totally masculine world—strikes a sympathetic chord in many women. In the Jungians we find an appreciation of the feminine in and of itself. But if we want to raise the value of feminine attributes, it is problematic to identify the female essence with a feminine "principle," for such a move subordinates the feminine to the masculine at the outset. In a traditional theoretical framework, we must remember, principles are discerned and formulated under the guidance of Logos, not of Eros. But there is an even greater difficulty. The feminine principle, Eros, *defines* woman and commands submission and obedience, whereas the masculine principle, Logos, sets man free to define himself through rational thought and action. We are reminded once again of Aristotle's insistence on man as a causal agent in the world and woman as a creature with potential powers that remain "ineffective." In the Jungian framework feminine powers are not ineffective but rather *unconscious.*

One might object at this point that even if the Jungians seem to allow man to define himself and restrict woman to obedience to the feminine principle, religions that draw on earlier views often seem to deny self-definition to both sexes. Although most religions have technically denied this self-defining power even to man, they compensated for this apparent denial by creating God in man's image and depriving woman of her earlier sacred images. This move effectively restores to man his powers of self-definition. As the "image of God," man is expected to exercise his rationality in self-determination, but woman is doubly deprived—no longer the complete image of any recognized god and powerless as the subject of one who finds her inferior. This deprivation has induced a longing in women that cannot be filled by masculine religions. Christine Downing expresses that longing:

> To be fed only male images of the divine is to be badly malnourished. We are starved for images which recognize the sacredness of the feminine and the complexity, richness, and nurturing power of female energy. We hunger for images of human creativity and love inspired by the capacity of female bodies to give birth and nourish, for images of how humankind participates in the natural world suggested by reflection on the correspondences between menstrual rhythms and the moon's waking [*sic*] and waning.[14]

Here we see a longing that reflects partly woman's biological nature and partly her internalization of male-created archetypes. It anticipates a return to early female religions and a substitution of female rituals for the dominant male ones. If we see this return as but one of many options, we may properly consider it with a whole range of other possibilities. But if it is part of a feminist manifesto, it might well lead backward. We might, after all, decide after careful study that we should abandon ritualistic religion entirely. Downing, it seems to me, more nearly captures rational female longing when she continues:

We seek images that affirm that the love women receive from women, from mother, sister, daughter, lover, friend, reaches as deeply and is as trustworthy, necessary, and sustaining as is the love symbolized by father, brother, son, or husband. We long for images which name as authentically feminine courage, creativity, loyalty, and self-confidence, resilience and steadfastness, capacity for clear insight, inclination for solitude, and the intensity of passion.

Here again we see images of a powerful female model, but Downing's paragraph finishes on a note that may arouse concern: "We need images; we also need myths—for myths make concrete and popularize; they give us situations, plots, relationships. We need the goddess and we need the goddesses." [15]

Many women agree. Carol Christ wrote a powerful essay explaining why women need the goddess. First, she says, "Religions centered on the worship of a male God create 'moods' and 'motivations' that keep women in a state of psychological dependence on men and male authority, while at the same time legitimating the *political* and *social* authority of fathers and sons in the institutions of society." To establish new moods and motivations, the symbols and rituals of the goddess might be useful. "The 'mood' created by the symbol of the Goddess in triple aspect is one of positive, joyful affirmation of the female body and its cycles and acceptance of aging and death as well as life." [16]

This is an attractive argument, but do we need the goddess? Edward Burton Tylor reminded us long ago that "myth is the history of its authors, not of its subjects; it records the lives not of superhuman heroes, but of poetic nations." [17] What should worry us here is that a reliance on myth may lead us to reconstruct masculine history. Perhaps we do need goddesses, but perhaps we do *not* need them. To make concrete and popular is an extremely important function in building any sort of foundation, but we might choose to do so through biography, phenomenological anecdote and analysis, and ordinary fiction rather than myth. The problem here is that myth has a way of becoming tied to an implicit view of reality. Sheila Greeve Davaney contends that several prominent feminist theologians risk repeating a basic error of masculine thinking:

Thus it can be seen that the two representatives of the "reformist" perspective [Schüssler Fiorenza and Ruether] propose as a critical norm for evaluating truth claims the furtherance of women's full humanity, but that accompanying this norm and giving it ontological status is the assumption that such female becoming corresponds to and reflects divine purpose and will. Hence, visions supporting feminist aspirations are not simply compelling human views, conditioned and relative, but indeed "true" if not absolute in that they bear the mark of divine validation and reflect the "true nature of things." [18]

We have seen that even Mary Daly refers to masculine views as a distortion of reality—suggesting that she too considers feminine vision a more genuine reflection of the true nature of things. At this point I want to confess some ambivalence on this problem and its solution. My method will require setting aside the quest for spiritual certainty, but I will return to discuss spirituality at the end of the investigation. At any rate we can see why the Jungian frameworks are so attractive to women seeking their roots and desiring to reclaim their earlier powers.

Myths do exist, however, and we need to analyze the most powerful of them to see whether they conform to feminine experience. The myths and descriptions of the classical feminine especially need careful analysis in our search for female perspectives on good and evil. The Jungian-classical view of femininity is deeply embedded in the analysis of myth, legend, and ancient religions. Because woman is entirely defined by the "feminine principle," her virtuous attributes are not so much attainments as they are manifestations of a superior force working through her. She is essentially unconscious. Erich Neumann, another Jungian, explains:

> It is no accident that in the symbols we have cited as examples consciousness is identified with the figure of the male hero, while the devouring unconscious is identified with the image of the female monster. As we have elsewhere shown at length [Neumann here cites his own work], this coordination is general; that is, in both sexes the active ego consciousness is characterized by a male symbolism, the unconscious as a whole by a female symbolism.

We can trace this sort of thinking to Plato, and in fact Neumann quotes from Plato's *Menexenus:* "In fertility and generation, woman does not set an example to the earth, but the earth sets an example to woman." [19] On one level this statement seems exactly right; we are part of the earth, and the earth has its own forms of evolution and generation. But on another level to accede to it is to indulge in a Uriah Heap–like humility. Have not women set an example to the earth in their rational motherhood, in their steadfast compassion for their own kind? Men have not hesitated to declare themselves masters of the earth, but women have been timid in asserting their strengths and true virtues. As we explored women and evil in the last chapter, we saw what forces have acted to maintain women's humility. Among these we found the story of Adam and Eve and the doctrine of original sin.

But the identification of woman with original sin has not alone kept women from speaking out on moral matters. The "unconscious" feminine essence has helped keep women silent on moral matters even though over the centuries many have suggested that women are naturally better endowed than men with the moral virtues already mentioned. Simple motherly goodness is not denied woman—she has it if she remains in touch with her inner nature—but if she begins to think about or talk about goodness, straightaway she becomes inferior. Even Immanuel Kant believed this, saying of a contemporary woman thinker and of women in general:

> Deep meditation and a long-sustained reflection are noble but difficult, and do not well befit a person in whom unconstrained charms could show nothing else than a beautiful nature. Laborious learning or painful pondering, even if a woman should greatly succeed in it, destroy the merits that are proper to her sex, and because of their rarity they can make her an object of cold admiration; but at the same time they will weaken the charms with which she exercises her great power over the other sex. A woman with a head full of Greek . . . or . . . mechanics . . . might as well even have a beard; for perhaps that would express more obviously the mien of profundity for which she strives.[20]

Thus women have been trapped by the classical feminine: to think like a man is to be unfeminine, but to think like a woman is to think not at all! Contemporary Jungians are aware of this problem in Jung's thought, and many are calling for revision. Estella Lauter and Carol Rupprecht, for example, say:

> Revision is necessary because of Jung's tendency, despite the remarkable range, complexity, and fluidity of his system, to think in terms of rigid oppositions. For example, he posited that Eros, or the principle of relatedness, was not only associated with females but was dominant in the female psyche; conversely, the analytical principle, or Logos, was dominant in males. Despite all our efforts toward individuation, he said, Eros would remain weaker in most males and Logos weaker in most females. Thus he set arbitrary limits on the development of both sexes and reinforced the stereotypes of man as thinker, woman as nurturer.[21]

The model of woman as nurturer is clearly subject to a variety of descriptions and interpretations. An interpretation that will be useful for my analysis must include an account of female rationality and not found itself simply on maternal instinct. Many Jungians recognize the problem and want to insist on a distinctive female rationality, but they fall into the master's way of talking when the subject is not the direct revision of concepts of consciousness. Ann Belford Ulanov, for example, acknowledges that our culture "has been fashioned primarily along the lines of masculine values" and that "consciousness itself is often characterized in masculine terms," but in discussing the stages of animus development, she does not dispute the characterization. A woman in stage three of animus development is fully conscious, but she is saved from stage two by a man:

> Thus either "a 'real' man and partner assumes the freeing role of consciousness and dissolves the old form of encompassment in the unconscious, or else it can be an 'inner' man, a power of consciousness in the woman herself, which accomplishes the freeing." In either case, the feminine ego feels incapable of freeing itself under its own power from the paternal uroboros and thus establishing a more equal relationship with the masculine. The feminine ego feels dependent upon the masculine and in need of help from it. Outwardly, this is illustrated by a man, say a husband, helping a woman free herself from her original family circle.[22]

Irene Claremont de Castillejo underscores this sort of dependency when she says, "I personally like to think of my helpful animus as a torchbearer: the figure of a man holding aloft his torch to light my way, throwing its beams into dark corners and penetrating the mists which shield the world of half-hidden mystery where, as a woman, I am so very much at home." When Castillejo denies the long-standing association of man with spirit and woman with earth, insisting that woman is not "blind with nature and life force," she aggravates the split by describing woman's spiritual awareness as diffuse and inarticulate: "Her innermost feminine soul is as dumb and shy as any man's anima. But her awareness is there, diffuse and all pervading. She can walk in the dark and place her feet as delicately as a cat without any light from her animus's torch." [23]

Even though some current disciples of Jung have rejected the spirit / earth dichotomy and have even attempted to redefine archetypes, they have a long and dramatic tradition to overcome.[24] Statements like Neumann's emphasize and particularize the central symbolism of the feminine *as material and unconscious* in classical views: "This central symbol is the *vessel*. From the very beginning down to the latest stages of development we find this archetypal symbol as essence of the feminine. The basic symbolic equation woman = body = vessel corresponds to what is perhaps mankind's—man's as well as woman's—most elementary experience of the Feminine." [25]

If this is man's experience of woman, it is unlikely to capture anything substantial of woman's actual experience. At the latest stages of development, in the present—and this is the only time truly known to us as women—woman's experience of herself is hardly that of vessel. Willingly, happily pregnant, she is an intelligent agent, careful in every aspect of her life to nurture and protect the growing child: careful in what she eats, how she exercises, how she rests—even in straining at a bowel movement lest she dislodge the beloved child. As she rests, her hand touches the momentary protuberances in her belly: *Is this hand, or knee, or foot?* she wonders. *Soon I will hold you, see you, feed you, teach you, come to know you.* Far from an unconscious and pure fecundity, pregnant woman is relational consciousness at its most intense and reflective stage.

It is fair to say, however, that feminists differ in their evaluation of the image of woman as vessel. Although I express dissatisfaction with it because it connotes an unconscious and pure fecundity, Adrienne Rich confesses some sympathy with it. Speaking of the woman potter, she says, "It does not seem unlikely to me that the woman potter molded, not simply vessels, but images of herself, the vessel of life, the transformer of blood into life and milk—that in so doing she was expressing, celebrating, and giving concrete form to her experience as a creative being possessed of indispensable powers." [26] Rich points out rightly that such images give woman an invaluable sense of herself. But that value was attached to a historical period—one in which the creation of human beings and of vessels for food and drink was honored in a world not yet split into public and private. There was then no need to consign natural creation to the unconscious. As we will see, when the split came even pottery making was taken away from women.

Difficulties with the older Jungian views are numerous, but the fundamental difficulty is that although those views capture something of the feminine that is convincing to many of us who are women, they seem to represent at bottom an emptying of male consciousness *about* the feminine. Somehow even though they purport to capture the essence of femininity, they miss the heart of female experience. We cannot help but feel that they perform an inversion of monumental significance: they make female experience a product of feminine nature rather than feminine nature a product of female experience. The latter view is of crucial importance because it holds open the possibility for both men and women to develop the best of the feminine; it is also crucial because it logically rejects the notion that traditional female experience derives from, and thus acquires legitimacy from, something called feminine nature.

Neumann's work demonstrates how natural it is for the male to regard the feminine as "unconscious," as that which he cannot make explicit and articulate, and how equally natural it is for him to equate ego consciousness—creativity and basic ethicality—to male experience, to "consciousness." The damage that this view has done to moral philosophy, to moral action, to human relations in general, and to female self-esteem would be hard to exaggerate. We observe on the one hand an enormous admiration for the female essence, the Great Round or life-producing vessel, and on the other hand a fundamental distrust and contempt for the feminine "nonrational" insistence on the primacy of relation and its role in guiding ethical action.

When Neumann describes what he labels the "elementary" character of femininity, he recognizes both a protective encircling function and a devouring encompassing quality. Again we see in this description a reflection of male consciousness—an appreciation for early protection coupled with a fear of being contained, held down, attached. Whereas Neumann and other Jungians see this enveloping tendency as part of essential femininity, we might well analyze it as a set of compensating moves to alleviate the pain of exclusion from the productive public world. We might with warm sympathy excuse a woman for pushing her husband and sons too hard and demanding that they appreciate her efforts when we recognize that she has been totally defined in relation to them. Their success has been her only success, their goodness the only manifestation of her goodness. Still, we must label this peculiar tendency an evil likely to arise in women's experience.

A paradoxical difficulty with the Jungian view is its inextricable bond with religion, myth, and legend. In one sense, of course, this rich cultural perspective represents a great strength of Jungian analysis; it certainly carries considerable authority. But does it capture authentic female experience? We might readily acknowledge the voluminous documentation on male heroes, female monsters, and sleeping (unconscious) beauties without agreeing that the universality of these images tells us anything about female nature. Here again we confront a stubborn problem of cause and effect. Certainly male projections into female experience have influenced women as well as men, and so it is difficult to sort out which features of the Archetypal Feminine are responsible for female experience and which are contingent products of that experience as men have designed and interpreted it. The archetype may well be a masculine mold for subordinate woman.[27]

We must of course acknowledge that the archetype is not intended to be the image of any concrete woman. Jung and his associates do not deny woman rationality. But it is not her essence. Again we feel torn because on the one hand Jungians at least recognize that intellect alone is not supreme and that feeling is powerful, and many of us would agree with this assessment; but on the other hand they do *not* recognize that the relational mode of female being involves both thinking and feeling and that in human relations this mode may be the ultimately rational mode of being—one that feels with others and acts generously on their behalf. All through the works of Jung and his disciples we find admiration / distrust, worship / contempt, dependence / fear in statements about the feminine and about women. Harding inadvertently highlights Jung's ambivalence when she discusses his analysis of the feminine mode in art and literature:

> In his essays on Picasso and the *Ulysses* of Joyce, Jung has discussed two such art creations, and has shown how these follow a law, but not the law of reason, the masculine Logos. Instead they turn aside from the rational and the consciously controlled and go by the path of the left, which leads down to darkness, into the primordial slime from which life first emerged. In these depths are the dark, sinister, feminine beginnings, in a region ruled over, not by the bright Logos of intellect, but by the dark Eros of feelings.[28]

This attitude toward the feminine pervades myth, religion, and legend as men have created them. The female has been both worshiped and feared and so has the "feminine" when it has appeared in men. Even when it is admired, it is seen largely as an emergency resource—a set of capacities to invoke if the "later," "more conscious," "masculine" mode of reasoned intelligence should fail. In chapter 1 we saw how Jung attempted to integrate body and spirit, feminine and masculine, evil and good in his theology. But the feminine role is always auxiliary, or "complementary."

Before leaving this exploration of Jungian views, we might speculate on the likely success of current attempts at revision. I will concentrate here on one main concept, the archetype, because one such idea—that of the shadow—will prove useful in a later analysis. The notion of archetype, to which so many feminists object, is shot through with difficulties. It also seems appropriate to give some attention to the concept here because, despite feminists' objections, the notion has achieved considerable acceptance in current works on women and spirituality.[29] What is an archetype? John Welch gives a standard Jungian definition: "Within the collective unconscious are pre-existent forms which Jung called *archetypes*. The archetypes are primordial images common to all humankind. By 'primordial image' Jung did not mean specific images or ideas, but predispositions or patterns." [30]

Archetypes, although themselves but a pattern or form, have in effect several components or aspects. The material component is the set of manifestations of each archetype, for example, the Virgin Mary as Good Mother. The symbolic aspect contains the meanings of particular manifestations both in relation to the archetype and in relation to the individuals who experience the manifestations. In chapter 2, for example, we explored the meanings attached to the juxtaposition of the Virgin Mary and the serpent in art and legend. The dynamic-emotional aspect of the archetype reveals the archetype's power to motivate, control, or influence individuals or groups; "animus possession" is an extreme example of the dynamic aspect of the Animus Archetype. Finally, the structural component of archetypes describes the relations among archetypes and their development in persons and cultures.

The first two components are perhaps less problematic for feminists than the last two. Even within Jung's framework we could seek new material examples and reinterpret the meanings of various symbols. But the other two features of the archetype contain normative elements and principles that constrain reinterpretation. The dynamic component suggests that there are archetypes that we should accept and cultivate and other archetypes that we should resist. Neumann writes of their power: "The archetype is manifested principally in the fact that it determines human behavior unconsciously but in accordance with laws and independently of the experience of the individual. . . . This dynamic component of the unconscious has a compelling character for the individual who is directed by it, and it is always accompanied by a strong emotional component." [31]

The one archetypal word I have used and will continue to use is *shadow*, but as I will explain shortly I am not convinced that we need to regard it as an archetype—that is, as something that precedes and controls experience. Insistence on the power of archetypes to direct consciousness has induced considerable criticism. Alasdair MacIntyre, in his description of Jung and his work, remarks, "Sometimes he seems to have treated the archetypal images as autonomous agents and the collective unconscious as a realm in which they dwell." [32] Although Jung did not regard the *images* as autonomous agents, he did grant such power to the archetypes themselves.

Recognizing feminist objections to Jung's view of feminine archetypes, the contemporary Jungian school sometimes suggests a view of archetype as process, particularly as the *valuing of an image*. [33] Although this revision may facilitate the recovery and elaboration of female consciousness, it causes a serious difficulty for Jungian perspectives of the spiritual. Jung did regard the psyche and its archetypes as real. He was careful to separate, at the theoretical level, archetype from manifestation and allowed for all sorts of manifestations of a particular archetype. But the archetype as a participant in psychic reality was *real*. Jung made this point again and again, nowhere more clearly than in *Answer to Job*:

> I have been asked so often whether I believe in the existence of God or not that I am somewhat concerned lest I be taken for an adherent of "psychologism" far more commonly than I suspect. What most people overlook or seem unable to understand is the fact that I regard the *psyche* as real. . . . God is an obvious psychic and non-physical fact, i.e., a fact that can be established psychically but not physically. Equally, these people have still not got it into their heads that the psychology of religion falls into two categories, which must be sharply distinguished one from another: firstly, the psychology of the religious person, and secondly, the psychology of religion proper, i.e., of religious contents. [34]

This fundamental statement makes it difficult to treat archetypes as mere processes of valuing—if, that is, one wishes to remain a Jungian. For Jung, as for Plato, values are part of an existing reality in which we individuals find ourselves. To redefine archetypes as "valuing" destroys a major foundation of Jungian thought. But even for those who merely acknowledge a debt to Jung and are willing to radicalize his program, a major problem arises. If the psyche and its archetypes are not a source of actual values but only predispositions to value and find patterns in images, then what *is* the locus of value? What have we achieved when we reach "insight," and what authorizes our claim? These questions are vital for the present study, and I will face them squarely in the chapters on female experience and evil. We have already seen that the lack of an authoritative and convincing alternative to relativism in masculine traditions has led many thoughtful writers to reembrace serious conceptions of God and Satan.

The structural aspect of archetypes is perhaps the most troublesome. The difficulty is pronounced in the structural (hierarchical) treatment of masculine and feminine. A possible way of avoiding the Jungian identification of *masculine* with cultural progress and *feminine* with the primitive unconscious is to regard the structure of archetypes as "processional." Hillman, for example, says:

> Their tales and their figures move through phases like dramas and interweave one with another, dissolve into one another. Whether expressed as instincts or as Gods, archetypes are not definitely distinct. . . . Their process is their complication and amplification, and each individual's psychic process involves attempting to follow, discriminate, and refine their complications. . . . All we can say is that the archetypes are structures in process; this process is many-formed and mythical.[35]

Even though Hillman warns that we must not regard the movement of the archetypes as "progression or regression," the writing of Jung and his disciples clearly reveals a belief in a progression both in the cultural transformation of archetypes and in individual psychic development in relation to the archetypes. Erich Neumann, for example, describes the Great Mother as a primordial archetype.[36] A primordial archetype lacks differentiation; it contains positive and negative, good and evil, light and dark, all in one entity. As consciousness develops, the Great Mother is differentiated into archetypal polarities: the Terrible Mother and the Good Mother. It is important to note as we discuss progressive differentiations that Neumann associated the earliest stages—the stage of uroboric unity and of the uroboric Great Mother (the primitive female circle)—with the feminine, whereas he identified the progress toward differentiation and consciousness as masculine. This way of thinking and talking has all the earmarks of a masculine project. It is as though Jung and his male followers asked: How did *my* consciousness develop? How did I first view woman? When was I most dependent on the feminine? The Great Mother, for male consciousness, is the Great Round, the vessel of primordial life.

It is difficult to look at all this from women's perspective. We are so completely submerged in masculine consciousness that it is hard even to discern the right spot at which to start questioning. Would we not also locate our origins in the Great Round, in the primeval sea of maternity? Of course. But we need not project our own initial unconsciousness onto the mature female that incubated us, and we need not characterize our developing consciousness as masculine or base our description of differentiation in the psyche so heavily on polarities, hierarchies, and stages. Far more sophisticated schemes of differentiation are possible when we think of physical others as related—as psychic "parts of me"—and "I" as a set of relations with others. The construction of a feminine alternative perspective is clearly possible, but it may not be possible to produce it within a Jungian framework.

Jung's notion of integration, however, contains a promising idea. When good and evil again recombine in one entity with full consciousness, we have a realistic opportunity to control the evil that is part of all of us. When I use the word *shadow,* I will refer not to an element in the realm of archetypes, but rather to a set of desires, inclinations, and behaviors that are observable in human experience. Some appear obviously in a given individual; those of which the individual is unaware are part of his or her shadow. Similarly, a group, institution, nation, or culture may have a shadow. Sometimes the traits belonging to the shadow are vehemently denied, even despised, and then we may predict projection. Hence integration is essential. This is a feature of Jungian thought to which I will return repeatedly.

I have not dwelt on problems with the material component of archetypes,[37] because I believe that they can be resolved if we work out the deeper problems of dynamic and structural aspects satisfactorily. Estella Lauter sums up the reasons for retaining the notion of archetype, and her reasons are interesting even for those unattracted to Jung's framework:

> The reason for retaining the concept of the archetype at all is to accord recognition and dignity to certain widespread developmental tasks, and to confirm the connection between the imagination and the biological

and psychological process of development. The patterns that imply the existence of an archetype, then, are the ones that deserve investigation in behavior studies and other kinds of psychological research. And archetypal images can be used to corroborate such research, or to test its validity. The search for archetypal images should present no problems for feminist theory as long as we regard the process as a virtually endless search for insight into human experience, which is constantly evolving while we are searching.[38]

This statement seems *methodologically* faithful to Jung, but normative problems may vitiate his program to study religious contents. Clearly it is possible to investigate developmental tasks without invoking the notion of archetypes, and it is also possible to give adequate attention to symbolic processes in other conceptual frameworks. The process of valuing that Jungians want to emphasize might gain strength from a concentration on experience—both cultural and individual—and from an imaginative reflection that leads to insight.

In summary, Jungian views of the feminine, for all their power and beauty, seem to prescribe female experience on the basis of a fascinating analysis of women's nature as it is revealed in myth and ritual. Although we will want to look more directly at women's experience as women have lived and described it, Jungian descriptions have contributed much to concepts of the feminine that many women have internalized. Further, although Jung's insights on how human beings manage their evil, or shadow, sides will prove valuable, we will see that his archetypal treatment of evil lends itself easily to a belief in an evil being and possession. It does not give us great insight into the *content* of evil.

VICTORIAN VIEWS

Although the Victorian age predated important Jungian writings, its influence overlapped and exceeded that of Jung. Certainly it flourished in the early 1900s and was bemoaned (though far from dead) by 1920. The popular view of Victorian woman held the public imagination well into the 1950s and, one might argue, still exerts considerable power. On the surface at least—and the surface is all the vast majority of people ever see or hear of—Victorian woman and her female progeny lost all the demonic power of the classical unconscious. Beneath the surface, hidden in subtleties and fictions, much of the earlier power remained.[39] Here we will first look at the popular conception. The early goddesses are now entirely gone, washed out in service to Christianity, and woman's powers are diverted to the service of husbands, fathers, and sons.

Neumann, in his Jungian-classical description of the feminine, named four polar points as locations of archetypal figures of the feminine: "the Good Mother, the Terrible Mother, the negative anima (or, more simply, the seductive young witch), and the positive anima (or, the Sophia-virgin)."[40] The Victorian view, in its better-known forms, reduces the female to the last two. True, Victorians extolled the mother, but the Victorian mother is no longer the powerful Moon Goddess or earth-mother or bestower of all fertility and abundance; she is no longer the magnificent sexual figure with great nourishing breasts and generous hips. Nor is she the powerful Terrible Mother, capable of tearing her children asunder if they displease her or depend on her too long or in too much weakness. She has become the pseudo-virgin, pregnant again and again, yet pure and innocent. Mary Daly comments on this impotent image:

> The "goodness" attributed to a few is not the goodness of a self-actualizing person but of an impotent creature, lacking in knowledge and experience. . . . In the case of the ideal of goodness foisted upon women, there is a special aura of glorification in the ideal, as symbolized by Mary, for example. This impossible ideal ultimately has a punitive function, since, of course, no woman can live up to it. (Consider the impossibility of being both virgin and mother.) It throws all women back into the status of Eve and essentially reinforces the universality of women's low caste status.[41]

It is not surprising that men and women have reacted with some disgust to the sickeningly sweet and impossibly unselfish image of the Victorian mother. In a sociological study of motherhood Jessie Bernard uses a series of sentimental Victorian quotes to start her attack on the restrictive vision of the mother model:

> Of all women in the world, the most pure—and the most useful as a sanction for adolescent chastity—was Mother. Every young Victorian heard his father's voice, sounding in his conscience, "Remember your dear, good mother, and never do anything, think anything, imagine anything she would be ashamed of."[42]

And:

> Genial, sunshiny, happy. Hers is life's sweetest and tenderest love, a love beautiful and loyal and true, love that never fails. A halo of purity rest-

ing on her saintly brow—her face abeam with joy the world cannot give or take away. Such mothers, though uncrowned, are the real queens of the earth.[43]

We see here that the father gets the credit for the explicit verbal instruction of his son; the mother is, we may assume, a sort of natural innocent who would be shocked by any discussion of the physical. Further, she lives in a hallowed state of subjugation. *Good* women are supposed to be filled with joy in their lives as unselfish wives and mothers; they are to be angels—confined, of course, to the house. Both Protestantism in its renewed appreciation of marriage and motherhood and Catholicism in its reverence for Mary as the virgin mother of God contributed to this set of expectations for women.[44]

The Victorian myth had to be exposed, and the Jungians deserve credit for doing so in part. But just as Harding succumbed to the Jungian notion of unconscious feminine obedience to a "principle," so Bernard gives way to sociology and declares motherhood a "role"— "Mother is a role, women are human beings."[45] Reducing mother to a role seems to me a monumental error. If we study feminine descriptions of motherhood in biography and fiction, we may want to insist that "mother" is a basic relation and not a mere role and that we must study the relation phenomenologically to see just how it connects to the virtues and distinctive consciousness we seek.[46] Just as male philosophers studied *The Iliad* to identify male virtues, we need to study the marvelous new works on the mothering experience to identify womanly virtues.[47] To reduce mothering to a role is to risk losing important elements of women's experience entirely. Bernard's ideas on mothering as a role seem perilously close to those of Plato's *Republic*—that women can be entirely equal to men in an essentially masculine world and that either sex may fulfill whatever roles society offers. It may indeed be more desirable, as Bernard acknowledges later (without endorsing the view), to use women's traditional experience to transform the world. If we agree, we do not want to change women's experience entirely. In particular we may not want to undervalue the universal experience that women have undergone, resisted, affirmed, and refined. "Essence," from this perspective, is the product of centuries of experience, and we should not unreflectively discard it.

Today many of us hold the popular Victorian image of women in scorn. Even though historical and interpretive works challenge the Victorian myth, we see for ourselves what remains in contemporary life, and we doubt that literary interpretations, fascinating as they are, do much to influence ordinary women's lives. But there is in these interpretations an echo of older, more mysterious and effective, powers. Nina Auerbach comments:

> In those two popular romances [*Trilby* and *Dracula*] and the romantic beginnings of modern science [Freud] we see the image of prone womanhood at its most dispiriting. Personal and cultural disinheritance, we see, could go no further than these tabulae rasae, all selfhood suspended as they are invaded by the hyperconscious and culturally fraught male / master / monster. But when we actually read *Trilby, Dracula,* or *Studies on Hysteria* we are struck by the kinds of powers that are granted to the women: the victim of paralysis possesses seemingly infinite capacities of regenerative being that turn on her triumphant mesmerizer and paralyze him in turn. Dispossessed and seemingly empty, the women reveal an infinitely unfolding magic that is quite different from the formulaic spells of the men.[48]

In other depictions of Victorian women we find something beyond the magical—a realistic steady goodness that reminds us of the best women we have actually known. In *To the Lighthouse* Virginia Woolf describes Mrs. Ramsay, a post-Victorian mother of eight who manages her household competently, dispenses charity and educational advice with compassion, and sustains all those around her in an order of tranquillity. Through all this she remains almost convincingly human and beautiful. An observer remarks:

> With stars in her eyes and veils in her hair, with cyclamen and wild violets—what nonsense was he thinking? She was fifty at least; she has eight children. Stepping through fields of flowers and taking to her breast buds that had broken and lambs that had fallen. . . . Charles Tansley felt an extraordinary pride; felt the wind and the cyclamen and the violets for he was walking with a beautiful woman.

Mrs. Ramsay comes across to us as excruciatingly real, even if somewhat like the angel, in the sense that she embodies what we have been taught is possible and even expected for women. It matters only intermittently that her keen intellectual powers are entirely confined to the private domain. There she is marvelous—a force to reckon with and depend on. We hardly know how to continue life without her. Her death hits us like a physical blow. Woolf knows how it will hurt us, and she channels our cry through Lily Briscoe: "In the midst of chaos there was shape; this eternal passing and flowing (she looked at the clouds going and the leaves shaking) was struck into stability. Life stands still here, Mrs. Ramsay said. 'Mrs. Ramsay! Mrs Ramsay!' she repeated. She owed it all to her." [49]

But Victorian heroes had to die, Woolf suggests, if a realistic image of woman were to develop. We all want Mrs. Ramsay for our mother and guide, but few of us want to *be* Mrs. Ramsay. Thus Victorian womanhood fell into scorn—an impossible ideal. And what became of Victorian woman's "virtues"? Thanks to an active and "realistic" social message in novel and film, the classical virtues of compassion, receptivity, and human understanding have been transferred from mother to the "whore with a golden heart." In an important sense this transferral keeps the mother model alive, but such compensating moves further alienate both men and women from the feminine. Further, whereas the angel in the house provided a model of moral behavior, she was a silent and captive model, and her goodness could not survive transfer from the private domain to the domain of public affairs.

The popular Victorian dichotomy of perfect mother or whore (with the "old maid" in limbo) distracted attention from real activism among living women. Indeed, the Victorian era teemed with paradoxes and artificiality. In discussing the demon-woman as the center of Victorian-romantic interest, Auerbach remarks: "The preternaturally endowed creature who taunts conventional morality as angel and demon, old maid and fallen woman, seems alien to the approved model of womanhood Victorians were bred to revere. Officially, the only woman worthy of worship was a monument of selflessness, with no existence beyond the loving influence she exuded as daughter, wife, and mother." [50]

Not only was there deep fascination with the femme fatale and other nonconforming women, but also the era produced politically active women. In this country Elizabeth Cady Stanton, Susan B. Anthony, Lucy Stone, and Antoinette (Nette) Brown all defied the traditional custom of women's silence. But women who dared so much often paid dearly in public ridicule and indignation. Page Smith quotes an early (1840) statement of such indignation; the chairman of the Connecticut Anti-Slavery Society expressed outrage that Abby Kelley had received permission to speak:

> "I will not sit in a chair where women bear rule. I vacate this chair. No woman shall speak or vote where I am moderator. I will not countenance such an outrage on decency. . . . It is woman's business to take

care of children in the nursery. She has no business to come into this meeting, and by speaking and voting lord it over men. Where woman's enticing eloquence is heard men are incapable of right and efficient action. She beguiles and blinds man by her smiles and her bland and winning voice." [51]

This indignant speech could have taken place at almost any time during the Victorian era. It sums up dramatically the paradoxes of the age: the power / powerlessness of women, their charm and guile, their political activism in opposition to well-entrenched norms, their eloquence in the face of commands to keep silent. It points up too the conflict between expectations and the actual experience of women.

RELIGIOUS VIEWS

Although I cannot present here a comprehensive discussion of religious views on women (I covered some of the material important to this study in chapter 2), we need to take note at least of the long tradition that has provided authority for man's speech and woman's silence in the public domain.

Religious views of the feminine are hard to separate from the social contexts in which we find them. When I discussed religion and evil in chapters 1 and 2, I spoke almost entirely of Judeo-Christian religious views. These are the ones that support and are supported by the Western patriarchal system. But clearly we have earlier religions to consider, and, as I suggested earlier, we should be cautious in recommending an active reclamation of them. Many of us would reject such a move because we think we must seek a female perspective that stands a chance of transforming the modern world—not virtues that will work toward the displacement of one tyrant and the rise of another. Yet we need to familiarize ourselves with ancient religions and goddess worship to see what men so greatly feared and why they felt it necessary and desirable to subdue and possess women.

Women did not necessarily have significantly greater actual power in the times when society recognized female gods. Indeed, little evidence suggests that the presence of female deities in a culture reflects higher social status or greater political power for women,[52] and we should not assume that a restoration of goddesses would increase women's social power. If women were to seize great power or to share equally in it, they could, of course, establish their own deities, as they seem to have done occasionally in history.[53] But it may also be that the worship of female divinities increases in times of great fear and uncertainty, when people seek the nurturance and protection of the mother, as seems to be the case with Marian worship. Across all cultures we find the virtues of nurturance, relatedness, compassion, and protection extolled as aspects of the feminine. Our task eventually will be to give voice to those attributes and behaviors we wish to maintain and to speak out against those that seem to be mere manifestations of a slave mentality.

Accounts of ancient religions and their deities do not come to us firsthand. They come wrapped in perspectives and explanatory schemata. J. J. Bachofen and Robert Briffault, for example, associated the divine feminine with matriarchy, but they also looked on matriarchy as an inferior if necessary stage in the evolution of human civilizations.[54] This association was, of course, one of our reasons for rejecting Jung's structural archetypes. The notion that femininity is basically inferior to masculinity pervades these studies. For example, occupations are enhanced when males enter them, and culture is said to "advance" as it becomes more and more patriarchal. Neumann quotes Briffault as saying "The art of pottery is a feminine invention; the original potter was a woman. Among all primitive peoples the ceramic art is found in the hands of women, and only under the influence of advanced culture does it become man's occupation."[55]

Here we see man seize the art Rich extolled—one that meant so much to woman as a potter, molding her own images—in the inexorable march toward "advanced culture." Even Neumann, a Jungian who expresses enormous appreciation for the feminine and for the balance of feminine and masculine qualities in all human beings, reveals this prejudiced joining of the male to advanced culture and consciousness and of the female to primitive life and unconsciousness. The balance he seeks tilts heavily to one side. For the male the "feminine" is a "primitive" resource: "But when consciousness and reason cannot, as in later human development, be drawn upon to decide a situation, the male falls back on the wisdom of the unconscious, by which the female is inspired; and thus the unconscious is invoked and set in motion in rite and cult."[56]

It is precisely this ritualistic restoration of the "feminine" that many women wish to avoid. Perhaps *all* ritual—whether retained for aesthetic reasons or for reasons of community spirit—should be sharply separate from the feminine as we seek to establish it. Certainly it is high time to separate women's experience from the unconscious. If we examine our own Western, Judeo-Christian tradition for its wisdom on women's virtues, we find the theme of "unconsciousness" reinterpreted and reinforced. As we saw in the diminished Victorian image, woman was stripped of her earlier powers—both beneficent and demonic. The religious tradition of which we are speaking is not innocent in this diminution. Woman's virtues in this tradition are "properties"—qualities more properly associated with things than with human beings. Even the lovely chapter 31 of Proverbs (vv. 10–31) in the King James Version is entitled "Praise and properties of a good wife": "Who can find a virtuous woman? For her price *is* far above rubies. The heart of her husband doth safely trust in her, so that he shall have no need of spoil" (vv. 10–11).

We know that the text mirrors the times and the "woman" here is probably a metaphor for "tribe" or "people," but there is no mistaking the import of the language. Woman is *property*, and her "virtues" are the sort of goodness we might attribute to a good car, a sound horse, or at best a worthy employee. There are two lines that speak to the possible moral initiative of women: "She stretcheth out her hand to the poor; yea, she reacheth forth her hands to the needy" (v. 20); "She openeth her mouth with wisdom: and in her tongue *is* the law of kindness" (v. 26).

But, as we know, both the poor (who are "always with us") and the "law of kindness" are thought to be markedly inferior in a patriarchal scheme of justice and entitlements. For men the "law of kindness" is no substitute for a hard-headed rational solution of the problems of equity, and it must always be carefully constrained. When the warrior model is invoked, the law of kindness is violently rejected. It is important to record the virtues that Western religions have recognized and cultivated in women: obedience, poverty, patience, charity, compassion, praise (adulation), truth, humility, prudence, and purity.[57]

Like many earlier and Eastern religions, Christianity universally extols virginity as a feminine virtue. But virginity in the Christian tradition means *virginity*—that is, complete abstinence from sexual intercourse. In earlier religious traditions powerful and independent women and goddesses were referred to as virgins without regard for their sexual virginity. Indeed, the Christian tradition forced a painful contradiction on women by extolling both virginity and motherhood. By remaining virgin, the Catholic woman can become "more like a man" in her service to God, but, in contrast, the most venerated woman in Catholicism is Mary, the mother of God. Many have noted the contradiction between motherhood and virginity in female divinities. Paul Hershman and others have explained it as only an *apparent* contradiction.[58] Writing of Hershman's solution, James Preston says:

> The virginity of a goddess is a symbolic statement of her spiritual purity, not to be taken literally or confused with human sexuality. The divine mother should not be understood as a mere projection of human motherhood. In many societies the process of giving birth, with its associated blood and placenta, is considered to be a polluting event that requires the practice of elaborate taboos for women.[59]

Surely the contradiction for real women in search of their essence is more than "apparent." It is real. It reveals again the conflict between female model and female experience. Human female reality must be denied in the quest for "spiritual purity." That men should choose these two virtues—motherhood and virginity—for women is not simply a symbolic effort to place spiritual purity above earthly life. It denigrates women's essential experience. Women elevate earthly love above all symbols by bringing real joy and smiles and tears and loving hands to the childbed itself—blood, sweat, pain, and all. The explanation that forces itself on us is that men wanted their wives to be virgin properties, their own properties, and their mothers to be asexual service machines. That explanation reveals a different interpretation of the symbolism.

Further, even though we might blame the early Christian church for the great emphasis on the moral superiority of virginity and the second-class goodness of motherhood, motherhood was not really exalted even in the Old Testament. Motherhood does not, for example, figure in the biblical story of creation. Indeed, Eve is "born" of Adam. As Susan Brownmiller points out, "With this unusual reordering of biological birth, the submission of woman to man was given a firm theological basis."[60] Women had to achieve motherhood in the Old Testament to be worth anything at all, but the physical functions that made motherhood possible were considered "unclean" and "polluting." Thus motherhood was valued as a commodity, and women who met the standards set for them were held up as models to be emulated, but the mother model that appears in the Bible was not designed by women—as, for example, the warrior model was by men. We will have to look further for the authentic contribution of women to mothering.

We catch glimpses of genuine female experience in the Bible—but little more than glimpses. The beautiful story of Ruth extols women's emphasis on relation. Because she loved her mother-in-law, Naomi, Ruth insisted on staying with her rather than returning to her own people after the death of her husband, Naomi's son: "And Ruth said, Intreat me not to leave thee, or to return from following after thee: for whither thou goest, I will go; whither thou lodgest, I will lodge: thy people *shall* be my people, and thy God, my God" (Ruth 1:16).

This story has several points worth considering. First, a decision of this sort *made by a male* would not have been considered so admirable. A male ought first to devote himself to *his* god and *his* nation, forsaking even family to prove his loyalty to them. Ruth—being a woman and having made her decision in the direction of the "right" god—is admired. But it is her unselfish devotion and not her courage that the verse admires. Second, the story and its beautiful language transposed into contemporary music convey the message that it is virtuous for women to follow their husbands as Ruth followed Naomi. How many young women have chosen this beautiful music for their own weddings, not realizing the prediction it embodies? Through how many corporate (and often unnecessary) moves will she follow him? Thus have men used a woman's "virtue." Finally, we must remember that Ruth is a small book of the Bible—just four short chapters—and it ends this way: "Now these are the generations of Pharez: Pharez begat Hezron, / And Hezron begat Ram and Ram begat Amminadab. / And Amminadab begat Nahshon, and Nahshon begat Salmon, / And Salmon begat Boaz, and Boaz begat Obed, / And Obed begat Jesse, and Jesse begat David." (4:18–20).

Where is Ruth? Ruth was "purchased" by Boaz to be his wife and to "raise up the name of the dead upon his inheritance." Nowhere does the Bible really extol the love between women, the unconditional love of mother for child, the steady insistence on relation over principle. The feminine virtues along with the females are gone. They are depended on, feared, surreptitiously admired, jealously subdued, and

ultimately co-opted. If we look at traditional religion for an elaboration of female virtues, we must undertake the task of radical reinterpretation, for everywhere we find the ideal of silence and service.

LEGACIES

The traditional feminine reaches right into the heart of today's society.
Perhaps the most pervasive manifestation is a legacy of the "unconscious" view of femininity. Whereas few today would deny that
women are capable of attaining virtues in the true or conscious sense,
"femininity" for many still points to a woman's success in capitalizing
on "natural" charms. These natural charms are not attainments but
gifts—natural attributes—and they center on face, body, voice, and
the like. Indeed the chapter titles of Brownmiller's book, *Femininity,*
reveal a current and popular emphasis: Body, Hair, Clothes, Voice,
Skin, Movement, Emotion, Ambition. Under this view of femininity,
a real woman gives careful attention to all but the last, and this she
carefully shuns.

Trying to present a balanced account, Brownmiller says:

> We are talking, admittedly, about an exquisite aesthetic. Enormous
> pleasure can be extracted from feminine pursuits as a creative outlet or
> purely as relaxation; indeed, indulgence for the sake of fun, or art, or
> attention, is among femininity's great joys. But the chief attraction (and
> the central paradox, as well) is the competitive edge that femininity
> seems to promise in the unending struggle to survive, and perhaps to
> triumph. The world smiles favorably on the feminine woman; it ex-
> tends little courtesies and minor privilege. Yet the nature of this com-
> petitive edge is ironic, at best, for one works at femininity by accepting
> restrictions, by limiting one's sights, by choosing an indirect route, by
> scattering one's concentration and not giving one's all as a man would
> to his own, certifiably masculine, interests.[61]

A significant number of women accept and even defend a blend of
this cosmetic view of femininity and its counterpart of woman as obedient helpmeet. Indeed, women like Phyllis Schlafly extol the comforts
and privilege of female life "in America" and go so far as to endorse
the most frightening measures to maintain their lives as men now direct them. Schlafly has even been quoted as saying that the nuclear
bomb is "a marvelous gift that was given to our country by a wise
God."[62] We see here an enormous faith in the patriarchy as men have
represented it through presidents and generals to God himself. Is

Schlafly in touch or out of touch with her "inner femininity"? It would be hard to say, on the basis of what we have discussed so far, that she is not in touch with the feminine principle. But as we begin to peel away the layers of masculine storytelling about women, we will find that women's complicity in this mystification is itself a great evil.

Now is a good time to remind ourselves that women have religions and histories—even though Simone de Beauvoir declared that we do not[63]—and that we have *experience* out of which we, like Sartrean men, can define ourselves. Of course we vary. We are not cast in the mold of archetypes. All around me as I write are stacks of books testifying to the authenticity of women's lives that we must examine, evaluate, and connect to our present experience. The mother model that has been forced on us is clearly a half-truth at best and radically incomplete; what women have made of it will give us important insights into good and evil.

In direct opposition to Schlafly, we find women who are seeking liberation from the cosmetic-slave view of femininity. Germaine Greer asks herself why she objects so strenuously to the sheltered cosmetic view and answers her own doubts in a powerful statement:

> So what is the beef? Maybe I couldn't make it. Maybe I don't have a pretty smile, good teeth, nice tits, long legs, a cheeky arse, a sexy voice. Maybe I don't know how to handle men and increase my market value, so that the rewards due to the feminine will accrue to me. Then again, maybe I'm sick of the masquerade. I'm sick of pretending eternal youth. I'm sick of belying my own intelligence, my own will, my own sex. I'm sick of peering at the world through false eyelashes, so everything I see is mixed with a shadow of bought hairs; . . . I'm sick of being a transvestite. I refuse to be a female impersonator. I am a woman, not a castrate.[64]

The view Greer expresses was once caricatured as "bra burning." "Women's lib" gained a narrow definition in opposition to the cosmetic view of femininity, and everywhere we heard people poke fun at women with hairy legs, no makeup, men's haircuts, unattractive clothing, and a distasteful odor resulting from their rejection of deodorants. But just as the "peaceniks" of the 1960s had a message far more important to the world than the discomforting unattractiveness of their appearance and social behaviors, so Greer and other feminists promoted a message beyond bra burning: Be yourself. Define yourself. Make something thoroughly human of yourself. Speak your own ethic.

Other women, while endorsing Greer's call to responsible person-hood, have taken a dim view of "women's lib" and have insisted that women already have all the opportunities they need but fail to use them. Midge Decter, for example, blames women for their lack of knowledge and even for the emotional patterns into which they have been socialized. Speaking of the ill-informed "libber," Decter writes:

> To judge from what she says and does, however—finding only others at fault for her predicaments, speaking always of herself as a means of stating the general case, shedding tears as a means of negotiation—the freedom she truly seeks is of a rather different kind. It is freedom demanded by children and enjoyed by no one: the freedom from all difficulty. If in the end her society is at fault for anything, it is for allowing her to grow up with the impression that this is something possible to ask. Even the good fairies that attended her birth would never have dared so far.[65]

Besides the problem that seems so obvious in the pages from which this passage is taken—that of setting up a likely straw woman—we might respond that even if society were responsible *only* for the deficiency Decter suggests, we should indict it for gross neglect. And once we have admitted that our society has allowed—even encouraged—many of its women to grow up as perpetual little girls, we have opened the door to an examination of many other forms of neglect. Decter calls for a bootstrap operation that, if successful, might well produce a generation of tough and unsympathetic females. We are reminded once again of Plato's female guardians. Our search for women's standpoint has another purpose in mind.

SUMMARY

I have tried in this discussion to sketch a compendium of important views on women and femininity to show that women appear as angels or as innately moral and beautiful as long as their sphere of activity remains severely limited. They have won admiration occasionally, but more as properties than as courageous independent agents. The views we have examined are sometimes terrifying, sometimes ludicrous, almost always disappointing. Together they sketch a portrait of the good woman, but it is not a self-portrait.

Before returning to the topic of evil, let me reiterate my fundamental purposes: to explain why women have not been heard in moral debate and to lay the groundwork for a critique of evil from the standpoint of women. Clearly, traditional descriptions of women contain elements of prescription, fantasy, and fiction along with snatches of reality. Women have internalized many of these expectations and have often participated enthusiastically in maintaining the layers of mystery that cloud their existence. How much of the transmitted female model should we retain and affirm? As we reflect on the model and make authentic choices for our lives, how will we describe good and evil?

4

Toward a Phenomenology of Evil

So far we have seen that evil became associated early with disobeying the father and his representatives. The roots of that association stretch far back into antiquity when early human beings felt contaminated by a preexisting evil. Ricoeur began his study of the symbolism of evil with an analysis of defilement. Already two things have happened that we must now set aside. First, evil is firmly associated with sin, guilt, impurity, and fault; there has been a move beyond pure terror to ethical terror. Second, thought already focuses on the symbol rather than on the experience. "By beginning with a symbolism already there," Ricoeur observes, "we give ourselves something to think about." [1] But even though we cannot separate ourselves entirely from symbols, my purpose is different from Ricoeur's. This study does not fundamentally concern the origins of the religious sense of evil in myths, but rather the basic affects associated with evil and the experiences that give rise to these affects. For this purpose I must take all the material so far discussed—material that is so much a part of our culture that it forms part of our natural standpoint—and set it warily aside. I will bring it back into the discussion from time to time for contrast and analysis.

This study started with a vague definition of evil as that which harms us or threatens us with harm and destruction. We have seen that the traditional view of evil concentrates on evil as disobedience to the patriarch. The harm that we do to each other is not primary. Although traditionalists consider that harm, they describe it as *evil* only when it transgresses the laws of God, state, father, or chief.

Now it is time to look at evil from the perspective of women's experience, to adopt the standpoint of women. In each section that follows we will focus on the basic occasions of evil and the feelings that accompany these occasions. We will see that the sensations and feelings we often associate with evil—pain, for example—are not always evil in themselves, and we must also differentiate between the feelings or affects and the conditions in which they arise. We must then ask whether these conditions are always evil in themselves, and we will see that the answer is again no. Running beneath this analysis like a subterranean stream will be the question, What *is* evil? What is this thing that we have discussed for three chapters, the prior descriptions of which must all now go into brackets?

I will start the analysis by looking at evil—that which harms or threatens harm—in the setting of old age. I have chosen this period of life not only because it combines a view of completed life, elemental needs, and unending longings, but, more important, because it is also a period of life in which gender is less salient than in earlier periods. Both women and men confront the imminence of death and the basic need to make sense of daily life. I will not study old age, but rather use fictional descriptions to launch my analysis of evil. I will show that the basic fears we experience in old age arise in infancy in the fear of pain, separation, and helplessness present shortly after birth. But the examples I choose for analysis will not confine us to a gender-less old age—if indeed there is such a thing. I choose them because they also include the stories of women who are testing their identities and learning a great deal about evil and good in the process. Although the analysis proceeds from women's standpoint, it attempts to show just how inclusive such a perspective can be.

The analysis of evil manifest in old age should provide some categories and indicators to use in analyzing evil in other settings. I will turn then to look at domestic experience to see if those categories are indeed useful, if they reveal anything new, and if the new questions that arise throw light or doubt on the preceding analysis.

EVIL AS REVEALED IN OLD AGE

In *The Diary of a Good Neighbor* Doris Lessing (through her diarist, Jane Somers) describes the slow death of an old woman, Maudie, whom Jane (Janna) has befriended. The friendship is incongruous. Jane is middle-aged and elegant, a successful writer of novels and editor of a high-fashion magazine; Maudie is a skinny, dirty, lower-class old woman. They have known each other but a short time. Although Maudie is past ninety, she sees her coming death as a "tragedy." She sees both her death and the present final events as evils from which she would escape if possible. First, there is pain: "She has so little energy, because of the pain, which is much worse. The sister, without words, showed me the glass she took in last night, with a gesture that said, You see? I did. It's the potion they use when the pain is really bad, though it is a killer, a mixture of morphine and alcohol."[2]

This pain accomplishes nothing. It is not the sort we endure to have straighter teeth or to deliver a child or to prevent a death that may be postponed. It is gratuitous and inexorable. We are tempted to say that *it is evil*. But here the question arises whether we want to label something evil if there is no agency involved in its occurrence. If we want to insist that God is somehow involved or could be involved if he so chose, then we immediately stray from the present suffering to its meaning or purpose. So let us set the idea of God aside for the moment. Without God, is there a point to calling this pain or the mortal ailment that causes it "natural evil"? We may have no compelling reason to reject the well-known label as long as we understand that the term does not imply the existence of an agent who wills the pain or a necessity or purpose for the pain. It is just a contingent, gratuitous, and inexorable pain that accompanies sure and final bodily destruction. Mercifully the people around Maudie—the sisters, Jane, the tired female helpers—do not muse on the necessity of this pain or on its role in soul making. They relieve it as best they can. So with the understanding that I will not attribute pain to supernatural causes, I will continue to use the expression "natural evil."

But pain is not the only, or even the greatest, evil Maudie suffers. There is helplessness. Even before her final illness Maudie hated the people who could force her to move out of her dismal but beloved apartment, hated the stiffening of her body that prevented her from bending to wash herself, hated even more the loosening of muscles that caused a run of filth that needed washing. To have control of one's body and mind is to be alive. Hence she puts off as long as possible taking her pain killers, and her understanding nurses "do not force her, or jolly her into taking it. 'In your own good time,' they say. 'Take it when you need it.'" To Jane she says repeatedly: "'Lift me up, lift me up.' I stand by her, lifting her so that she is sitting straight up. But no sooner have I done it and I have sat down, she whispers, 'Lift me up, lift me.'"[3] Maudie strives to look the world straight in the eye. She does not want to be helpless, to be at the mercy. It seems to her that people are trying to steal her autonomy, her very humanity. And yet helplessness is not an unrelieved evil. It too has positive features. To be temporarily helpless in the presence of loving strength can be a relief. One is not responsible; one can accept the efforts and the gifts of others. But to be helpless when one wants to act or, worse, when one feels that one *must* act—that is an evil. So, recognizing the need to avoid helplessness, Jane and Vera (the social worker) and Bridget (the home helper) work hard to sustain Maudie's sense of efficacy in the world.

If we probe our consciousness deeply enough, we can find a fear of helplessness at its inception. What if mother leaves me? What if this wetness engulfs me? What if food never comes? What if this pain never ceases? And so we cry and howl as infants. How fortunate we are if help comes promptly and our sense of helplessness subsides: I *can* bring relief; I can summon this other who comes to me with smiles and soft words and gentle hands. Helplessness is not total.

In both pain and helplessness we see gradations from evil to almost good. We are not ready yet to make final judgments, but even now we can see significant variations. There is the gratuitous and useless pain of Maudie's dying. This pain we have tentatively flagged as evil, and we must come back to it. But pain also serves as a warning of damage and thus often saves us from greater harm or even destruction. (In the religious mode, of course, this kind of pain is still problematic, because we have to ask why an all-good creator would endow us with such a painful warning system. But we have put God in parentheses.) In addition to what might be called a biological purpose for pain, we have already noted ordinary human purposes; we accept pain to avoid crippling, death, and disfigurement. There are also times when we seek physical pain and use it to overcome psychic pain. I may walk twelve miles suffering some emotional agony and finally, blessedly, become aware of a blister on my heel. Now the trick is to get home without doing real damage to my foot, or leg, or hip, and I overcome mental anguish by the practical necessity to reduce the present physical pain. Similarly, we might reflect on the story of a young man who burned himself with cigarettes. His father had recently died in an industrial fire, and this young man was trying "to find out how it felt." In part, I believe, he was trying to overcome his emotional suffering with physical pain. I am not labeling this kind of pain "good" (we are not ready yet for labels), but I note that it comes to us as a sort of good. Something worse fades away.

Similarly, helplessness—the feeling of helplessness—runs a range of valuations. One sort of helplessness affects us as evil—the helplessness that thwarts our emotional sense of being able to or wanting to accomplish something. This helplessness generates anger, frustration, and anxiety; we cannot recognize our true selves in the situations that induce this feeling. But another sort of helplessness relieves us of responsibility, allows us to relax while someone else takes over. Further, there seems to be something called "learned helplessness." This sort is probably a condition rather than a feeling, but we may induce it by a conscious or unconscious desire to maintain the feeling of helplessness. When we are helpless, after all, things are out of our hands; we cannot be held responsible. We can rest, stay at ease, feel certain that any efforts we might make would be ineffectual anyway and thus wasted. Is this helplessness good or evil? In the effort of writing this account (or reading it), I (or you, reader) may be tempted to say that learned helplessness is evil—something to get rid of. But we must resist the temptation to evaluate from the outside. How do we feel *in* the situation? We cling to our helplessness. It feels better, apparently, than some available alternative.

In addition to pain and helplessness Maudie suffers not only from a *fear* of separation but from the actual feeling of loss induced by real separation. Her husband and siblings deserted her long ago. Her only friend is Janna, and although she refuses to acknowledge what Janna means to her, she clearly fears separation from her. "I go up every day after work, for a couple of hours," Janna writes. " 'Oh, there you are at last,' says Maudie. And when I leave: 'Going, are you?' And she turns her face away from me." [4]

Maudie fears not only separation from Janna but separation from life—from active engagement with the clatter and daily turmoil of living. "Noise! I said to Maudie, 'Let's shut the door,' but she said, 'No, no, no,' breathlessly shaking her head. She is afraid of being shut in." But perhaps her fear of being shut *out* is even greater. Maudie wants to remain a part of active life. She resists her medication because it increases her helplessness and at the same time separates her from normal life. " 'They are taking my mind away from me, they are deadening my thoughts,' she has whispered to me, reproachful, sorrowful, angry." [5]

We feel separation and loss as evils from the very beginning of our conscious lives. Two- to three-year-olds feel "separation anxiety" acutely. The absolute terror on the face of a child lost in a supermarket tells us that this fear is basic and pervasive. Wise pediatricians and child psychologists now even advise mothers not to plan extended absences during this crucial period unless they are unavoidable. The dreadful, elemental terror returns in old age.

But separation is not in itself evil. Some separations are clearly good—even to the extreme captured in the expression "Good riddance!" We feel some separations both as losses and as matters of pride, as when our children go off to college or marry or take positions that carry them away from home. And we feel some separations both as losses and as reliefs, as when someone in great pain or simply aching with the burden of years finally dies.

The fundamental evils seem to be combinations of physical and emotional pain—what we might call psychic pain, a pain that threatens our sense of being. Physical pain accompanied by hope or happy anticipation (as in childbirth) is not evil; only if physical pain overwhelms the more joyful aspect would we evaluate the occurrence as evil. Physical separation that induces emotional pain uncompensated by a sense of fulfillment, relief, or other positive affect is clearly evil to the one who experiences it. Similarly, helplessness unrelieved by a carefree sense of happy dependence is evil. Thus pain, helplessness, and separation are the basic conditions of evil, and as the analysis proceeds we will see that the great existential anxieties male writers have identified—Paul Tillich's anxieties of death, guilt, and meaninglessness, for example, and Sartre's anguish of freedom[6]—can either be derived from these basic senses of evil or (in Sartre's case) denied as inaccurate descriptions of female existence. Even in the case of these basic candidates for evil, we have seen that they are not evil in themselves. Sometimes they appear to us as good, or at least better than what they replace. Further, we will see perversions of each—cases that appear good to a few individuals and evil to a healthy majority.

In this chapter I take a woman-centered view of evil by asking, in the words of Gerda Lerner, "If women were central to this argument, how would it be defined?"[7] It is difficult work, because all of us—men and women alike—live in a symbolic world that men developed and that we cannot ignore even if we strive mightily to do so. Thus I plan to move deliberately and dialectically between descriptions of women's experience and traditional accounts of evil.

In chapter 1 we saw that the traditional theodicies advise us to find meaning in pain and suffering. But having put all gods temporarily aside, we find no meaning in Maudie's suffering. Further, neither

Maudie nor any of her female caretakers mention God's will or an ultimate purpose in her misery. They work to relieve her pain, alleviate her loneliness, and preserve—as nearly as they can—her autonomy. To these women evil is the deliberate or negligent failure to combat these great natural catastrophes, and the willful induction or aggravation of these ills would surely be unregenerate evil. Describing the atmosphere of the Old Hospital, in which Maudie is dying, Janna notices the emphasis on kindness. The sister in charge

> is middle-aged, rather tired, has thick legs that seem to ache, and a broad sensible pleasant face that gives confidence. She is always on the watch for the slightest sign of unkindness or impatience by her nurses. She does not mind that they are slapdash, casual and—apparently— sometimes inefficient, forgetting to do this or that, recovering the situation with a laugh and an apology. . . . But when I saw one of the more brisk nurses using a sharp edge on her voice to old Maggie, Sister White called her over and said to her, "This place is her home. It's all the home she's got. She's entitled to be silly if she wants. Don't hurry her and harry her. I won't have it, Nurse!" [8]

Sister White's use of the word *entitled* has nothing to do with the standard treatment of entitlement in theories of justice. It derives, rather, from a tradition that treasures and guards personal relationships, a tradition women have fostered for millennia. She did not mean that old Maggie had a right to be nasty or to abuse others. She meant that Maggie had a basic longing to be treated with loving kindness regardless of her shortcomings and that the first obligation of caretakers is to convey the gentle assurance that they will continue *to care* as they perform their duties. [9]

Lessing (through her diarist, Janna) contrasts the attitude of Sister White with that of the physician in charge of Maudie's case. In using this contrast, I do not imply that physicians are generally uncaring or that women are superior to men in their devotion to caring. (Maudie's sister, for example, treats Maudie abominably.) Rather, I am trying to bring to consciousness and analyze the moral wisdom often embedded in women's conversations and in the attitudes they bring (or feel they should bring) to their work and to their relationships. [10] The women tending Maudie treat her as a sister human being in pain. The "big doctor" who attends her treats her as a case. Recognizing how irrelevant she is to him as a person, Maudie fails to discuss her pain with him at all, and Jane knows that she will receive no direct word from him. He would communicate only with Maudie's "personal" physician, who in turn would talk to Vera, and Vera would tell Jane what really ailed Maudie. Jane then would have to agonize over what to tell Maudie. In this chain of mystification we see the power of authority to maintain and increase helplessness—even to make the whole performance seem somehow necessary—and we see the ambivalence of women caught up in the web of mystification unsure whether to dust it away or leave it undisturbed.

In chapter 2 we discussed dramatic differences in the way Pearl Buck's parents approached good and evil. Recall that Andrew would not allow Mr. Ling or his second wife (a "concubine") to join the church. He insisted that according to Christian law he must send her away. In contrast, Carie wanted to welcome the woman, who, Carie saw clearly, was not at fault for the social arrangements that made her a concubine. Years later, when Carie was close to death, she seemed to realize that the view of good and evil under which she had been forced to live was somehow mistaken. She then wanted music, dance, and beauty in her life.

> She turned quite against Andrew these days and would not have him beside her. . . . So we kept him away, and he was bewildered but willing enough, for he had never understood her nature and the changes of which she was capable, none greater than this at the end, when she deliberately put from her all thought of religion and God and chose the beauty of life and creation in this world that she loved and knew richly.[11]

In contrast, Andrew never learned to participate in ordinary human life. Yet toward the end of his life he seemed to need people as a shield against the coming silence.

> Sometimes at twilight he would seem timorous of being alone, as though he remembered the old ghost stories he had heard as a child. He wanted the lights early, and he wanted to hear human voices, to have people about him. Carie's daughter stayed near then, and spoke to him cheerfully of small things, and sat by him with everyday sewing in her hands, and encouraged the children to run in and out. He was comforted by such small ways, and warmed, though he never knew how to share in the life of home or children. But he sat and watched and the look of fear went out of his eyes and after a while he could go up to bed.[12]

So even this spirit-man who worked with enthusiasm into his eightieth year and really lived for and through his work needed, at the end, to feel the warmth of human relationships. In contrast, during his gender-salient years sometime earlier, in writing a brief account of his life at the urging of his daughter, he told "the story of his soul, his unchanging soul." He mentioned his wife and children only once and "forgot entirely a little son who lived to be five years old and who was Carie's favorite child, and he made no comment on any of them." [13]

We see something of the same sort of turning toward ordinary life in the last confessions of Cyprian, the priest in Mary Gordon's *The Company of Women.* Cyprian considers himself a failure because he never achieved objectivity or neutrality in his human relationships. First, he berates himself for leaving his parents and siblings for the priesthood; he might have helped them, he thinks, but instead he sought glory and higher things. But these too he failed to realize. He turned bitter and disgusted at worldly changes in priests and the priesthood. Then he encouraged the company of women to whom he became spiritual adviser. For so many years he thought that *he* was giving to *them,* and now at the end he realizes that they sustained him and gave him the love he sorely needed. Even before his turning to the company of women, he found himself "too warm" for the priesthood, unable to "disappear inside [the] office." His elders seemed to forgive him this sin, which he assesses now as pride.

> They referred to it as warmth of heart, my ardor for the souls who came to me. They did not understand that I loved those souls not in God but for themselves, that I wished to talk to them not only for their salvation but for the pleasure of words given and taken, personal gifts. I have not learned the great lesson of these men: the lesson of silence, the lesson of forgetfulness. [14]

How strange these words would seem to Carie (and yet how familiar). Is it a sin to love human beings for themselves? Can we really love them in any other way? Here we see a man striving for what his male-dominated and abstract religion says is good but all the while feeling inside himself a need to love particular human beings. From a woman's perspective the neglect of relation that he found so hard to achieve is itself a candidate for evil, something that induces both separation and a feeling of helplessness in those who accept it. One must cut off one's love, direct it to God, and redirect it impartially to the human beings one encounters. Those nonpriest humans in turn become helpless in their passionate efforts for one another and must pretend that their strength and love come from God through this special other. How odd all this seems when we examine it through the clear lens of female experience.

Nearing the end of his life, Cyprian clings to his faith; he still longs for the face of God. But he allows himself to see the truth about his dependence on people: "I think it is unbearable that one day I will not see their faces. I fear the moment of death when one longs only for a human face, that beat, that second between death and life eternal. . . . I fear the moment of longing for a human face." Cyprian at the end suffers the pain of separation so well known to women but, like most of us, fails to see how the world could be changed if he took a different attitude toward that pain: "Love is terrible. To disentangle oneself from the passions, the affections, to love with a burning heart which demands only itself and never asks for gratitude or kindness. In that I have failed. I have hungered for kindness; I have hungered for gratitude." [15]

What is wrong, women might ask, with a desire for kindness and gratitude, particularly if one has devoted one's life to giving them? Is it the *hunger* that makes him wrong? If so, we must ask what creates such a hunger, what deprivation or counterstriving triggers the perpetual gnawing. As we get closer to the source of this deprivation, we draw closer to evil itself.

Let us see now if we can draw out of the discussion so far a preliminary analysis of evil. Our first candidate for evil was pain, but clearly pain is not always and in itself evil. Useless and intractable pain we have called natural evil, but it might be even better simply to call it useless and intractable pain. Real evil—moral evil—occurs when some agent causes such pain or fails to alleviate it when he or she is clearly in a position to do so. From this perspective moral evil is not sin, because there is not yet a god to offend or sacred rules to disobey. Morality is entirely bound up with how our best reflective experience tells us we should meet and treat each other, and this reflection demands a clear look at evil as that which harms us. Because female experience has been so often and so intimately confined to persons for whom we must care (or for whom we do care), the feeling should arise in us that we *must* relieve pain when it is in our power to do so, and certainly we must not inflict pain unless we have an excellent reason—which we will see, is not easy to produce.

We must carry out a detailed analysis of pain, then, in two directions. First, we must explore what we may do and what we must do to relieve pain; we must ask also about the sources of permission and obligation. Second, we must investigate the conditions, if any, under which we can justifiably inflict pain. Among the topics we will discuss in the first direction are euthanasia and abortion; in the second, physical and psychic violence, war, and sadism. We will pay special attention in this analysis to practices such as torture that induce not only pain but helplessness and separation as well.

The three occasions of evil we have identified so far resemble other analyses of fear and anxiety. Paul Tillich, for example, identifies three existential anxieties and the fears in which they culminate. The first of these, anxiety over bodily well-being and fear of death, relates usefully to the analytical scheme I am trying to develop on evil. We fear the pain that often precedes death, but even more (as we saw in the earlier anecdotal accounts) we fear separation from loved ones and acquaintances. Perhaps most terrible of all is the ultimate helplessness of death—a state in which we can do nothing, think nothing, feel nothing. Since death threatens us with all three great potential evils, the willful or negligent causing of death is a great moral evil.

The anxiety of guilt and fear of condemnation clearly relate to the evil occasions of separation. Tillich's categories arise, of course, out of a religious framework; ethical terror is already a reality in his account. But an existential aspect of guilt arises necessarily out of our desire to be in caring relations with other human beings.[16] Our fear of separation gives rise to an ethical concern. If we treat another badly, he or she may desert us, and we will deserve this abandonment or at least bring it on ourselves. Moreover, even if we are blameless in our relations with loved ones, they may withdraw from us if they learn that we have treated others badly. Thus the neglect of relation—the failure to maintain positive relations when possible and desirable and the failure to attend to the quality of negative relations—is another great moral evil.

Finally, the anxiety of meaninglessness relates to the evils of separation and helplessness. The loss of meaning does not begin in a separation from ideas, as Tillich suggests, but in a separation from people and ordinary life. Intellectual life, which in an important sense gives meaning to our lives (since it gives us the capacity for meaning), also threatens the loss of meaning, for ideas wipe one another out ruthlessly, and only a connection to active life gives thought the stability it needs to sustain meaning. Pearl Buck discusses the perils of intellectual detachment in *The Good Earth*. She has her main characters, Wang Lung and O-lan, observe the melancholy of their eldest son with mixed feelings. O-lan thinks that he needs a sexual outlet. Wang Lung sees a deeper truth in her observation that the boy is like a young lord:

> Wang Lung was surprised, after he had pondered for a while, for he saw the truth in what she said. It was true that when he himself was a lad there was no time for melancholy, for he had to be up at dawn for the ox and out with the plow and the hoe . . . for if he [indulged in melancholy or ran away] there was nothing for him to eat on return, and so he was compelled to labor.[17]

The boy was separated emotionally from his father by a gulf of education, and the elemental striving that gave meaning to his father's life was unnecessary for him. Perhaps the son was not so much sensitive and filled with deep thoughts as deprived of the experiential qualities that hold back the realization of separation and helplessness. An important problem for us will be to see just how the neglect of relation, separation from ordinary life, and the loss of meaning are related.

One of the errors of the Christian tradition, as we have seen, is to locate evil in bodily human life and to posit good in a spiritual realm vastly separate from ordinary human relations. In this tradition the neglect of human relations rarely appears as evil because it is so often held to be justified by the search for God. Indeed, an undue interest in ordinary life has a close association with sin. But from the perspective of women's experience we will see that the neglect of relation is in fact a basic evil. Existentialist writers sometimes make an error similar to the traditional one. Sartre, for example, certainly does not condemn the earthly or exalt the heavenly, but he clearly fears the bonds of ordinary human life. He wants his human relations to cluster around pleasure or great causes and not to become causes or projects themselves. He expresses his concern in this revealing passage:

> Such is the present paradox of ethics; if I am absorbed in treating a few chosen persons as absolute ends, for example, my wife, my son, my friends, the needy person I happen to come across, if I am bent upon fulfilling all my duties toward them, I shall spend my life doing so; I shall be led *to pass over in silence* the injustice of the age, the class struggle, colonialism, Anti-Semitism, etc., and, finally, to *take advantage of oppression in order to do good*. Moreover, the former will be found in person to person relationships and, more subtly, in my very intentions. The good that I try to do will be vitiated at the roots. It will

be turned into radical evil. But, vice versa, if I throw myself into the revolutionary enterprise I risk having no more leisure for personal relations—worse still, of being led by the logic of the action into treating most men, and even my friends, as means.[18]

But does devotion to intimate human relations induce descent into radical evil, or is this a bit of mystification? If there were never a turning away from family, friend, neighbor, or proximate stranger, how many of Sartre's great causes would remain? And as Sartre himself noted, great causes have a way of proliferating evils as they move inexorably toward eliminating the one great evil that they aim to overcome. Sartre is right, however, when he warns against the temptation to maintain oppressive structures so that we can act as philanthropists or "helpers." Many citizens hold positions that we might do well to try to eliminate.

Sartre is right again when he points to the dangers of deluding ourselves. Mystification is an evil in which women have participated rather too fully. We may make excuses. Forced helplessness and the need to gain recognition out of serving can lead to self-righteousness, and that state provokes the need to rationalize. What better reasons can be found than ones that will at least produce some kindness and praise from those in charge? Mary Gordon's characters Cyprian and Muriel recognize at one level that they have wrapped their lives in self-serving mystery, but neither can face the ultimate responsibility for this condition. Cyprian knows that he has used Muriel and that his coming death will devastate her:

> For Muriel it will be worst, her I have most failed, most wounded. I should have warned her that her love was dangerous, born of fear, the damaged and possessive love that turns on itself. And yet, when I was lonely, I fed off her love. I allowed her to come and live here, for I was afraid, in the solitude that did not serve me, of falling into despair. I did not like her company, but I required her presence. . . . [He speaks next of repentance and forgiveness for his "cowardice" and "smallness of heart."] Only faith can save us from self-hate. In faith I leave it all behind me, in the hands of God, in the hands of a girl.[19]

Here we see the old priest in and out of authenticity. In his evaluation of Muriel's state he is honest and accurate; in his assumption of total blame for her misery, however, he fails to credit her with full autonomy. Again in his leaving it all to faith—instead of talking to Muriel, for example—he falls back on a lifetime of mystification. In leaving things "in the hands of God, in the hands of a girl," he still does not see or appreciate the great strength in the extraordinary company of women with whom he has worked for so long. He picks the least autonomous—a child—as one through whom God will work.

Muriel, the weakest and least lovable of the women, suffers from the same longing for human affection that Cyprian expressed. Absorbed by the church's mystification but never really satisfied by it, she has loved Cyprian—a safe, religiously acceptable love—but now it turns out that she loved and needed *him*, not the mystery he represented. Thus she admits to herself, "For me, his death will be the end of life." In the company of strong women who have known one another for a lifetime, she still feels alone and unloved: "They have one another," she observes.[20]

Both old people suffer from a helplessness that derives in part from personality defects but in perhaps greater part from a socialization that depends heavily on mystification—a continuous veiling of central issues and building up of elaborate rationales and magical rituals, all compounded by inducements to believe and conform and disincentives to shake loose and live authentically. It is not their being religious in and of itself that makes them victims of mystification (the other women in the group are also deeply religious), but rather their inability to demystify the issues that affect their capacity to live fully and freely.

So far I have identified three conditions and the evils associated with their deliberate induction or neglect: pain and the infliction of pain, separation and the neglect of relation, helplessness and the mystification that sustains it. I need to say much more about each, of course, but this identification provides a framework in which to continue to analyze evil from the standpoint of women's experience.

DOMESTIC EXPERIENCE AND EVIL

In this chapter we are searching for the phenomenological roots of evil—for that which we would name as evil if we were not caught up in its surface or conceptualized manifestations. The analysis has proceeded from an examination of old age and dying with appropriate parallel comments on infancy and on women's attitudes toward the evils so manifested. From psychoanalytic perspectives the psychological problems of young and mid-adult life are so different from those of infancy and old age that we might require an entirely different scheme to grapple with evil in mid-adult life. But a different scheme does not seem to be necessary when we work from the perspective of women. Women do not need to tear away from the mother and relatedness to achieve individuation, and so their old age does not require a re-turning to the tranquil domestic scene.[21] A central concern of this study is to separate and evaluate carefully the elements of good and evil in this experience. Further, we should be interested in controlling our future experience to preserve good and minimize evil. Such a task requires carefully analyzing women's experience. What strengths have arisen from traditional domestic life? What parts of domestic life ratify evil?

In the preceding chapters we saw that *woman* has been defined in a way that serves men. In the early days of patriarchy, men actually exchanged women as property, a practice reflected today in the ritual wedding question, Who *giveth* this woman? Even the prohibition of incest represents, according to Lévi-Strauss, "a rule obliging the mother, sister, or daughter to be given to others." It is, he says, "the supreme rule of the gift."[22] Surely using human beings as objects of exchange is evil. The practice induces pain, separation, and helplessness; it is thus a prime candidate for assessment as a moral evil.

But now we see that in addition to natural evil and moral evil we may need another category. Human beings frequently participate in the practices of their culture without reflective evaluation. A man living in the early days of patriarchy almost certainly did not intend to inflict pain, separation, and helplessness on the female members of his family—as long as they were "good" women. He did not consider the possibility that he was committing evil. His evil deeds in this arena were not the deliberate acts of an individual agent. Rather, they were accepted and respectable acts that we must now evaluate as *cultural evils*. Neither Aristotle nor Kant—giants of moral philosophy—saw the evils they participated in by denying the rationality and autonomy of women. Will we be able to see the evils and potentials for evil in our own culture and in the solutions we suggest for current problems? My aim is to use what we learn from an analysis of traditional views not only to identify practices that seem obviously to be evils from today's perspective but, more important, to apply the framework thus constructed to current and future situations so that we can avoid generating evil even as we struggle to overcome it.

Cultural evils have a way of embedding themselves in the tissues of society. They resist elimination and instead undergo transformation; sometimes the transformation is merely cosmetic and sometimes it is moderately significant, but the evils remain potent. On the topic of man's oppression of woman Gerda Lerner remarks: "Traditionalist defenses of male supremacy based on biological-deterministic reasoning have changed over time and proven remarkably adaptive and resilient. When the force of the religious argument was weakened in the nineteenth century the traditionalist explanation of woman's inferiority became "scientific." [23]

As our discussion of Victorian women revealed, this explanation acknowledged women's potential but insisted that the work of perpetuating the species drained women of the creative energy they might use for other purposes. Those who accepted the mandate of species survival and threw their energies selflessly into that task were verbally honored but, of course, still tightly controlled. The need for honor and praise in addition to explicit commands and threats almost certainly increased with the spread of literacy. Moderately well-to-do Western women, at least, could read and begin to question the evil practices of the supposedly good societies in which they lived. Therefore they required more to make them content with their positions.

The historical parts of Ken Follett's fictional *Man from St. Petersburg* illustrate both the degree of control and the power of incentives. Charlotte, the wealthy young heroine of Follett's story, lives the extremely protected life of well-to-do post-Victorian females. But she is intelligent, sensitive, and headstrong. When she sees the misery of poverty and exploitation on the city streets, she challenges her wealthy parents to defend their ways. The sight of people sleeping in the streets particularly offends her. When her mother tells her that the "people on the pavement are idlers, criminals, drunkards and ne'er-do-wells," she responds sharply, "Even the children?" Her mother then reprimands her for impertinence, a reminder that the greatest sins are disobedience and disrespect. As this conversation is about to close, Charlotte decides to take a closer look at one of the street sleepers outside her own gates and recognizes Annie, a former housemaid in her parents' hall. "Annie, what happened to you?" she cries.[24]

Charlotte's parents discharged Annie without a reference, it turns out, because she was pregnant and unmarried. Her seventeen-year-old lover ran away to sea. The fate of women in this situation was dismal and seems incredible to us today. They could give up their babies and live in the workhouse doing menial labor, or they could take to the streets with their infants as beggars or prostitutes. Many infants died. Their mothers were "ruined" women who were often ostracized by members of their own class. Thus Charlotte's parents were not alone in turning a judgmental eye on Annie and preventing her from getting "decent" work; her former coworkers had also internalized the rules of behavior for good women and would have been scandalized if she had rejoined the household. Women's sexuality in the early twentieth century was controlled by keeping upper-class females in ignorance until they were safely married and lower-class females in terror of ostracism and physical misery.

In the fictional account of Annie we read what really happened to a multitude of women and children.[25] The evils of pain, helplessness, and separation appear obvious to the uncluttered consciousness, and the traditional custom of condemning such women and children as sinful begins to look like a monstrous ratification of evil. We see something else, however, in Annie's story. In Charlotte we see the horrified reaction of a young woman who has learned to believe in and live by the law of kindness; as her ignorance disappears she sees that her society lives not by this rule but by one of power. Her compassion and desire to alleviate pain lead her to consider joining the suffrage movement, which, among other goals, strives to relieve the dreadful conditions of lower-class mothers and children.

The traits and attitudes that appear in Charlotte and in many actual women correlate intricately with society's expectations for mothers (what might be called the mother model) and with the actual experience of mothering. Jane Addams, for example, came more directly under the influence of her father than of her mother, who died when Jane was only two years old. But she knew that her mother had been eulogized as someone who would be "missed everywhere, at home, in society, in the church, in all places *where good is to be done and suffering relieved.*"[26] She did not herself become a mother, but neither did she reject the "ideal of womanhood."[27] In her life, as in the lives of so many others in the nineteenth and early twentieth centuries, we see lively intelligence working diligently for the relief of basic evils. Whether this compassionate behavior springs from biology or social custom is a question that intrigues many feminists and anti-feminists, but pursuing that question, like so many of the traditional questions I have pointed to, might be another enormous distraction. For whatever reason, women have fed, nursed, soothed, served, and attempted to relieve suffering. This is an empirical claim for which so much evidence exists that we need not waste time citing it.

Paradoxically, however, women have also allowed themselves to support the infliction of suffering, particularly in their endorsement of great wars thought to be necessary to defend a cherished way of life. Women have sometimes expressed pride in the sacrifice of their sons, an attitude the male-dominated nation-states encourage. Domestic experience contributes to this peculiar attitude—one so much at odds with women's basic tasks of preservation—in at least two ways. First, the idea that one's only sphere of autonomy and security may be threatened is a powerful incentive to mount defenses, and so in a sense the sons who will die are sacrificed to maintain a way of life designed to preserve and nurture them. Second, women confined to domestic life might naturally welcome any opportunity to belong fully to a cooperative venture that promises glory and recognition. Women fall prey to mystification and work against the logic of their own lifework. I will return to this theme in chapter 7.

Well-educated women who see and share human suffering, like their male peers, often seek solutions in alternative ideologies. In particular, because women's literacy and interest in social affairs grew rapidly in the late nineteenth century, women reformers sometimes considered Marxism a program that might alleviate both their own oppression and the general misery of poverty.[28] The difficulty in this view—at least for the present examination of evil—is that it addresses only those evils that have an economic base. Indeed, it insists that all evil stems from unfair practices in the production and distribution of goods for the sustenance and transformation of life. Although Marxism is historical in its method, it is peculiarly masculine in its phenomenology, valuing the actual production of material goods over affectionate human relations, the nurturance of children, caring for the ill and aged, and like activities. Where attention turns to these activities, Marxism describes them as wage-earning tasks and entirely ignores the special attitude that has accompanied such tasks as women have performed them.

More will be said on the relation between economic theories and humanistic studies in chapter 6; in the present brief discussion I want to make clear why I must say something about Marxism and other political and economic theories. All of them either totally neglect or give a dangerously narrow interpretation of human relatedness. The evil of separation is aggravated by their adoption. In this important sense fascism, liberalism, capitalism, communism, and even socialism all miss the fundamental qualities of human life as women experience them. They do not explore and discuss fully what I will refer to as life-sustaining and life-enhancing activities and relations. Having mentioned these terms—*life-sustaining* and *life-enhancing*—I must make clear that they apply as well to activities other than those to which I refer. Architecture, medical science, the composition of symphonies, the invention and manufacture of home appliances, and many other activities in the public world may all properly be described as life-enhancing. When I use the terms in connection with female experience, I mean life-enhancing in a direct and personal way. We will be interested in activities directed to particular concrete others for their own sakes, and then we will consider whether we can extend such activities into the larger domain without losing the characteristic attitudes that accompany them in the personal domain.

Current feminism shows a good deal of interest in the activities women have traditionally performed, but writers have generated much confusion by describing these activities in terms that belong to a different domain of discourse. Jane Roland Martin, for example, uses the Marxist terms *productive* and *reproductive* to describe the major activities of men and women. Reproductive activities, she says, "include not simply conception and birth but the rearing of children to more or less maturity and associated activities such as tending the sick, taking care of family needs, and running a household." We can view and discuss all these activities in economic terms; from a materialist point of view they are convertible to productive functions, and some feminists discuss them in just such a fashion. But this treatment misses the human heart of these activities. Martin certainly does not intend this result. On the contrary, she wants to make "nurturance, caring, concern, and connection goals of education." [29] Clearly, however, these are not mere *activities;* they are activities characterized by certain attitudes or ways of being that support both productive and reproductive functions. Therefore we must probe these functions deeply from the standpoint of those who have performed them.

To motivate a more thorough analysis of women's life-giving, life-sustaining, and life-enhancing activities, I should say a bit more about the weaknesses of political and economic ideologies. Historical materialism is wrong not in its emphasis on history, but in its emphasis on *man*'s history and its sole reliance on masculine phenomenology. Further, we need not condemn it for its materialism, so far as that term describes human beings as bodily creatures; but it is wrong to put such great emphasis on the crasser connotations of *materialism*. Human beings are creatures who love, fear, grieve, long for, play, have tender memories, and make commitments to each other as well as to causes. We need not regard humans as embodied spirits or as dual beings (mind and body) to acknowledge these aspects, but any description that does not account for them fails in a dramatic and fatal way.

Some feminist theorists, of course, embrace Marxism. Sheila Rowbotham, for example, advocates both communism and an emphasis on women's consciousness, but the aspect of consciousness she relies on is a consciousness of oppression.[30] This choice shows the inevitable narrowing of human *being* that occurs in Marxist thought. It may be possible to repair and revise the Marxist framework to take greater account of women's experience, but such changes are likely to destroy the basic structure of Marxism, for any adequate description will have to include the human quest for spirituality, the longing for individual human attachment, and even the conscious commitment to empower others.

Feminist-Marxist thinkers have examined women's activities, but they have not carefully investigated the whole experience that accompanies such activities. Indeed, Marxist studies sometimes charge that domestic life itself is evil or that certain tasks within it are evil in their effects on women. Charlotte Perkins Gilman, for example, analyzed sex life and homemaking tasks such as cooking—seeing the latter as an especially pernicious part of women's subjugation. She was right to have looked at cooking and feeding, because they are fundamental life-sustaining and life-enhancing functions, and the expectation that women will perform them has affected all women, but she abstracts her analysis away from women's actual experience. Proceeding through Marxist concepts, her study is not a phenomenological analysis but an illustration of perceived evil in the form of social and economic oppression.[31]

There is also some humor in this story (and this is something else that is forgotten in ideological analyses—human beings play and laugh, and sometimes even chuckle while reading historical materials). Page Smith, in his account of Gilman's work, expresses some dismay at her attack on cooking: "The vehemence of Mrs. Gilman's attack on cooking (the 'unutterable depravity of gluttony and intemperance') and her intermingling of food and sex suggest either something a bit pathological in her own background or her sense that she was assaulting an almost impregnable redoubt." He gives her the benefit of the theoretical doubt in his continuing historical account. But in his introduction we get a hint of what dismayed him in Gilman's attack. He refers good-humoredly there to his wife, who during the course of his writing the book "seduced me from my labors with delicious meals (so that my girth grew with my book)."[32] This statement illustrates exactly the relation between sex, food, and labor that Gilman so vehemently attacked. What she missed, however, is the genuine tenderness, the delight in pleasing and being pleased, the appreciation of each partner for the other's ill-understood work.

Cooking for a family has been central to women's work, and when we look at it without the lens of abstract ideology, we are hard put to categorize it as an evil. In cookbooks such as *The Vermont Year Round Cookbook* we find a description of life from a woman's perspective along with the recipes, celebrating the partnership of hardworking women and men. Mrs. Appleyard (the author's pseudonym) comments on the old story that Vermont farmers regularly ate pie for breakfast:

> Mrs. Appleyard happens to know from personal observation that it was true fifty years ago and that there was nothing ridiculous about it. The man who was enjoying a good slab of pie at seven-thirty had been up milking cows since four o'clock. He had already done what most men would consider a day's work, and he would still be working twelve hours later. He very likely had pie twice a day and he needed it.[33]

We hear in this statement a warm sympathy for male partners whose work—like woman's work—was often tedious, backbreaking, and apparently endless. There is a hint of autonomy in the statement and certainly in the accompanying recipes. Women managed their larders and kitchens; they made significant choices about the use of family resources. Baking pies and feeding a family were necessary and important work. Although this work involved an element of drudgery (as did men's work), it also yielded extrinsic and intrinsic rewards for many women. *The Grass Roots Cookbook* (which includes biographical sketches along with recipes) tells the story of a seventy-eight-year-old woman, Mary Rohrer, who was still active in the domestic tasks she enjoyed.

> She now does allow herself an afternoon catnap, but within half an hour or so she is up and about again, hoeing her vegetable garden (which she calls "going to the doctor," because gardening, she believes, is good medicine for both body and soul); simmering giant kettles of Chicken-Corn Soup or Chicken Potpie; helping a neighbor "put up" peas; baking berry pies for a Mennonite fund-raising sale; refinishing a set of chairs she has picked up at a county auction; adding another coil or two to a huge braided rug she is making to order.[34]

The women who perform such life-sustaining and life-enhancing work frequently derive strength for their own lives through an appreciation of culture and nature. Here Mrs. Appleyard describes summer in Vermont:

> Sometimes it is warm enough, if you have a camel's hair robe, to lie out on the front porch and read the complete works of Jane Austen. Mrs. Appleyard knows them so well that she often sandwiches in a look at the landscape between sentences. She can look across her covered bridge, the smallest in Vermont, and see the wind making green and silver waves and ripples in the uncut hay. In the pasture Jersey cows are conscientiously nibbling down the grass to green velvet. Hummingbirds are emeralds and rubies among the larkspur spires. Sky roses of cloud drift by. She can hear the brook dashing down the valley.[35]

The performance of life-sustaining and -enhancing functions is not in itself a sign of oppression. There is a good deal of autonomy, pride, and delight in the stories we read in cookbooks. But even though many women have experienced challenge, satisfaction, and delight in preparing meals for their loved ones and guests, there is another side of the story. Sylvia Plath's autobiographical heroine, Esther, imagines herself married to a man whom she finds attractive, but shudders at thoughts of the life that would follow:

> It would mean getting up at seven and cooking him eggs and bacon and toast and coffee and dawdling about in my nightgown and curlers after he'd left for work to wash up the dirty plates and make the bed, and then when he came home after a lively, fascinating day he'd expect a big dinner, and I'd spend the evening washing up even more dirty plates till I fell into bed, utterly exhausted.[36]

Mrs. Rohrer and the other women *The Grass Roots Cookbook* describes would find Esther's complaint amusing. Imagine being exhausted by managing two meals for a mere couple! But Esther's fears reveal an important element of modern female consciousness—the recognition that women are *coerced* into their role as caretakers by the universal demands of the mother model. This recognition causes psychic pain: Why should I not be able to choose what I will do in life? Why should my life be subordinate to another's? Today we can reject the mother model, but opposing its coercive power brings a fear of separation and loneliness. Rejecting it requires a woman to redefine relationships and work creatively to build and maintain them. Finally, the very thought of rejecting the mother model may induce helplessness in many women. Those whose families, friends, and communities work together to sustain the mother model are indeed trapped in mystification. Do happy women like Mrs. Appleyard and Mrs. Rohrer, then, ratify a fundamental evil?

Questions concerning who ratifies evil and exactly where the evil is located require meticulous analysis. Women whose basic consciousness reveals beauty, love, and contentment in their nurturing roles are certainly not engaging in or supporting evil by remaining committed to the work that brings them deep satisfaction. Women who attempt to coerce others into a similar commitment are clearly supporting the evil inherent in the mother model—a set of expectations that threatens us with pain, separation, and helplessness if we reject it. But this analysis leaves the status of cooking for one's family (however we define *family*) unclear. Gilman saw it as an evil from which women must be freed, and she clearly thought that men too would be healthier and happier if home cooking were abolished, since it all too often produced "fat, greasy" husbands afflicted with indigestion and gluttony and trained to exchange affection for food.[37] But home cooking and domestic life do not appear as evils in themselves when we examine women's experience more carefully.

In this discussion the old dilemma rises anew. Will we create new evils or aggravate old ones in our attempts to overcome evil? By concentrating on freeing women from homemaking tasks, we evaluate these tasks as menial and demeaning, as tasks made respectable only by wages. But this way of thinking surely suggests we have succumbed to a new mystification. When we read the personal testimonies of women from every class, region, and century, we find over and over again a deep appreciation and sense of responsibility for their life-sustaining and -enhancing activities. These are the fundamental activities of life, those that connect us to the earth and to each other. Our attempts to overcome evil must not culminate in solutions that make us helpless in new ways and separate us further from each other.

In *The Bell Jar* Esther suffers from a sense of separation and isolation. Indeed, this sense is a clear sign to the reader of her impending mental illness. She wants to be self-defining but is unable to separate the loving functions associated with women's experience from the coercion by which all women either commit themselves to these functions or accept the sanctions of a cruel society. Esther does not want to be a female slave. She still doubts her own worth, however, and the more she fights against the mother model, the more unhappy and confused she becomes. In striving toward freedom and trying desperately to protect a self already deeply wounded and fragile, Esther turns her back on Doreen, a friend with whom she had spent a miserable evening—an evening of drinking and watching Doreen's wild sexual activities with Lenny. Doreen turns up at Esther's door in the middle of the night wretchedly sick. As Doreen sinks to the floor in the hall of their residence hotel, Esther considers what to do: "I decided the only thing to do was to dump her on the carpet and shut and lock my door and go back to bed. When Doreen woke up she wouldn't remember what had happened and would think she must have passed out in front of my door while I slept, and she would get up of her own accord and go sensibly back to her room." Doreen vomits violently as she faints, but Esther leaves her, steps back into her room, and shuts the door. In the morning, she dresses and even applies lipstick before opening her door. "I think I still expected to see Doreen's body lying there in the pool of vomit like an ugly, concrete testimony to my own dirty nature." [38]

In rejecting Doreen, Esther rejected part of herself. In trying to overcome both sexual evil as it was defined for her in adolescence and the evil of slavery as it appears in the mother model, she fell into real evil. Denying her relation to Doreen, she deliberately separated herself from the sick woman in the doorway. This is evil—to inflict or ignore pain, to induce separation or deny relation, to aggravate or ignore helplessness. But I am not suggesting that we condemn Esther. Her acts are clearly symptoms of mental illness, an illness traceable at least in part to prior evils. But committing evil for whatever reason seems to press us into further evils, and this multiplication of evils is surely part of the terrible pain of mental illness. Jungians might locate Esther's problem in her separation from the feminine principle, but I am more inclined to locate it in the demand that women define themselves by a principle they have not freely chosen. It would be hard to find a more powerful contemporary illustration of the role traditional evil plays in engendering real evil, but, as we will see, examples abound.

Another domestic task that makes great demands on women is childrearing. Here again, as we noted earlier, women disagree on the value of childrearing as an individual woman's function. Just as Perkins attacked cooking, Shulamith Firestone attacked childbearing and raising.[39] When we first look out on the world and on evil from women's standpoint, we claim to see a variety of things, because women—like men—differ from one another. Our concern is not, however, with differences of taste and opinion but with the logic of each phenomenon as we examine it. Should childrearing be considered an evil because it has been and still is associated with women's oppression?

The experience of mothering has been a source of great joy for many women, and, like cooking, mothering has given rise to opportunities for autonomy, creativity, and the sort of thinking that is generous and other-oriented. Nineteenth-century feminists often expressed the idea that mothering engendered in women a moral superiority over men. Elizabeth Cady Stanton, for example, spoke regularly on this theme.[40] Contemporary feminists who care deeply about children scarcely consider mothering an evil. But the logical test is whether mothering necessarily inflicts pain, separation, or helplessness of the sort we have described. Pain, we might say—both physical and emotional—is necessarily involved, but it is pain we accept for growth and joy; it is neither gratuitous nor inexorable in its direct association with mothering, and the point of most of it comes clear in observable events in this earthly life. Far from inducing separation, mothering is the function par excellence for maintaining relations and strengthening them. Finally, the basic aim of mothering is to empower, to teach the young how to be happy and independent adults; thus mothering acts to overcome helplessness, not to create it.

One could argue, of course, that the structures revealed in the mother model are so oppressive that women in fact cannot engage in mothering as I just described it. Because the mother model oppresses women, they often behave in ways that separate children from fathers and that bind children to mothers in pathological ways. But this line of argument will not do. The recommendations that follow always involve the desirable aims already attributed to mothering but assign them to persons other than individual mothers. It cannot be the experience of mothering that is evil, then, but something in the oppressive expectations of society that spoils the experience. If we could show that this something is individual mothering itself, we might establish Firestone's case, but that conclusion is clearly not true.

Readers might complain at this point that I have missed the point of Firestone's attack. We should focus on the separation of women from the public world and the induced helplessness that brands them ineffective in nondomestic life. *That* is the evil Firestone has in mind. Our earlier discussion now becomes important. If mothering is a relation—one often characterized by joy and companionship—and if we recognize that *someone* must do the tasks traditionally assigned to mothers, the answer to Firestone's demand must be to make mothering more manageable. Other people, society in general, cannot give children the special affection and attentive love that parents can give. Therefore society must restructure the pattern of work and support so that mothers and fathers can both parent effectively and hold down paying jobs.

Whereas nineteenth-century feminists extolled the virtues of good mothers and attempted to transpose those virtues into the public world, some contemporary feminists are exploring the nature of maternal thinking. Sara Ruddick, for example, discusses three great interests of maternal thinking: preserving the life of the child, fostering its growth, and shaping an acceptable child.[41] Each of these interests is subject to interpretation, of course, and one mother's description of an acceptable child may differ from another's, but each concerns enabling the child to live in respected and respectful relations with whatever group or community has established the standards of acceptability. The three interests may conflict with one another, as Ruddick admits. A mother who wants to preserve the life of her son, for example, may find that she needs to reexamine her desire to establish him as acceptable and honorable in time of war. Often, as we saw in the discussion of Esther Harding's judgment of the woman who distracts her man from his duties as a warrior, women have chosen in favor of keeping their sons acceptable and honorable rather than alive. Jean Grimshaw and Jean Elshtain analyze this conflict directly in some depth.[42] When I discuss war in chapter 7, I will return to this conflict. For the moment it is perhaps sufficient to note that war is as logically incompatible with the basic aims of mothering as it is with the fundamental precepts of Christianity, but both mothers and Christians have found ways to participate in it.

The important points for the discussion at hand are these: mothering is not evil in its effects on women, nor need it work evil on others through its practices. Rather, the practices and thinking associated with it strengthen our conviction that we can characterize evil by the presence or infliction of pain, separation, and helplessness. Mothering, by the logic of its aims, strives to avoid all three.

If we can argue that cooking and childrearing are not in and of themselves oppressive to women but, on the contrary, suggest a view of evil radically different from the traditional one, what of other domestic chores? What of dishwashing and housecleaning, for example?

In *The Exile* Buck writes of Carie:

> There was for her beauty not only in a pool of mountain water under moonlight, but as well in a room made still and clean and fresh, in dishes newly washed and shining. I remember her saying that one of her pleasures in the austere times after the Civil War was that there were no dishes to be bought and so every day they had to use the blue and white willow-pattern china and the thin crystal wine goblets that her grandparents had brought from Holland. Every day she chose to wash them, above every other household task, so that she might feel their delicacy.[43]

The family Buck describes in these lines was not wealthy and was suffering from a common postwar hardship, but it was rich in comparison with families who had no china and crystal to keep shining. But the theme of caring about beauty and personal dignity echoes in the stories of poor black women as well. Alice Walker tells how her mother put on a newly received secondhand dress before going to a Red Cross distribution center to obtain the flour to which her voucher entitled her. The woman in charge refused her the flour, saying, "Anybody dressed up as good as you don't need to come here *begging* for food." In spite of her mother's protestations of real need, the angry woman behind the counter continued to refuse her and, worse, humiliated the poor woman for her attention to beauty and cleanliness. "Niggers" were not supposed to have such sensitivities. What did the family do for flour that year? "Well," said Walker's mother, "Aunt Mandy Aikens lived down the road from us and she got plenty of flour. We had a good stand of corn so we had plenty of meal. Aunt Mandy would swap me a bucket of flour for a bucket of meal. We got by all right." Reminding the reader that she does not intend to glorify poverty, Walker says, "Southern black writers . . . have a heritage of love and hate, but . . . they also have enormous richness and beauty to draw from." [44] Women have created and maintained much of the beauty of everyday life.

To women who find beauty as well as love in well-kept homes and gardens, whatever threatens to destroy them is a prime candidate for evil. Violence that leaves women helpless to protect their loved ones and cherished belongings is clearly evil, and the usual explanations—that some great abstract evil must be overcome—sound shallow rather than profound. A woman might well ask why the preservation of the nation, union, or state should necessitate the destruction of her children or even of her willow pattern china. What, after all, is the point of a "state" if it cannot preserve its members from violence?

In this brief look at domestic life, described as yet too simply, we have seen that we should not be hasty to label things evil. The oppression of women is obviously evil because by definition oppression harms and threatens to harm. When we examine the domestic tasks and functions associated with women's oppression, however, we find that women have developed considerable autonomy and creativity in performing them and that they may undertake many domestic tasks with great love for partners who are also working hard. We see also that the direct concern for others that develops in maternal thinking is likely to strengthen our conviction that the traditional view of evil is wrong and itself contributes to evil. What we see from this standpoint are the basic evils of pain, separation, and helplessness. None of this discussion means, nor can it logically be construed to mean, that women should be confined to domestic tasks or that they should be the only persons to perform them. Such a move would be evil, because the demand for subservience and obedience would inflict pain and layer on layer of mystification would encourage helplessness.

If all domestic tasks became paid work, the burden of oppression would shift from gender to class. Some women, like some men, would be free from work that brings little public reward. But the alienation that Marxists fear would in all likelihood increase with such a solution. Women and men have a special concern for their own children, their own homes, and each other's welfare that hired strangers rarely have. Caring for loved ones is not alienated labor. Thus Marxist arguments to abolish the usual patterns of domestic life fail in their recommendations. Domestic activity is so vital for the growth of fully human rationality that women and men should share it. To induce occupational helplessness in women is, of course, evil; to induce separation and encourage the neglect of relation in men is equally evil. A solution must not ratify evil.

THE SENSE OF EVIL

We may recall Simone Weil's comment that real evil is "gloomy, monotonous, barren, boring," whereas imaginary evil is "romantic and varied." In describing pain, separation, and helplessness as the trinity of elemental evils, we feel none of the excitement conveyed by stories of devils, witches, demons, spells, and possession. Evil does not have a stomach-turning stench, nor does it signal its presence with palpable cold and darkness. We do not fall into it haplessly, nor does it entrap (possess) us. Rather, we often act willfully in complicity with it.

If we set aside the myths and stories that have fascinated us for so long, we see that our sense of evil is activated when we become aware that something is harming or threatening to harm us or others. Too often we move directly from this awareness to a judgment that the thing or event itself is evil, or we ignore the actual evil in the event and move to some abstract entity or alien other that is said to be responsible for it. We make mistakes in locating and labeling evil.

The most basic form of evil seems to be pain. Physical pain, when it does not promise a better end state (right here on earth), is an evil we should avoid or relieve. Separation is evil because of the deep psychic pain it causes, and the fear of separation makes human beings vulnerable to all sorts of further evils. Helplessness too is associated with psychic pain, and we must consider its deliberate infliction a great moral evil.

But what should we say about the traditional senses of evil—its filth, ugliness, power, craftiness, stench? What should we do with the familiar categories of defilement, shame, guilt, terror, anger, obsession? What should we say about vice? We can discuss each, I think, within the perspective of women's experience.

What is filthy and ugly is not some bodily function or contamination by some unseen entity of great power. It is, rather, the harm that we do to one another and our fearful refusal to alleviate great pain when we encounter it. From this perspective a woman who is raped is not defiled but hurt, wounded. The man who rapes her is the one defiled; it is he who is dirty, unclean, sullied, dishonored. In fairness I should say that Augustine made this point clearly. Although he can hardly be considered a champion of women and his legacy has brought misery to untold numbers of "sinners," he deplored the violence that human beings do to one another, and he insisted that it was the rapist and not the woman who was shamed by the act.[45] The pain and terror that a woman experiences in rape compound the shame that a cruel society makes her feel about her body and who should have access to it. In the act itself she suffers the physical pain of violence and the psychic pain of helplessness, but both become infinitely worse if she must also fear separation from those who should love and support her. It is not sex that is filthy, then, but the infliction of pain and the use of physical force to satisfy selfish purposes.

Shame, an affect associated with the public disclosure of errors, faults, relations, or evil acts, seems to be part of our fear of separation. When we are ashamed, we fear the loss of esteem of those whom we regard as important. Unlike guilt, shame is pressed on us by the opinions of others. Guilt and shame do not necessarily go together. One may suffer public shame and escape a feeling of guilt entirely, or one may escape shame and suffer deeply from inner guilt. To shame another is to inflict deep psychic pain, and we must ask ourselves whether some good is likely to accrue to the one shamed in our act of public disclosure. Sometimes, of course, we must disclose the wrongdoings of another publicly, but shame is not the aim in such cases. Indeed, one who is likely to feel shame can usually be persuaded by other means.

Guilt is also associated with evil and is an important affect to understand in a morality of evil. In particular we have to understand that guilt can be healthy if it leads to restitution. If we can undo an act or soften it or make up for it, we can relieve our guilt and at the same time help heal the separation that occurs when we wrong another. This is another area in which the traditional view has led us astray. Doing penance for wrong acts does not necessarily address the victim's pain; making restitution, giving an apology, and asking forgiveness of the one wronged are more effective in avoiding evil. As we will see, guilt is a powerful precursor of scapegoating. When we have hurt another person, it is comforting to convince ourselves that he or she deserved it.

Anger too is associated with evil. Indeed, anger is a popular theme with feminists, many of whom call on women to feel and express rage at their long years of exploitation and oppression. Women who resist this move sometimes encounter suspicion within feminist circles. Judith Stacey, for example, considers the recent work of Betty Friedan and Jean Elshtain to be "conservative" precisely because it takes the anger out of sexual politics; both look toward a reconciliation with men and an effort to promote the well-being of all human beings, not just women.[46] To be sure, Stacey does not oppose making the world a better place for all people, and she agrees with Friedan and Elshtain that feminism must pay more attention to the needs of children. What Stacey fears is that "social feminism" as Elshtain (and many women before her) described it will encourage women to abandon sexual politics. What we need, Stacey believes, is a passionate sense of being wronged if our society is ever to be a just one for women.

Mary Daly also speaks of rage and the necessity to maintain it.[47] From the standpoint I have taken, however, rage seems to be counter-indicated. Rage creates separation and causes new pain. It is yet another example of risking the actual commission of evil in well-intentioned efforts to overcome it. As we examine several great evils in the following chapters, we may find effective alternatives to rage. We will ask, What have women learned about overcoming evil, avoiding it, turning it aside?

SUMMARY

We have now begun the difficult work of defining and describing evil from the standpoint of women's experience. Starting with a discussion of evil in old age—regarded as a less gender-intensive period of life—we looked at women's reactions to the ordinary events of life. Three great categories of evil emerged: pain, separation, and helplessness. Of these three, pain seems to be the most basic, and indeed both separation and helplessness are regarded as evil because of the psychic pain that accompanies them.

We have also found it useful to distinguish among natural, cultural, and moral forms of evil. The pain of illness and death are natural evils; poverty, racism, war, and sexism are cultural evils; the deliberate infliction of physical or psychic pain—unless we can show convincingly that it is necessary for a desirable state in the one undergoing pain—is moral evil.

We also briefly discussed the affects associated with evil to make connections with the next set of analyses. Having a sense of evil as that which induces pain, separation, and helplessness allows us to focus on what we can do to avoid evil or, if we cannot avoid it, how we might reduce its effects. We are now ready to examine some important natural, cultural, and moral evils from this new perspective.

5

Pain as Natural Evil

The main topic of this chapter is pain and suffering. Since the psychic pain of separation and helplessness often accompanies physical pain, all the fundamental evils will necessarily enter into the discussion. Even though we have already covered quite a bit of the topic in the criticism of theodicy and in the attempt to identify various evils phenomenologically, we have not yet explored the implications of a feminist analysis. If suffering itself has no purpose and if we see separation and helplessness as states that increase suffering, what recommendations can we make about the social management of pain?

The exploration will begin with a discussion of pain as natural evil and then proceed in the next chapters to its analysis as cultural evil and moral evil. Earlier we considered the reasons men have given for harming other human beings and noted that these reasons often seem alien to women. Becker and others are not necessarily wrong when they say that men hurt one another out of fear and the desire to overcome evil, nor is Nietzsche necessarily wrong when he claims that the capacity to suffer and to inflict suffering is a prerequisite to power. But people looking at the scene from the perspective of women's experience should logically be unlikely to seize on violent solutions or to put a high value on power. Thus the behavior so lavishly and eloquently explained remains to us inexplicable. Women too are afraid, yet we rarely explode into physical violence.[1] Perhaps our experience has taught us the futility of such behavior, given our powerless condition. As our power grows, so might our inclination to violence. I will take a different line of argument, however, and suggest that the life-enhancing tasks for which we have been responsible and the virtues we have learned to admire in ourselves are instrumental in forming our views on good and evil. It is illogical from this perspective to inflict pain or fail to alleviate it. The investigation will continue, then, in the setting of women's experience: protecting and teaching children; feeding a family; tending the sick, wounded, and helpless; maintaining a home. But first we must consider an alternative perspective that shares much with feminist views; it sees the cold reality of life on this earth, but it misses the great joy of everyday living and loving.

PAIN AND PESSIMISM

Pain and suffering pervade the world. As Ernest Becker remarks:

> Existence, for all organismic life, is a constant struggle to feed—a struggle to incorporate whatever other organisms they can fit into their mouths and press down their gullets without choking. Seen in these stark terms, life on this planet is a gory spectacle, a science-fiction nightmare in which digestive tracts fitted with teeth at one end are tearing at whatever flesh they can reach, and at the other end are piling up with fuming waste excrement as they move along in search of more flesh.[2]

This sort of observation has made pessimists out of many strong men and women. Schopenhauer and Tolstoy, for example, both considered suicide to be the only logically consistent response to life as Becker describes it. Even those who reject pessimism recognize the reality of accounts of melancholiacs and those William James calls "sick souls." Acknowledging this reality, James says: "The normal process of life contains moments as bad as any of those which insane melancholy is filled with, moments in which radical evil gets its innings and takes its turn. The lunatic's visions of horror are all drawn from the material of daily fact. Our civilization is founded on the shambles, and every individual existence goes out in a lonely spasm of helpless agony." James goes on to refer to the great carnivores of prehistoric time and their bloody flesh tearing. But the carnage continues: "Here on our very hearths and in our gardens the infernal cat plays with the panting mouse, or holds the hot bird fluttering in her jaws." He concludes his description of natural pain and horror by remarking, "[The] deadly horror which an agitated melancholiac feels is the literally right reaction on the situation."[3]

The pessimists' account is not so much wrong as it is incomplete. It either fails to see the savage lion tenderly nursing her cubs and the cubs playing energetically in the sun, or it discounts these activities as foolishness. Failing to see how the human mother's activity builds rationally on the animal instincts to live and nurture young, Tolstoy classifies women with children in their irrational acceptance of the happiness life offers. But it is Tolstoy and the pessimists who are irrational, for they cannot act on what they prescribe as logically required. In the last chapter of this book I will discuss (and confess to) a tragic view of life that accepts a large part of the pessimists' description but is based on the more complete picture I am trying to develop in these chapters on the three arch evils.

When we look closely at the lives of predators, we see the contrast immediately. Bloody jaws belong to the same creature who licks her young with such affection. The lion and tiger have no choice in what sort of creatures they will be; they simply are as they are. But human beings can to a large degree choose their way of being in the world. If we choose to build our lives and our conceptual models on the natural facts of affection and protection of the young, we construct a different human being from the one modeled on the bloody hunter. I do not suggest that all bloody hunting—all pain and suffering—will then vanish, but rather that we will question the occasions for violence in the light of an alternative ideal and will chip away the apparent need for violence to some perhaps irreducible core. We will not build violence into our conceptual models simply because it occurs naturally, but rather demand that it be justified whenever it is chosen.

Properly refusing to give way to pessimism, religious thinkers nevertheless often see the horrible side of ordinary life and long for something better. Even the Old Testament, filled with the cruelty of God and men, records the hope that benign life will prevail. In Isaiah 65 we hear that "the voice of weeping shall be no more heard in her [Jerusalem]," that newborn infants will not die and, finally, that "the wolf and the lamb shall feed together, and the lion shall eat straw like the bullock" (vv. 19, 25). But as so often happens in these accounts, the desire for good and the promise of earthly well-being are directed to a particular people. The prophecy favors one people and threatens others: "They shall not build, and another inhabit; they shall not plant, and another eat: for as the days of a tree are the days of my people, and mine elect shall long enjoy the work of their hands" (v. 22).

One can suppose that a tender mother might also make such promises to her children, but we would hope that her devotion to them need not imply ill for other children. But the Lord of the Old Testament does not set a motherly example. We read in the last chapter of Isaiah that "the Lord will come with fire, and with his chariots like a whirlwind, to render his anger with fury, and his rebuke with flames of fire"

(66:15). The book closes with a promise (or prediction) from God to his chosen people: "And they shall go forth, and look upon the carcases of the men that have transgressed against me: for their worm shall not die, neither shall their fire be quenched; and they shall be an abhorring unto all flesh" (v. 24).

Although the message may relieve us of pessimism with respect to our own fate, it encompasses promises of power, threats of destruction, images of conquest, justification for the infliction of lasting pain, the threat of separation, and a continuous stream of mystification that begets obedience or helplessness. These, among other reasons, are why I have bracketed God and sin—so that we can investigate how best to relieve each other of pain, separation, and helplessness. What we want to avoid is a solution to the problem of our own suffering that merely displaces it onto others. We must avoid especially the vicious notion that our relation with some deity justifies the direct infliction of pain and deprivation on others or decisions that inflict pain even as they purport to uphold some great or sacred principle. Not only must we reject the cruel partisan god of the Pentateuch, but we must also set aside the optimistic, misty-eyed vision of an all-good and all-loving god. There *is* dreadful suffering in the world. Setting aside all gods for the moment, how should we respond to it?

SUFFERING IN FEMININE EXPERIENCE

How should we act in the presence of pain and suffering? Let us briefly reconsider Lessing's character Maudie. Maudie is in great pain from what we call a natural cause—a cancer. But her *suffering* goes beyond physical pain to include the fear of separation and her awareness of increasing helplessness. Jane and the nursing sisters respond to all three aspects of Maudie's suffering, but the physicians—whom we barely mentioned—take a different approach.

The doctor who cares directly for Maudie in the hospital, says Jane, "is nice, and she likes him—I can see she does, though he could be pardoned for believing she hated him." The Big Doctor, in contrast, increases Maudie's sense of helplessness by treating her as a case, inviting his students to prod and push on her belly. Maudie complains that he does not look at *her* but only at *them*. She feels like a thing or an idiot. After Maudie is moved to the hospital for terminal cases, the Big Doctor's insensitivity increases. When Maudie shuts her eyes stoically to endure a group examination, the Big Doctor decides against it and takes his students into the hall. There, in full earshot of Maudie, Jane, and the nurse, he tells his students that Maudie is "now in a coma and will slip away in her sleep." But Maudie is not in a coma, and her physical pain is deepened in psychic suffering by the treatment of this doctor who is in charge of her case. Jane and the nurse exchange sympathetic and helplessly outraged glances.[4]

Maudie, of course, is a fictional character, but her story reflects a multitude of real-life cases. The separation—neglect of relation—from which Maudie suffers is pervasive. Lessing has her diarist comment on "the utter and absolute gap between doctors and nurses," and she asks, "How did this extraordinary system grow up, where those who issue orders don't know what is really going on?"[5]

Not all doctors are insensitive to their patients as persons, however. In sharing this chapter with a physicians' seminar, I was surprised at how many agreed with Lessing; they indicted their training as grossly negligent in sustaining the humanistic ideals with which they entered medicine. But several insisted—rightly, I think—that physicians ought not to be accused of insensitivity merely because they "come in, check up, issue orders, and leave." They described persuasively how deeply they really do care about those they treat.

One problem is that physicians do not participate in the extended intervals of direct caring that nurses see as the heart of their work. Thus they do not have an equal opportunity to show their caring. But perhaps more important, many of them do not *develop* genuine attitudes of caring, because they do not do the hands-on work that engenders such attitudes. Touching is central in the work of nursing, but not in the work of doctoring. Paula M. Cooey remarks, "Touch as an act of valuing that exemplifies the unity in reciprocity of language and body, culture and nature, communicates the complexity and diversity of women's values, women's worth in different contexts, and therefore an individual woman's identity as 'woman.'"[6]

The tasks that women are called on to do involve many opportunities for human contact, and the law of kindness is legitimated in these situations. Childcare workers, teachers, and nurses spend much of their time in the company of people who need their personal attention. Daniel Maguire claims that the moral sensitivity of women has been enhanced in several ways—for one, "women have historically had more opportunity to 'go to school' on children and thus to be

more identified with the moral rhythms of minimally corrupted human life." [7] Direct contact with the helpless and needy stimulates care,
and centuries of such experience may well have induced in females a
predisposition for caring.

But the picture is complicated. Not all nurses—female or male—
are considerate and compassionate. Big Nurse, the fictional monster
of *One Flew over the Cuckoo's Nest,* comes to mind as a dramatic
counterexample.[8] We do not yet know enough about the interactions
among sex, personality factors, task, and setting to make confident
empirical pronouncements. But we have some evidence that the tasks
themselves help trigger caring responses. In an ethnographic study of
disabled people attempting independent lives, Carole Anderson
quotes a former minister who became an orderly in a nursing home.
Even though his orientation had always been theoretically one of caring, hands-on activity taught him something. "I learned my perception as a minister in a nursing home and as an orderly in a nursing
home were two different games. I saw things very differently. And one
of the things I became involved in was patient's rights. They had
none." [9]

Clearly we need empirical work in the area, but I am interested here
in the logic of descriptions and recommendations we might make and
in the possibility of alternative formulations. Kari Waerness argues for
"the rationality of caring." Her account emphasizes again that any
social theory resting its entire argument on an economic base is defi-
cient. She refers to caring, for example, in terms of "both labor and
feelings":

> Caring is about relations between (at least two) people. One of them
> (the carer) shows concern, consideration, affection, devotion, towards
> the other (the cared for). The one needing care is invaluable to the one
> providing care, and when the former is suffering pain or discomfort, the
> latter identifies with her/him and attends to alleviating it. Adult, healthy
> people feel a need to be cared for by others in many different situations.
> Worn out, dejected, tired, depressed—there are many adjectives to de-
> scribe states in which what we need or desire is for others 'to care for
> us'. In such situations we may feel that we have a *right* to our need for
> care being met. This means there must be others who feel that it is their
> duty or desire to honor this right.[10]

Waerness discusses the need for both private and public caregiving,
and she emphasizes the need to maintain in public caring the attitude
of love that characterizes private caring. As we have seen, nurses often

share this concern. Their training differs from that of physicians, and the theoretical perspectives that guide training are now articulated in a way that underscores the difference between human caring and medical science.

In a chapter entitled "Nursing and Metaphysics" Jean Watson writes:

> The previous chapters have attempted to set forth a view of nursing that is consistent with nursing's tradition of human caring, rather than the tradition of medicine. In advancing such a view there is a call for a revaluation of humans and caring. The alternative world view of nursing that is being suggested will place nursing within a metaphysical context and establish nursing as a human-to-human care process with spiritual dimensions, rather than a set of behaviors that conform to the traditional science/medical model.

Watson emphasizes the *actual caring occasion* in which the nurse and patient meet. "The moment of coming together in a caring occasion presents the two persons with the opportunity to decide how to be in the relationship—what to do with the moment." [11] Such a philosophy of nursing reminds the nurse that pain and physical disability do not sum up natural evil. A large part of human suffering derives from separation and helplessness and the fear of these states. Not only the separation from loved ones presents itself as evil, but also the separation from caretakers created by enormous differences in power—differences that are not "natural" but cultural. Understanding that the fear of separation and helplessness increases human suffering and that human beings in positions of power may abuse others in the exercise of that power, Watson insists on an appropriate mutuality in the caring occasion. Subjectivities must be shared and respected. Caretakers must not treat patients by a recipe of uniform and artificial cheeriness.

The training of nurses, then, may affect their attitudes and ways of being on the job. But clearly nursing tasks and centuries of experience in tending the ill have molded and refined the view Watson expresses so eloquently. We might predict that nurses, working closely with patients and seeing many aspects of their personhood, would be strong advocates of healing and maintaining life. When these goals are feasible and humane, of course, nurses are such advocates. But unlike physicians, nurses often concern themselves more with suffering than with the mere maintenance of life. Because the medical science model does not drive them so forcefully, they are less likely to see patients as cases, and although their training includes large doses of problem solving, their proximity to sufferers prevents their being distracted by technical and scientific problems. Holding a small child who vomits repeatedly, mopping the child's tears, wrapping trembling limbs to restore warmth, distracting the child with toys, watching the shadow of pain cloud a young face—all these tasks touch the heart and deepen a concern for the suffering individual.

Nurses tend desperately ill people—aged or adult or infants—more closely than do physicians. Indeed, physicians sometimes avoid contact with dying patients because, as Frederick Abrams puts it, "the doctor considers failure to cure to be a personal failure." [12] The suffering of separation and helplessness then compounds the patient's pain. Abrams urges physicians to recognize that they can do much for the patient even when they have lost the battle against the disease. Unlike physicians, nurses do not have the option of absenting themselves from patients. Because they share the suffering on a daily basis, they are apparently more often receptive to the idea of allowing death to end a patient's suffering. Even in caring for very premature and malformed infants, nurses often want to end the suffering, whereas physicians strive to maintain life against enormous odds. [13] How much of this maintenance is motivated by scientific interest and rationalized as a valuing of life is uncertain.

When we set aside propositions about God, sin, and science, we find at the bottom of each suffering event pain that cries for relief, a threat of separation that triggers an increased need for connection, and a dread of helplessness that begs for empowerment. Further, these evils spread through the sympathetic attending company. One who moves a pain-racked body begins to feel a sympathetic pain; psychic suffering springs up in the helper; fear of loss plagues the affectionate attendant who is or becomes attached to the sufferer; fatigue induces a frightening wish for separation; and guilt and fear pass back and forth from sufferer to caretaker. We will have to consider in a bit whether the compassionate instinct to let die is in part a desire to save the self as well as the patient from further suffering, a question we will face squarely in a discussion of euthanasia.

Both doctors and nurses at their humane best (Abrams and Watson, for example) consider that it may be part of their task to help patients find meaning in suffering. This way of casting the problem is a religious legacy and may be appropriate and comforting for those who participate with reflective consent in such a tradition. But a better response, given what we have found at the heart of suffering events, is to ask, What can I do in the face of this reality? Suffering can—like any other affective event—act as an impetus in a search for meaning, but that meaning must go beyond the suffering itself, for everything we find there is evil. It is in our response to evil that we find an opportunity to enhance meaning in our lives. Suffering is not *required* to bring out the best in us or to teach us the meaning of its opposite. Caring for young children, growing plants, teaching those who wish to learn, feeding the healthy hungry—all call forth tender responses. We do not need suffering to build our souls; we need only opportunities to care and to empower, together with a well-developed sense of obligation and the skill to do what is needed. If we have souls, this sort of caring activity is sufficient to develop them, and indeed this conclusion seems reasonable when we look at life through the eyes of those charged with caring for physical human beings.

EUTHANASIA

So far I have discussed attitudes toward pain as natural evil and shown how the tasks we perform and the relations in which we perform them affect those attitudes. I could say much more about the forms and manifestations of pain, but my principal purpose is to reveal the logic of thinking that arises in female experience and the resultant attitudes toward evil in general and toward pain in particular. To do so the analysis has had to avoid the distractions of God, sin, symbol, and medical science and remain fixed on human-to-human interaction. We must now consider what many regard as the greatest natural evil—death—and its connection to the natural evils we have identified so far. In doing so we will need to bracket still another body of thought, legal thought, to see eventually what attitudes sustain it and whether those attitudes are consonant or dissonant with those that feminine experience engenders.

What should be our attitude toward euthanasia? Euthanasia is commonly defined as the painless killing of one who is hopelessly ill, injured, or in great pain. It is important that the killing be merciful in both its method and its motivation. In the discussion of pain we have already uncovered a basic attitude. We do not ask, guided by some symbolic body of thought, what this pain and suffering mean. Rather, we ask the far more direct and open question, What should I do in the face of this reality? In particular, the question before us now is, What should I do in the face of extreme suffering when there is a well-grounded judgment of hopelessness?

I have purposely ended the guiding question in a way that will allow us to consider the widest possible range of cases. There must be extreme suffering to justify our reasons of mercy; there must be an element of hopelessness to justify our choice of killing as the merciful means to end or alleviate the suffering. But I will not insist at the outset that the extreme suffering must be in the one who is in a hopeless condition. The suffering may be in those attending or responsible for the individual whose condition is somehow hopeless. By making this choice we walk along the precipice, but we must do so if we wish to describe fully the agonies of those who have been led to the brink through the tasks they perform and the relations they cherish.

Traditionally the case thought to be morally easiest is one in which an individual is terminally ill, is in great pain, and wishes to die. In current practice "letting die" has become largely acceptable in such cases, but active killing is still forbidden. Indeed the Joint Commission on Accreditation of Hospitals has recently announced that all hospitals must formulate a policy on resuscitation and withholding medical intervention for terminally ill patients. Further, the directive states that physicians, nurses, and patients' families must all have roles in those important decisions. But since the process of letting die usually takes much longer than, say, killing by lethal injection, one might conclude that passive euthanasia is less merciful than active euthanasia. After describing horrible cases of letting die, James Rachels draws just that conclusion. "To say otherwise," he remarks, "is to endorse the option that leads to more suffering rather than less, and is contrary to the humanitarian impulse that prompts the decision not to prolong . . . life in the first place." [14] We must recognize, however, that medical science has made it possible to alleviate most of the physical pain associated with terminal illness, and Cicely Saunders and Elizabeth Kubler-Ross have written eloquently about the possibilities of serenity and even growth in the final episodes of life. [15] We can expect further advances along these lines, and so active euthanasia may become less and less necessary as a way to end physical pain. In this view the patients remain valuable in themselves as whole persons capable of relating, responding, and expressing preferences. But psychic pain may still overwhelm a patient, and in that event active euthanasia might be a reasonable and compassionate choice. The possibility of making this choice may also reduce a patient's sense of helplessness.

Why do the medical and legal professions (and a large segment of the population at large) retain their absolute rule against active euthanasia? Philosophers have concentrated on the peculiarities that may arise in such cases—mistakes, coerced decisions that only seem voluntary, and the like—but I want to suggest that two underlying ideologies powerfully restrict our thinking. The first, clearly, is the Judeo-Christian religious tradition, which we have already discussed at length. In this tradition the giving and taking of life are prerogatives reserved to God, and life—*because* it is God-given—is sacred. Those who profess such a belief often apply it capriciously, however, and largely ignore it in their discussions of war and capital punishment. Further, this tradition's attitude toward suffering is at bottom cruel. It elevates suffering to a sacred status; in some instances it even treasures suffering. Although feminist and liberation theologies are changing Christian thought, the changes have not yet effected equivalent changes in our social structures.[16]

The second ideology that works against a change in policy is the tradition of individualism. We suppose that a moral agent must decide as an individual what is right and that he or she must do so in roughly the way we expect schoolchildren to solve geometry problems—alone and dispassionately working from universally accepted principles through valid chains of reasoning to irrefutable conclusions. Philosophy is nearly mired in this tradition, and the language that has developed in it makes escape difficult. In a discussion of euthanasia Philippa Foot, for example, repeatedly asks whether and under what conditions *one man* may opt to end the life of another.[17] But why must one person make the decision, and why should we suppose that the best of such decisions should be capable of codification?

The relational ways of thinking characterized in female experience offer an alternative. When someone is suffering and wishes to die, all affected parties should take part in the decision. A support group consisting of physicians, nurses, family, patient, and perhaps a trained advocate of sorts could talk with each other about what is best for the patient and for everyone else who is suffering. It is especially important to include nurses on such a committee, because as Daniel Maguire has pointed out, "The nurse enters into the patient's drama not only at the professional medical level, but also in a more personal way. She provides a personal context that the intermittent appearances of the doctor cannot."[18] Decision making that grows out of open and compassionate dialogue is not likely to fall into the errors that Foot so greatly fears; mistakes of fact will be less likely, and mean motives will be hard to hide. In the case we are now discussing—that of active voluntary euthanasia—the patient should be the initiator. He or she might request a meeting of the support group and indeed should be the main agent to decide on its constitution. Is all this too much for a dying patient? It may be. But in so many of the stories with which we are familiar, the greatest suffering connected with dying lies in the dreadful separation from others that occurs even before death, in the helpless exclusion from autonomous action and from community life. We must talk to each other about pain and death and separation.

The procedure discussed above should provide adequate safeguards against the main worries philosophers have expressed about voluntary euthanasia. Extended discussion among interested parties should enable the participants to decide whether a request for euthanasia is well informed and not capricious. We do not, of course, wish to respond to every voiced desire to die with a cheery assurance that we will immediately cooperate. Just as we will continue to try to dissuade people from all unreasonable attempts at suicide, so we should in many cases encourage a decision for continued life for those who, although terminally ill, can live with some comfort, dignity, and pleasure. The same spirit of genuine concern, open discussion, and loving sympathy should govern the decision to help live and the one to help die.

Jonathan Glover too sees "thorough discussion" as the means to "identifying which requests signify a stable and thought-out preference for death," but although he recommends trying an experimental program, he continues to worry about the possible side effects of lifting the ban on voluntary euthanasia.[19] Such side effects include the possibility that terminally ill people will feel coerced into choosing death to relieve their relatives of financial and emotional burdens. There are two directions from which to approach this problem. As Waerness pointed out in her discussion of the rationality of caring, there are private and public aspects of caretaking. From the public perspective medical care should not be an intolerable financial burden on individuals and families; this is a problem for the collective. If a person wishes to live or might wish to do so in the absence of this pressing concern for others, medical services collectively financed should be available. From the private perspective there can be no absolute assurance that unloving relatives will not suggest strongly to an elderly person that he or she has a duty to die and be done with it. But no form of law can relieve the suffering that this sort of human cruelty represents. Law can protect the physical life of one who is emotionally abandoned, but it cannot make that life worth living. If everyone around me wants me to die, that may be sufficient reason for me to choose death.

The worry expressed above is part of our failure to think relationally. Because we fail to build the relations required to explore our own needs, guilt, and fears openly, many of us may suppose that those around us will be only too quick to do us in if they have the right to do so. But loving family life, supported by public financial commitment, should alleviate this concern. In the case of those who have no family or loved ones and wish to die, we can be sure that nasty relatives are not coercing the decision. Indeed, it seems likely that more people without loved ones will make the decision than will people who have family about them. Maudie, for example, found her impending death a "tragedy" because she valued her new friendship with Jane so highly. From the perspective of female experience death is not the ultimate evil against which we need protection. We have laws to protect us against death at the hands of others, but none protects us from separation and helplessness. Softening existing laws against euthanasia might force us to think more deeply about the human relations that make life worth living.

A relational way of approaching the evil of pain is, I think, an outgrowth of female experience, and several aspects of that experience are probably influential. One unpleasant aspect is the subordination that has forced women to consult, to seek guidance. For centuries women have raised sons, for example, tending their physical needs, teaching them, and even punishing them for household infractions. And yet at a certain time in the son's life, his mother was expected to submit to his rule and guidance. Before that she was expected to obey husband or father. But because males knew so little about her daily work and the moral stamina required for a life of service, she turned to other women for conversation, guidance, and support. Both of these conditions—the coerced acceptance of guidance from men and the compensating conversation with women—have made it seem natural and reasonable for women to seek and accept counsel. Today we want to escape traditional subordination, but perhaps we should not lightly discard every attitude and skill that grew out of that abominable tradition. Women have not had much experience with the "loneliness of command," and the present analysis suggests that no one *should* have such experience when lives are at stake and the pattern is avoidable.

Moreover, women have had enormous experience with repetitive work and informal ritual. The continuous cycle of preparing and serving food, cleaning up afterward, and planning for a new round of meals is just one example. Patience and creativity may develop in repetitive tasks undertaken for the sake of particular others. It is clearly not mere repetition that is salutary; repetition can be tedious and soul deadening. But when tasks must be done over and over, creative thought can convert basic necessity into life-enhancing events. Meals, then, are not made to be growled over and gobbled but to provide a setting in which family members talk to each other, savoring food, conversation, and the setting itself. Further, few events are more delightful for a mother than a gathering in the kitchen with her daughters as they prepare food, exchange recipes, analyze children, sort herbs (and perhaps pot them on the spot), and concoct favorite dishes in just the way loved family members enjoy them. The company need not, I hasten to add, include only mothers and daughters.

The rituals of food preparation and eating are an example of caring occasions. They are fundamentally different from food preparation as a paid occupation, and they illustrate (but certainly do not exhaust) the ways in which human beings can convert basic needs into occasions that sustain mind and soul as well as body. This sort of patience—the sort that faces the labor and the necessity as well as the possibilities that surpass immediate needs—is essential in the presence of pain and death. The creative effort that uses an unavoidable physical event to promote human well-being might profitably extend to the full range of human activity.

From the most recent discussion we can see that the tasks traditionally performed by women should logically affect attitudes and, more generally, a way of being in the world. But the tasks themselves, taken individually and out of context, are probably not the sole determinants. That the tasks are varied and directed at the welfare of particular persons seems to be of great importance. Attention is continually focused on the persons for whom the tasks are performed and not narrowly on the tasks themselves. Hence if we recommended that everyone be exposed to feminine experience, we could not faithfully implement the recommendation by giving everyone a turn at chopping vegetables in the kitchen or carrying trays in the hospital.

I do not suggest, however, that the masculine approach of problem solving and specialization is useless in caring situations, and I do not intend to associate *feminine* with good traits and *masculine* with bad. Many feminists become angry when they hear scientific, technological, and mathematical thinking associated with the masculine and want to insist that women have these capacities also. Many certainly do, and undoubtedly many men have the capacity to care. But until experience changes substantially, we simply cannot know whether the talents and skills now associated with one sex will prove to be as generously distributed in the other. What is important is that both modes of experience be available to persons of both sexes.

The usefulness of masculine experience in caring situations is typically technical. Disposable diapers and washing machines are marvelous technical aids in infant care, but we cannot solve once and for all the problem of diapering babies. The wise mother makes the necessity into a caring occasion; she plays with the baby, checks its body for rashes and bumps, gives it bodily freedom and exercise. Technical thinking has made it easier to devote time to play and tenderness. Washing machines, detergents, and disposable diapers are important supports in the caring situation.

The point of this renewed discussion of female experience is to emphasize the need for balance in our thinking. In the matter of euthanasia we succumb too often to the sort of technical thinking that arises out of masculine experience. We think that we must codify everything to make it rigidly clear and binding on all persons in similar situations. The machinery of technology and law has displaced the person who should be at the center of our thinking.

Having argued for the humaneness of active voluntary euthanasia when the process is protected by a well-constituted support group, I want now to consider nonvoluntary euthanasia. I do not suggest here that active euthanasia be performed on persons against their explicit wishes. Although under some unusual circumstances it might be permissible to take someone's life against his or her will to protect him or her from a demonstrably worse fate, such circumstances are hard to imagine, and I will not explore the possibility here. Involuntary active euthanasia will simply be ruled out. Here the language of rights and the language of caring both reflect the deeply held belief that it should be unthinkable to kill or deliberately let die one who wishes to live. We have already seen what the appropriate response is to persons like Maudie who are in pain, cannot recover, but want to go on living with as much pleasure and dignity as possible. Nothing so far in this discussion, however, would rule out passive euthanasia in the involuntary case. Perhaps we can allow the terminally ill to die against their wishes if the community does not have the resources to keep them alive. There is some question, however, whether such allowing to die can properly be called euthanasia. When it is peaceful and natural, when it simply occurs without intervention, it is just natural death. When it becomes the fate of some because resources are too scarce to keep all alive who require intervention, it is a case of social failure and can hardly be called euthanasia. Thus it seems that all forms of involuntary euthanasia should be unacceptable in a moral society, even though cases of this sort will occur as the community struggles to create the resources necessary to prevent them. The cases we will consider next involve the individual who cannot make his or her wishes known.

We will consider two major categories. In one set of cases an individual is either comatose or so badly afflicted by senility or some other irreversible mental incapacity that he or she cannot communicate. When the evidence is conclusive—when it is virtually certain that the condition is hopeless—there seems little point in prolonging life. Some philosophers, however, want to subject cases like these (and all cases) to a double test; not only must the case be hopeless, but our act of euthanasia must be done for the sake of the one dying. This requirement makes the decision problematic in the absence of suffering. If the victim has previously expressed a horror of being in a state of complete insensibility or has enacted a "living will," we may have grounds to act. If not, how can we be sure that euthanasia really is in the best interest of the victim?

Philippa Foot, for example, recognizes that such a life may no longer be a good to its possessor, but she is unwilling to label it an evil in the absence of suffering: "The connexion between *life* and *good* may be broken because consciousness has sunk to a very low level, as in extreme senility or severe brain damage. In itself this kind of life seems to be neither good nor evil, but if suffering sets in one would hope for a speedy end." [20] But who is this "one" who would "hope" for a speedy end? In real life, as opposed to abstract argumentation, actual people tend the victim, and these people are often suffering too. We must take their suffering into account. Haggard parents attend the bedside of a hopelessly comatose daughter for weeks, months, perhaps years, all the while incurring heavy debts and depriving themselves of activities that make life worth living. They are clearly suffering. Even if the community could remove the debt—as it should—their emotional suffering would continue. Or consider the case of a middle-aged woman who has children and grandchildren, a job, and community services that she has always performed. Now she also has a hopelessly senile parent to support, visit, and worry over. The parent does not even recognize her. Is this woman not suffering, and should not her suffering enter into the account?

I understand what Foot fears. She repeatedly states her concern about possible abuses:

> What we must consider, even if only briefly, is the possibility that euthanasia, genuine euthanasia, and not contrary to the requirements of justice or charity, should be legalized over a wider area. Here we are up against the really serious problem of abuse. Many people want, and want very badly, to be rid of their elderly relatives and even of their ailing husbands or wives. Would any safeguards ever be able to stop them describing as euthanasia what was really for their own benefit? [21]

Here Foot has an opportunity to explore the suffering of families and medical attendants, but instead she associates all acts of killing for the sake of others with Hitler's sense of euthanasia. The very mention of Hitler, Eichmann, and Warthgenau frightens us out of our arguments. But with courage and the empathy bred through centuries of female experience, we should persist in our investigation. We must consider all suffering. The suffering must be genuine, of course, and we must avoid abuses. That is the function of a well-formed support group.

But we cannot avoid abuses by simply *saying* that we must avoid them. Under what circumstances should we consider nonvoluntary euthanasia? We have been exploring the case of persons permanently comatose or so badly impaired by senility or the loss of brain function that they can no longer respond to normal human interaction. If a medical team—not "one man"—has verified that the case is hopeless and if the family is ready to let go, then euthanasia should be considered. Review procedures could be instituted, but they should not be lengthy. Our attention should go to those capable of suffering, and we should be sure that the recommended euthanasia will not cause them even greater suffering through regret and guilt. Foot wants to insist that euthanasia must always "benefit the one who dies,"[22] but in the cases we are here considering neither life nor death benefits the one whose body clings to mere biological life. The benefit is to the consciously living.

Any accusation that this type of euthanasia is just like Hitler's is clearly wrong. It is not permissible to kill people simply because they can no longer work or are mentally slow, old, of a different race or color, ill, or in our way. I have ruled out involuntary euthanasia. However, because a death relieves the suffering of some other than the one who dies does not make it immoral. Only an intensely guilty and sanctimonious society would insist that it does. As Maguire points out, compassion, not anger and selfishness, motivates mercy killing. "Compassion," he says, "is a work of love and love is a unitive force which resists separation."[23] Although Maguire refers in this passage to compassion directed toward the one dying, it is clear from his overall argument that he would include compassion for caretakers unless doing so would destroy compassion for the central victim.

But our discussion raises an important question about the nature of suffering. If, for example, a young man claims that he is suffering because he must visit an elderly grandfather who cannot respond to his greetings and whose continued life deprives him of an inheritance he could use to pursue his own happiness, we would probably not assess his misery as genuine suffering. What can we mean by this assessment? After all, even the utterly evil can suffer psychic pain in their desire to achieve evil ends or to enact evil means. In what sense, then, is such suffering not genuine? We encountered this problem earlier when we discussed attitudes toward pain, separation, and helplessness. We may regard suffering as pathological if a change in attitude alone would remove the cause of suffering; that is, we must ask whether the situation as described would be likely to induce suffering in any reasonably caring person. The case under consideration would have to convince us that the young man is either suffering in reaction to his grandfather's misery or is being forced to sacrifice a significant part of his own pursuit of self-affirmation. Neither seems likely.

There are situations, however, in which empathic observers can be quite sure that the suffering of carers is genuine. When a person needs continuous, long-range intimate care, the carer must sacrifice attention to his or her own projects to perform this task. Further, the task is difficult and unpleasant. By definition there is no hope for recovery, no response from the one afflicted, and a steady physical demand to do stomach-turning tasks. Women, who have met these needs for centuries, should understand the plight of those who find themselves in such situations.[24] As they find the voice to tell their stories, they can help each other realize that their suffering is worthy of consideration. But we should not rush to codify this sort of experience. We should not write into law the outcomes or decisions, but rather the possibility of making such decisions.

Consider now the second category of cases, and here we must press our analysis into the fearful territory from which Foot so quickly withdrew. What should we do with severely handicapped or deformed infants? These tiny creatures share with the senile and comatose the great handicap of being unable to communicate. In contrast, however, they are often conscious (although unreflectively so) and undergo enormous and obvious pain. As we saw earlier, nurses frequently suffer sympathetically with these small beings, and it is not surprising that they sometimes take the law into their own hands in ending the dreadful agonies that they must otherwise stand by and watch.[25]

Perhaps the best way to proceed in this difficult argument is to analyze Foot's chain of thought. She agrees that allowing some terribly afflicted children to die may really be in the best interest of the child (her crucial question is, "Is it for the sake of the child himself that the doctors and parents choose his death?"), but even in these cases she cannot bring herself to endorse active euthanasia, since the child "cannot ask that it should be done." She concludes: "The only possible solution—supposing that voluntary active euthanasia were to be legalized—would be to appoint guardians to act on the infant's behalf. In a different climate of opinion this might not be dangerous, but at present, when people so readily assume that the life of a handicapped baby is of no value, one would be loath to support it."[26]

Foot makes an important point in worrying about our attitudes and values. She is afraid that many of us may callously and even carelessly discard the life of someone who, if allowed to live, might come to cherish that life. But she does not explore the notion of guardians fully enough. In the scheme I have suggested, infants would have several layers of protection—more, I dare say, than they have now. First, medical personnel would be required to consult so that the prognosis of hopelessness (or profound and continued helplessness) would be well founded. Second, the support group would consider both the suffering and the available strengths in those who must care for the baby. If the parents can have other children or already have other children, if their religion permits the decision under consideration, if their ordinary support structures are thin, and if the handicap of their child seems to them insurmountable, the group may concur that it should provide a quick and painless death for the child. If the group cannot agree, then it must make all medical efforts to improve the child's condition and all human efforts to nurture and love it. That most horrible of decisions—to let it die of dehydration or starvation (leave it "in the hands of God"?)—must never be made.

I need to say more about the case in which a support group cannot come to agreement. If the parents resist euthanasia, it seems clear that the support group must enact efforts to help, described above. But if the parents vote for euthanasia and one of the medical team insists that the child can with help live a decent life, the problem takes on new and greater difficulties. Who should be responsible for the case of such a child? I cannot investigate that question fully here, but I can indicate a way of looking at it. It is certainly not—or should not be— a simple matter of rights. "The child has a right to life," some say. "Life is sacred, and we should not play God," others say. But we *do* play God when we sentence parents to years and years of lonely caring for badly handicapped children who cannot respond, will not grow, or live in such pain that the parents inevitably suffer too. Whatever the decision in such cases, the community that dares to make it must share in the care of the child. Those who insist that we should value the helpless and afflicted more highly are not always among the ones who offer actual care.

It is obvious to any thoughtful person that the constitution of support groups, the rules by which they should proceed, and the possible appeal mechanisms all require careful study. That work is not part of my present purpose, however, except so far as it requires a statement or description of attitude—a task I believe I have accomplished. Foot rightly worries about what will happen once we have one boot on the slippery slope of euthanasia. But many of us worry about the horror already rampant. Too often we take the rule-bound way out of life's most terrible dilemmas because it allows us to separate ourselves from suffering while retaining a fine feeling of righteousness. The law reflects this inclination to abstraction and separation, and one reason it has been able to do so is that those making the laws and those providing daily care to the afflicted have been two different sets of people. The discussion here represents an attempt to give voice to the caretakers.

In this discussion of euthanasia we have already moved from pain as natural evil to pain as cultural evil—our way of organizing and institutionalizing pain—and when we consider what is right (as opposed to what is legal or customary) we are looking at pain from a moral perspective. Women have for centuries been assessed as morally inferior for their attachment to physical bodies and their continuing concern for actual living beings. We saw it in the suffering of Carie, the exile. We saw it again in Maudie's nurses, who dared not speak out against the Big Doctor's faulty—and abstracted—conclusions. When we decide on the basis of law to preserve the life of a painfully handicapped person, we wash our hands of the guilt we might suffer by making a merciful decision (we are not like Hitler and Eichmann), but we heap great suffering on the human beings who must care for that person. Some parents' lives are scarcely worth living because of the demands they must meet to care for severely handicapped children,[27] and we often make matters worse for them by glorifying their selflessness and suggesting that God has somehow chosen them to do a great work. How easy it is to make the "right" decision and then either castigate those who must bear it for their moral weakness or praise them in words sickeningly like those of *The Angel in the House.* From the perspective of those who must feed, wash, lift, transport, puncture, watch over, and suffer with, the entire matter needs a thorough reexamination.

ABORTION

At first glance it seems odd to include abortion in a discussion of natural evil. Those who hold that abortion is evil would of course label it a moral evil; that is, they would accuse one who submits to it or performs it of committing moral evil and would consider a society that permits it guilty of sustaining moral evil. But if we begin our examination by studying the experience of women who are unwillingly pregnant, we see familiar signs of evil in that condition—the psychic pain of helplessness, for example. Before we decide that abortion is evil, then, we must ask what we might do in the case of an unwanted pregnancy—a natural event—that is causing its bearer great pain.

Abortion is a highly charged topic to which people often respond in extremes. As L. Wayne Sumner points out, neither the extreme liberal nor the extreme conservative view is convincing if pushed logically.[28] Most of us do not believe that early abortion is murder, for example, because an early spontaneous abortion is not considered a death. We do not hold funerals for lost embryos, and some of those events occur almost without definitive signs. On the other end of the continuum many of us feel deep revulsion at the thought of destroying a viable fetus. If someone must inject a chemical to stop a heartbeat, that sounds perilously like killing a human being. We are tempted, then, to follow Sumner in his argument for a third way—which turns out to be very like the one the Supreme Court ruling prescribes.

The question is how to argue for this third way. Most arguments to date use the language of rights, and questions about rights involve debates about the moral standing of those who are supposed to have rights. I want to argue that the language of rights is inappropriate in this area—as it is in the discussion of euthanasia—and that we can move directly from the perception of human response to a sense of our obligation.

Let me start by reconsidering some of the ground covered in the previous discussion of euthanasia. Suppose Ms. A has an elderly father whom she dearly loves. After an active, loving, and productive life, the father is stricken with a form of senility that incapacitates him. He can no longer dress or feed himself. Occasionally he shuffles about, but he does not know where he's going or where he is at any given moment. He is incontinent. His speech is incoherent—little more than grunts and moans. He rarely recognizes his daughter, and when he does—or seems to—the pain in his eyes overwhelms the daughter with suffering. Ms. A wants to help her father die, and I have already argued that it should be possible for her to do so. It is clear, however, that she would not argue that her beloved father had lost his right to live. When we insist on using the language of rights, we find it necessary to switch in this instance to an emphasis on the right to die. We cannot establish either right unambiguously, and the language is useless when applied to cases where the individuals under consideration can neither express the desire to claim their right nor benefit from it if it is accorded.

Michael Tooley, for example, argues that "an entity cannot have a right to life unless it is capable of having an interest in its own continued existence." [29] By this Tooley does not mean the blind will to live that Schopenhauer describes. On the latter account we could say that the vigorous plants that force their way through our sidewalks have an interest in their own continued existence. Tooley wants to define this interest by the following criterion: "An entity is not capable of having an interest in its own continued existence unless it possesses, at some time, the concept of a continuing self, or subject of experiences and other mental states." [30] Using this criterion, Tooley shows that neither a fetus nor a newborn infant has a right to live. This way of going at things creates great difficulties for the case of Ms. A and her father. Clearly, by this criterion the father has a right to live, and if we insist on this language we would have to say either that he is stuck with this right (since he did nothing to waive it earlier) or that his right to die somehow supersedes his right to live. A problem with Tooley's argument and with so many others that center on rights is that their authors plainly want a particular result and invoke all their philosophical principles and strategies to support that result. Hence they do not dig deeply enough, and the solution of one problem creates new ones.

The method that I have chosen requires us to return to the situation itself. We have a perspective in this situation, of course, and it is not free of assumptions. It is the perspective of woman, a conceptual creation that is in part described by the experiences of real women and in part constructed by the ritualized expectations of a culture. What we seek from this perspective is a unified approach to ethical life, particularly to the problems associated with evil.

Just as we would be unlikely to say of a beloved elderly father that he no longer has a right to live, we would probably not say of a fetus (our own) that it has no right to live. If we insist on the language of rights, we would have to emphasize our own right (to what?) and show that it somehow supersedes the right to life others claim for the fetus. It is hard to imagine a woman going to her physician with a request for an abortion couched in language like this: I want this fetus removed because it has no right to live. The language of rights springs from something deeper, and when we see what that is, we may no longer need that language.

Some feminists use the language of rights even though they acknowledge, as Alison Jaggar does, that "talk of rights is notoriously problematic." In part the common language of social and political philosophy directs this kind of talk. To have an impact on legal decisions, to be heard in political debate, one almost has to use such language. Jaggar argues that women in a society like ours must have the right to decide for themselves whether or not to abort but that, paradoxically, in a society that cared more honestly and adequately for all its citizens, women might lose that right. Rights are only important, she suggests, as long as

> every society is composed of individuals whose interests inevitably conflict. . . . Ultimately, however, when the community as a whole takes on the responsibility for fulfilling the needs of its members and the conflict between the interests of the individual and the interests of the rest of society is reconciled, this right will no longer be necessary. To achieve the legal right to decide about abortion is a first step on the way to women's liberation, but the last step may be the achievement of a society in which the whole notion of individual rights against the community makes no sense at all.[31]

Although Jaggar's final statement is compatible with the feminist de-emphasis on individualism and rights, her argument does not consider the moral status of abortion as an act in itself. Beverly Harrison also uses the language of rights. Confessing to be one of those pro-choice "extremists" Sumner mentions, she insists that her position is appropriate given the nature of our society. Her argument is for "women's well-being" and the "procreative choice" that is part of that well-being. But clearly Harrison—like Jaggar and several other writers whose positions we will consider—would prefer a world in which abortion would occur less often. In summing up, she moves away from the narrow language of rights to a broader consideration of what makes life worth living:

> Persons of authentic theological sensibility must continue to insist that every child who is born among us deserves to be embraced in a covenant of love and affirmation that includes not merely the love of a mother, or a father, but the active concern and respect of the wider community. . . . I noted at the outset that if women did not have to deliberate the questions relating to our procreative power in an atmosphere of taboo, we would be able to turn our attention to the positive moral

task I have commended: what it means for us to use our procreative power responsibly. In the present condemnatory atmosphere, such moral reasoning will go largely undeveloped.[32]

Much as I sympathize with Harrison's assessment of present conditions, I would be reluctant to enact a position that neglects the basic questions of when and why we may evaluate abortion as a moral act *in itself*. Surely even if social conditions changed radically for the better, the question would remain, for not all women think and behave morally. Ideally we would like the law to capture our best moral thinking as nearly as it can and not merely further our various political agendas, however just they may seem. The abortion of a viable fetus, except under the gravest threat to the life of the mother or the full humanity of the infant, is at least questionable morally. Further, adopting the position that the present conditions of society entirely determine the moral status of the act commits us to a thoroughgoing relativism at odds with the larger position Jaggar and Harrison espouse.

Robert Goldstein offers a view similar to Harrison's in its emphasis on the child's need for love. Presenting a closely argued legal interpretation, Goldstein proceeds from a neo-Freudian perspective. He too rejects the *individualistic* language of rights but wants to preserve rights language in a new setting; he directs us to consider the fetus as part of a dyadic relation. Having no life without its partner, the mother, the status of a fetus depends entirely on this relation. Wanted and loved, it has a special status as potential being conferred by this love; unwanted and unloved, it has no status at all. Goldstein's arguments are especially valuable because they resolve several apparent dichotomies and paradoxes. First, they blur an apparent difference, which Kristin Luker identifies, between pro-life and pro-choice activists.[33] For different reasons both may put tremendous emphasis on the love of the child and the importance of family. Second, Goldstein makes pro-choice arguments compatible with heroic efforts to save premature infants. Goldstein remarks:

> The dyadic perspective justifies with the same reasons both abortion-choice for a reasonable period of time and the protection that tort and criminal law afford the fetus. And it explains to us why our society and our physicians may be equally and simultaneously committed, at the request of mothers, to the heroic treatment of their fetuses and at-risk newborns and to the performance of an abortion.

Goldstein goes on to note that the perspective can also "emphasize the special status of women during pregnancy and the months after birth," because a decent society recognizes both the commitment required to bear and rear a fully human child and society's obligation to assist in this process.[34] His point has obvious implications for child care and education as well.

In contrast to Harrison, however, Goldstein would limit abortion in much the way *Roe v. Wade* now does. His test for establishing a deadline for choice is viability. This test raises some of the important problems with which we started this discussion. As we noted earlier, Tooley fixes the right to life not in viability but in a concept of continuing self. Sumner finds it in sentience, a weaker and broader conception of awareness that, as Sumner puts it, admits of degrees. To have moral standing and thus a right to life, a being must be sentient. Sumner's argument makes early abortion permissible because the embryo is clearly not sentient and late abortion not permissible because the viable fetus is sentient. There is, then, a "threshold area" in which the growing sentience of the fetus makes it necessary to justify an abortion. This argument, like Goldstein's, has the obvious merit of taking into account the vast difference between a zygote and a viable fetus or infant.

It also has the less salutary effect of creating a hierarchy of moral standing, and women—unhappily situated in Augustine's hierarchy—may express some concern not only about how entities are located in this hierarchy but also about who will do the locating. When we talk about moral standing and membership in a moral community, we create the mechanisms for both inclusion and exclusion. Sumner finds the criterion A. I. Melden uses—the capacity for moral agency[35]—too exclusive, since it makes moral agents and moral rights bearers coextensive. He wants—rightly, I think—to argue that entities can have moral rights even though they cannot fulfill duties as moral agents.

This approach leads us to search for the properties that give a being moral standing. Sumner says, "A criterion must connect moral standing with some property of things whose presence or absence can be confirmed by a settled, objective, and public method of investigation."[36] The great danger here is that we suppose that such a property can be defined without thorough contamination from the ones doing the defining. If we aim our definition at some form of cognition or perception, we find that we need to amend it when we consider criminals and enemies. Such people are, for example, sentient, capable of expressing interest in their own continued existence, and so on. Their status as criminals and enemies, then, somehow attenuates their rights. As we will see in the discussion of war, we become facile at dismissing people from the moral community (and thus relieving ourselves of respecting their moral rights) when we have reasons to regard them as enemies.

I think we must accept that the moral standing we accord various beings depends not only on properties they may have but, more important, on our relation with them. I do not mean that we *should* treat people as though they have a reduced moral standing simply because our relations with them have deteriorated to enmity. Rather, I am arguing that we must take into account the ways in which our own assessment or understanding of relations affects our descriptions of moral standing. When we understand this connection, we will be in a better position to say how we should behave toward each other. Consider, for example, the traditional devaluation of women's moral standing, which seems to derive from the power relation men wanted to maintain over women. Given that men wanted to retain their domination over women, it was logical to ascribe properties to women that would make this domination morally acceptable.

We need to consider, then, not only individual entities and their properties but also how entities relate to each other and the characteristics or properties of these relations, and throughout this sort of exploration we must remember that *we* are doing the exploring. We value certain properties, respond to certain forms of address, perceive certain reactions. Any hierarchy of sentience that we construct is bound to reflect our own properties and how we value them; the more a creature is like us, the higher it will stand in the hierarchy. But which properties of "us" will we use to determine the likeness?

Consider Ms. B, a philosopher who likes cats but dislikes rats. She accords to cats something very like moral standing; that is, she feeds strays, cares for her own pets, and contributes to an organization that promotes the well-being of cats. But she calls the exterminator if rats try to make their abode with her. As a philosopher Ms. B is disturbed by her own attitude. She allows herself a preference, of course, but she wonders whether in fact cats do have a moral standing superior to that of rats. Cats are sentient. Are they more so than rats? Ms. B's cat seems to miss her when she is away at conferences; the family reports that the cat does not eat well at those times. It seems that the status of cats, for Ms. B at least, derives from the kind of interaction that she has with them. The temptation for philosophical thinking is to reject this in intellectual horror. Surely moral status cannot depend on how we *feel* about entities. To avoid this dreaded possibility, we may begin to cast about for impersonal, objective criteria that can demonstrate that cats should be accorded a status superior to that of rats. (Or, of course, we could take an opposite tack and attempt to show that both cats and rats are *persons* on some criteria for personhood and therefore that we should treat both with respect.)

Let's resist for the moment the temptation to seek objective criteria in the form of properties belonging to either cats or rats. Ms. B knows that certain changes in rat behavior would give her a problem. Suppose rats were to seek food openly at the back door; suppose they started to rub against her leg affectionately; suppose they advanced expectantly toward her instead of scurrying away. One prefers not to consider the possibility. One prefers, of course, not to consider the parental tenderness of one's enemies, the pain of enemies' children caught in firebombing, or the idealism of people who use violence to promote their causes. In all these incidents, however, we are deeply affected by the sorts of response we expect, give, and receive.

None of this is to say, as yet, that we should allow ourselves to be so affected. Kant, among others, so distrusted human feelings that he actually devalued acts done out of love or inclination and insisted that only those done out of duty have moral worth. But let us face the centrality of feeling. We risk some idiosyncracy, to be sure. Whereas Ms. B loves and values cats, Ms. C may hate and fear them as greatly as most people do rats. Even in this rather odd case—seemingly detached entirely from the interaction of human beings—we can see that we are deeply affected not only by our personal preferences but also by a broader tendency in the human species. Because so many of us like cats and wish to protect them, we may consider one who hates and fears them phobic. We might even advise such a person to seek counseling. In contrast, most of us dislike rats and do not consider it at all odd to pursue their extermination.

My point is that our feelings are not wholly capricious and idiosyncratic. We have many basic feelings that are widely shared. These may be called intuitions, but we need not claim that intuitions are necessarily true or that they represent a form of knowledge comparable either to mathematical or scientific knowledge. This kind of move always leads to disappointment.[37] What we must do is acknowledge the existence of these basic feelings and ask how we might reflect usefully on them.

Tooley, for example, recognizes that feelings run deep on infanticide, and even though his logical argument leads him to allow infanticide in the first few days of life, he cautiously sticks to the first few days, and he implies that one should have good reasons for the decision. Why? If abortion in the ninth month is no different from abortion in the second month, if the infant is not different from the embryo in a morally relevant way, why recommend care or caution? Tooley cannot, understandably, be sure exactly when a human being has that first sense of continuing self, and should that sense be present, we would commit a grave moral error in killing that being. But such talk is largely rationalization. In all our moral pronouncements we have to come up with judgments and reasons that satisfy persistent and common feelings. Most of us are horrified by infanticide; that is a fact. Women, even menopausal women, often react to the cry of a newborn with tingling breasts. We (many of us) want instinctively to nurture. What lies at the bottom of this set of feelings is simply that we value the response of which a human infant is capable. The nuzzling, snuggling, sucking, grasping warmth of a human infant is something to which many of us respond emotionally and positively. That is a fact about value.

When we try to move away from the kind of strictly personal preference that would allow one person to kill an infant as one might a fly and that would lead another to gather lost infants in a circle of protection, we should take into account honestly the facts we have about our own values. I do not mean at all that we should endorse violence if it seems that many of us value violence or that we should ban infanticide just because many of us value infants. I do mean, however, that we should reflect on our values, search them thoroughly for consistency, and ask whether their rejection promotes or impedes the advancement of those values most basic to us. As an example of such values, we may posit the value almost all of us place on what Sumner calls the "paradigm person"—the fully sentient adult. As another example, we may name the universal desire to be cared for—to be helped in time of trouble, to be relieved of pain, to be regarded as special in the eyes of someone.

Philosophical writing cites most often the value of a paradigm human being. Needless to say, it describes this creature largely as a cognitive being. From a female perspective the value we place on being cared for looms much larger. It is the value that has called forth the best in women; it has produced, as we have seen, the paradigm woman. It is not necessary to decide between the analytic rationality of paradigm man and the caring rationality of paradigm woman to build a moral philosophy. Both attributes are present in both sexes, and we must consider, interpret, and use them as the grounds on which we base our judgments.

A creature that can respond to us in ways that call forth our desire to care is one that we will accord something like moral standing. Certain capacities of the entity itself are involved, but our own capacities and inclinations are equally involved in assessing the qualities to which we will attend. Thus to regard both our rationality and caring, we should respond to living entities in ways appropriate to their capacities to respond. Creatures that can feel pain should not be made to suffer. Creatures that can respond with affection should not be deprived of the opportunity to give and receive affection. Creatures that can plan and solve problems should not be reduced to slavish obedience. In all these recommendations we recognize the value we place on certain attributes and we affirm these values. Both moves are important.

From this perspective the capacity to respond is basic to considerations of abortion, just as it is to euthanasia. If an entity lacks the capacity to respond in ways that are both characteristic of its species and valued by us, there is little sense in constraining our behavior toward it with rules designed to codify intuitions that grow out of communicative experience. An adult human being permanently unable to respond to human communication is not, despite biological signs, truly alive; therefore we should direct our sympathetic caring to those who are actually suffering in the situation. Similarly, an infant who cannot and will never be able to respond need not be kept "alive" unless responsive human beings would suffer dreadfully from its killing.[38] Finally, since an embryo has no more capacity for human response than an egg or sperm, there need be no concern over removing it.

This way of approaching the problem of abortion has several merits. First, it is consonant with our ordinary response to natural experience. When a woman has an early natural abortion (a miscarriage), she may experience deep disappointment, but she does not experience grief; there is no beloved being lost. (I am not suggesting that we be unsympathetic toward one who exhibits grieflike symptoms in such a situation; we can feel with her, but she has lost a possibility—a dream—not a responsive child.) Second, it avoids the interesting but distracting problem of deciding whether the intention of abortion is death of the fetus or separation of the dependent fetus from its unwilling host, and this observation underscores a problem with the notion of viability. I will elaborate a bit on this merit in a moment. Last, we can generalize the approach to other encounters that have moral aspects; some of these we have already discussed, and others will arise when we talk about poverty and war.

Several writers have discussed abortion with respect to its intention.[39] Judith Thomson, for example, in essence turns the doctrine of double effect—usually employed against abortion—to a defense of abortion. She argues that the intention of abortion is to free the pregnant woman from a dependent being that has no right to the use of her body for its own maintenance and growth.[40] There are two significant aspects of her argument. One involves a discussion of competing rights, and I will not comment further on that, since I have already argued that rights talk masks the story of response that underlies our tendency to accord rights. The separation argument, however, is an invitation to mystification that we have not yet explored here.

As Steven Ross points out, if separation is the intention of abortion, one could not object to the maintenance of an embryo outside its original host's body.[41] A pregnant woman who claims that she only wants to be free of an unjustified use of her body would have to say, "If you can remove this entity without destroying it and bring it to viability in a bottle (or somewhere), that's fine; I only want to be separated from it and its demands." But as Ross cogently argues, this does not seem to be the primary intention of abortion. Most would-be parents who seek abortion do not want there to be a baby (a responsive being) who will be their biological child. They do not want to enter the intense relationship characteristic of parent and child, at least not right now, and they do not want to turn that responsibility over to an already overburdened society. They do not want a person to exist who, by its genetic makeup, will have a response-based claim on them. Ross concludes that potential parents really do desire the death of the fetus and not merely separation from it. I argue that this whole way of talking is a mistake. There is no death to consider if the entity whose biological processes are stopped is incapable of human response. It is precisely this capacity that early abortion is designed to prevent. Tooley's argument is essentially right in this regard, but he takes too narrow a criterion for establishing the appropriateness of our response to entities, and hence his claim that certain animals are rights bearers whereas infants are not strikes us as counterintuitive. Again a result that is counterintuitive is not necessarily wrong, but in questions of moral matters an argument that is consonant with our deepest intuitions and reflectively held values has greater merit than one that fails in consonance.

The separation argument would lead logically to scientific efforts to preserve the lives of embryos outside their hosts' bodies. Here pessimists with their tragic view of life might give us wise counsel. Everywhere we see the senseless proliferation of living things that will not achieve maturity—millions of frog eggs that will never be frogs, thousands of baby sea turtles that will never reach the sea, hundreds of tiny silk trees growing beneath a parent tree that will deprive them of sun and nutrients. It is pointless to fuss over the loss of every potential paradigm entity. Our attention should go to those already existing beings with whom we can establish a responsive relation.

The argument I have presented here has features in common with the arguments of several other writers. The notion of response is similar, for example, to that of sentience. But sentience has been used to establish hierarchies; it can be so used because the criteria of sentience are posited to be properties of the (sentient) being. In contrast, the concept of response embraces qualities both in the being encountered and in the one establishing the criteria. Instead of a hierarchy of sentience we describe a flexible array of responses. We reflect deeply on our reactions to entities and their capacities for response, and we recognize that our values and preferences change. This process does not land us in relativism, because we value highly at least two universal qualities or relational events—the capacity to reflect (thinking, reflective awareness, self-consciousness) and caring (doing the caring, being cared for). The former is a valued quality of beings; the latter is a characteristic of human relations. Caring requires a contribution from both carer and cared for.[42] As we reflect on the value we place on other qualities or relational characteristics, we must refer them to these two and to any others already established as consistent with them.

In questions of abortion, as in those of euthanasia, we need to remove the layers of mystification that render us helpless to assist ourselves and others. I do not at all suggest that every law, every religious tenet, every philosophical principle be cast carelessly aside. I mean, rather, that we should return to the basic events themselves and study our reactions as we live through them. We may then return to laws and recommendations somewhat wiser, and we will build into the laws we formulate a flexibility that reflects our intuitive grasp of address and response and our capacity to work things out in cooperative dialogue.

SUMMARY

In looking at pain as natural evil, we have seen that pessimism has a firm hold on one part of human reality but misses the part that makes life precious to us. When we include in our analysis our biological instinct to live and the small joys of everyday life, we see that our best course of action is to recognize caring occasions; in them we celebrate the satisfying rituals of relatedness and ease the suffering of pain and death.

We explored the possibility that there is something in the tasks to which women have been assigned that induces empathy and compassion. But after careful inspection we concluded that the tasks alone are not responsible for the feminine outlook. Rather, the attitude seems to flourish when we perform the tasks as a constellation of activities centered on known and cared-for individuals. There is both agency and continuity in this caring.

The attitude of caring desires to relieve suffering. It is concerned first with human beings and their suffering and only second with the problems and promises of science, religion, and law. Further, it counsels a careful look at the full range of suffering, including the suffering of loved ones and attendants. It is a relational attitude, one that posits the relation as more basic than the individual.

We considered euthanasia. From the feminine relational perspective we found euthanasia often justified. Arguments against active euthanasia in the face of terrible human suffering seem, from this view, to ratify evil—albeit with good intentions. Simple prohibitions protect us from traditional and legal charges of criminality, but the cocoon of righteousness in which we thus wrap ourselves has a worm inside and ugly crusts of age outside. We might charge that our culture has institutionalized practices that actually endorse great evils.

Finally, we discussed abortion. Again we found that extreme views (no abortion or abortion any time) derive from concepts that do not emerge from the phenomena under study. What does emerge is a story of human suffering that begs for relief and a clear understanding that we humans are deeply affected by certain valued patterns of human response. This understanding leads us to consider a reflectively established set of acceptable acts in dealing with entities that display an array of responses, which in turn trigger valued responses in us.

6

Helplessness: The Pain of Poverty

Sometimes individuals or groups deliberately or carelessly cause physical or psychic pain to others. This is moral evil—harm that individuals inflict on other human beings. We can prevent such evil, and it is one task of moral education to do so. Much of the pain that surrounds us does not stem from the intentions of particular moral agents, however, but seems to be the result of our customs and social structures. Evils thus induced are hard to see as preventable. Indeed they often go unidentified for long periods of time. When sensitive people finally see and name them, they become the objects of social reform. Then, when consciousness rises, resistance to reform often accompanies it, because most people find it hard to admit their roles in maintaining such evils. Who has caused them? Our long-standing predilection for seeking devils inclines us, on the one hand, to blame perpetrators other than ourselves for such miseries; on the other hand, our equally well entrenched belief in the retributive and pedagogical powers of suffering allows us to blame the victims for their unhappy condition. Sometimes, as in the long history of misogyny and slavery, we even insist that the sufferers enjoy their condition.

It is impossible to discuss comprehensively—or even to identify—every contemporary cultural evil. I have chosen poverty as an evil characterized by the feeling and often the reality of helplessness. In keeping with the method I have established, the analysis will begin with an attempt to understand the suffering experienced in poverty. Next will be a brief discussion of the sort of remedies by which, some say, the oppressed may liberate themselves. Finally, drawing on the experience of women in unequal power relations, I will suggest a pedagogy of the oppressor.

THE PSYCHIC PAIN OF POVERTY

There are many ways to look at the problem of poverty. We might select a lens from economics, sociology, or political science or from social work, pragmatic politics, or religion. Once again we will put all these views into brackets temporarily and try to understand what poverty means to those experiencing it and to those looking on.

As we saw in our earlier examination of Doris Lessing's Maudie, poverty involves psychic pain that aggravates the physical pain of growing old and being ill. The combination of old age, illness, and poverty resulted in dreadful living conditions for Maudie—a place that "was cold, dirty, smelly," and in several ways unsafe. Invited inside with Jane Somers, we experience the "sour, sweet-sharp reek," recoil at drinking tea from filthy cups, feel dismay at the empty cupboard and cold grate, and flinch at the thought of helping Maudie bathe from an enamel basin. Identifying easily with bright, articulate, and elegant Jane—whose favorite luxury is long soaks in a perfumed bath—we are horrified by Maudie's personal dirtiness. But Jane thinks, "Once Maudie had been like me, perpetually washing herself, washing cups, plates, dusting, washing her hair." [1] Maudie suffers now not only from cold and dirt but from the consciousness of being seen as helpless and dirty.

Poverty is a many-faceted phenomenon, and human beings take a variety of attitudes toward it. Often they regard it as the just desert of the lazy, stupid, or immoral. Annie, the fallen servant girl of Follett's *Man from St. Petersburg,* was condemned to utter poverty—joblessness and homelessness—because "she had been ruined by a man." She was in a hopeless and helpless state when Charlotte spotted her lying on the sidewalk. At Charlotte's urging, Lord Walden—against his sense of moral judgment—would recommend her for a factory job so that she would no longer be penniless, but she would never again obtain a household post. Men had absolute control over the virtue of women as their property, and the upper class had the lower class at its mercy in the network of references, implied respectability, and security. The pain inflicted for disobedience included the physical pains of hunger, cold, and illness, the psychic pain of helplessness, and the overwhelming pain of separation.

These pains form an interlocking structure of misery and mystification that works to maintain existing power structures. Lord Walden understandably hesitated to reduce any one of them lest the whole structure come tumbling down, but Charlotte's pleading brought him to consider some form of help. It is instructive to consider the one thing he would not do, however, even at the insistent urging of Charlotte. He would not restore Annie to a household post.

Poppa said: "Charlotte, we cannot possibly have a woman of bad character to live in this house. Even if I would allow it, the servants would be scandalized. Half of them would give notice. We shall hear mutterings even now, just because the girl has been allowed into the kitchen. You see, it is not just Mama and I who shun such people—it is the whole of society." [2]

In this short speech Lord Walden reveals the web of mystification on which society depends to control its subordinate members. Even most of the oppressed believed that Annie's treatment was justified. If they did not, fear for their own dependent status forbade direct action. It is not surprising that in the face of this ugly and total domination only a few relatively privileged women banded together politically to demand suffrage and to perform violent acts of resistance. Like Charlotte, these women did not often begin their campaign with a longing for full citizenship and expression of their rights. Rather, they reacted in sympathy to the physical and psychic pain they observed in other women and children. This awful pain induced in them a belief that only women's voting could change the cultural conditions of poverty and, when they were ignored, ridiculed, and put off they finally responded with violent acts. These acts are described in Mrs. Pankhurst's speech as recorded in Follett's story. The women (about a thousand went to prison during this period) burned putting greens with acid, cut telephone wires between London and Glasgow, broke windows in London clubs, wrecked the orchid houses at Kew Gardens, broke a showcase in the Tower of London, and bombed a house under construction for Lloyd George (being careful to do so before workmen arrived on the scene).[3] Much of the violence came in response to public goading "that women were not really committed to suffrage, that men would have fought harder." [4] So women responded, it would seem, in a symbolic language men could understand.

Because women's campaign for suffrage had such close ties to the desire to change living conditions for the poor—especially for women and children—it was easily derailed when other great causes arose. Again and again women were betrayed by male politicians who promised their endorsement of suffrage in return for women's help in liberal causes—against slavery in the United States and in support services during World War I in England. It was relatively easy to control people who already believed that service, cooperation, compassion, and fidelity were great virtues. Further, women remained for a long time victims of the mystification surrounding class and race. Those waging the war against poverty were largely educated women, and unfortunately these women maintained a separation between themselves and women of poverty and color. To a large extent this separation remains a problem today. Thus the three great evils interact to increase the suffering that is their common end.

The religious tradition that defined evil in terms of sin and disobedience has also added to the pain of poverty, but its position has been ambiguous. The Calvinist tradition emphasized hard work, righteousness, and prosperity as though the three were inseparable, but the nineteenth century brought a threat to religion in general and caused a rethinking of social attitudes in the light of secular knowledge. Christians, especially Christian women, were called on to relieve suffering, and, as we noted above, even the drive for suffrage had close links to social programs thought to depend on the enlightened voting of women. A hopeful strain of environmentalism sprang up between the older and harsher Calvinist reign and the later social Darwinism that would once again proclaim that the poor are poor in mind and spirit as well as in material things. The environmentalist spirit promoted the establishment of reform schools and other attempts at rehabilitation.[5]

But even while environmentalism flourished, the darker current that would welcome social Darwinism was not silent. In an 1855 report on insanity in Massachusetts, Edward Jarvis wrote:

> Poverty is an inward principle, enrooted deeply within the man, and running through all his elements; it reaches his body, his health, his intellect, and his moral powers. . . . Hence we find that among those whom the world calls poor, there is less vital force, a lower tone of life, more ill health, more weakness, more early death, and diminished longevity.[6]

A double fatalism operated here. The long-standing religious tradition made it easy to infer that the poor were either getting just punishment for their own sins or suffering for the general sins of humankind. In the latter case if they bore their suffering nobly and obediently their reward might come in heaven (although the Calvinist tradition found this result unlikely, since poverty was one sign that its victim was not a member of the elect, or saved). Antienvironmental scientific thinkers also blamed the victims. Their answer was to promote eugenics, since the core of the fault was not sin but defective genes. The two attitudes sometimes blended to posit sin as the ultimate cause of defective genes.

I said a bit earlier that the religious position on poverty was ambiguous. There was on the one hand a call to Christian charity and on the other a righteous judgment on the poor as sinners. But we might argue that the dogma, structure, and alliances of Christianity were not at all ambiguous. Even the call to service was an evangelical and self-serving program. Christians might earn stars in their crowns for serving the poor and converting the heathen. A self-righteous feeling of superiority often lay at the foundation of both attitudes.

Women often followed the overt message with real devotion, however. Did they do so out of stupidity—a lack of analytical capacity? Or was their behavior just a feminine form of social hypocrisy? More than likely some of each played a part for women as well as for men. But the experience of women, as we have seen, produces more *caring occasions,* and these occasions give rise to genuine personal feelings of sympathy for those in need. In the case of Carie, as Pearl Buck describes her, we saw a woman torn between her religious faith and her human love for the physical beings in her environment. Because she had borne children, tended other women in childbirth, aided mothers with ailing children, cooked for family and visitors, kept an "American garden" for her children (and her own peace of mind), cleaned house, and spent hours teaching children, she had countless occasions to develop a sense of caring for others for their own sakes. For Emmeline Pankhurst, contact with the poor and suffering preceded her militancy in the cause of suffrage. For Jane Somers, Maudie called forth a spirit of empathy and sisterhood. We might argue that religious institutions merely gave a verbal blessing to that which women would have done anyway. Indeed, it may be that without an emphasis on helping, the church could not have enlisted and held so many women.

From this perspective it is not surprising that priests who minister directly to the poor in Third World nations often adopt "liberation theology." They too enter caring occasions and are no longer able to see their parishioners solely through the church's objective office. Like Cyprian, perhaps, they struggle against the intimacy of understanding and loving individual human beings, but they find themselves responding more and more directly and with less dependence on the mediation of institutional dogma. The psychic pain of poverty touches those who enter caring occasions. The first reaction may be to reach out as an individual, to do something to help. The next, conditioned by a long tradition of abstract problem solving, is to formulate a wide-ranging solution—to adopt an ideological perspective, mount a concerted drive, join the oppressed in radical action.

PEDAGOGIES OF THE OPPRESSED

One set of responses to economic oppression consists of liberation theologies and pedagogies aimed at helping the oppressed liberate themselves. In authentic liberation theologies and pedagogies, we find many points of agreement with female thinking but also some important differences. Paulo Freire, for example, insists that the oppressed must free themselves and that an oppressor, desiring earnestly to help, must give up his or her privileged way of life and join the oppressed wholeheartedly.

> This, then, is the great humanistic and historical task of the oppressed: to liberate themselves and their oppressors as well. The oppressors, who oppress, exploit, and rape by virtue of their power, cannot find in this power the strength to liberate either the oppressed or themselves. Only power that springs from the weakness of the oppressed will be sufficiently strong to free both.[7]

But what is a power that springs from weakness? There is an understanding of suffering that only the sufferer can achieve, and there is a longing for freedom that only the unfree can know deeply. Beyond these, however, even though Freire insists that the liberation of both oppressed and oppressor by the oppressed "will actually constitute an act of love opposing the lovelessness which lies at the heart of the oppressors' violence, lovelessness even when clothed in false generosity," he gives us little reason to believe that radical action will be loving.[8] What in the history or in the experience of the oppressed leads us to suppose that they will be loving? Or is liberation an act of love simply by virtue of its result?

The role of the oppressor in this task is to join the oppressed in solidarity. "Solidarity requires that one enter into the situation of those with whom one is solidary; it is a radical posture." But clearly the oppressor can only approximate this solidarity. The oppressor will of necessity have a different consciousness from the oppressed and different instruments to express outrage. Striving to clarify the role of the repentant oppressor, Freire explains, "The oppressor is solidary with the oppressed only when he stops regarding the oppressed as an abstract category and sees them as persons who have been unjustly dealt with, deprived of their voice, cheated in the sale of their labor—when he stops making pious, sentimental, and individualistic gestures and risks an act of love."[9]

A full description of this "act of love" is not forthcoming, nor does Freire justify his belief that men can or will produce such acts. For him an act of love does not relieve the suffering of a single individual or group but rather transforms the objective conditions of oppression so that such individual acts of false generosity become unnecessary. It is unclear whether an act that transforms the objective conditions of oppression for an individual or group is an act of love. Freire works always at the extremes, at the level of all or nothing. He fails to explore fully the obvious danger in his recommendation to reject individualistic gestures, namely, that the oppressed will again become an abstract category—this time of another sort. The new category may require them to have a certain attitude, to adopt a uniform set of goals, to use prescribed means. He recognizes that the oppressed are likely to mimic the oppressor as they move toward liberation, and he counsels guarding against such mimicry, but because he does not consider the role of the oppressor in his pedagogy, he cannot suggest positive measures to prevent this tragic result. We need a more thorough examination of how those already free should behave, of how those uncommitted to total solidarity may yet avoid increasing their cruelty as oppressors. Both the nature of loving acts and a continuum of such acts need careful analysis and elaboration.

Not surprisingly, Freire's position reflects the paradoxical attitudes we have seen in religious perspectives. Traditional religion perceives a dichotomy in the spiritual status of rich and poor. Christianity sometimes suggests that the rich cannot enter the kingdom of heaven and that the poor will eventually inherit a kingdom of some sort. It has advised rich men to give all to the poor and follow Jesus. This is part of the ambiguity I mentioned earlier. On the one hand, the Gospels give reason to extol poverty; on the other, institutional religion has the good sense to recognize its dependence on benefactors and cannot offend prosperous, hard-working contributors without an adverse reaction. Middle-class religion ignores this dogmatic dichotomy to avoid offense; yet it springs up again and again in radical and fundamental religion. Even mainstream religion exalts poverty when saints freely choose it but hardly considers it an appropriate ideal for those who must maintain the church building, pay the minister's salary, and support good works.

Freire's point is, of course, that the doing of "good works" supports the structures of oppression by making them somehow necessary, and there is clearly more than a grain of truth in his perception. But by failing to treat in any depth the whole range of loving human activity, he risks the success of his project. Just as Christianity has had to take a pragmatic outlook on the virtues of poverty—not everyone can indulge in it, for someone must feed those who wait for God to provide—so a practical program to relieve poverty must go beyond the dichotomy of oppressed and oppressor, beyond a faith in the loving or spiritual power of the oppressed to liberate. There must be a pedagogy for the oppressor as well as a pedagogy of the oppressed.

Freire's call for solidarity echoes in the work of feminist Christian theologians such as Sharon Welch. Writing from a Foucauldian perspective, Welch sees the new Christian theology as a subjugated discourse. She rejects (as many feminist theorists do) universality and absolutism. The concern of liberation theology, she says, is

> not sin in a universal sense, but sin in particular, sin as the denial of solidarity. A liberating Christian faith addresses historical conditions of fallenness with a hope for and a struggle toward redemption in history. The faith that grounds theologies of liberation is intrinsically historical and particular, directed toward the denunciation and transformation of specific forms of oppression.[10]

Welch too accuses traditional theology of "trivializing suffering."[11] Liberation theology expresses faith in a God who really liberates— who in an important sense grows and learns with us how to liberate as we learn what liberation means. Welch retains Christian terminology. She quotes with approval Dorothee Soelle's reinterpretation of resurrection and liberation:

> Resurrection is the most encoded symbol of faith, and it resists decoding. It is the utmost yes to life. . . . The symbol transforms even death into an instrument of life. Different times will attempt different translations of this mystery. While the bourgeois theology emphasized the individual dimension, the new theology . . . will emphasize the social dimension of the mystery. Hence we bring together liberation with resurrection because our deepest need is not personal immortality but a life before death for all human beings.[12]

But what induces this deep need in the otherwise comfortable? What prompts the solidarity of which Freire, Soelle, and Welch speak? "Solidarity takes the place of traditional notions of redemption: it is evoked or enabled by the grace of God; it is the evidence and the result of God's incarnation; it is the fulfillment of creation." [13] This is a new and beautiful theological message that has had as yet little effect on our social and political structures. The people who speak it most convincingly have had direct experience with the oppressed and have felt their suffering directly. Understandably they put more hope in pedagogies of the oppressed—who, after all, have whole lives to gain— than in pedagogies of the oppressor. Welch confesses to both radical doubt and a deeply tragic sense of life: "I find, therefore, in liberation faith an intrinsic correlation with doubt and a deepening awareness of the tragic dimensions of life. For as conversion to the other grows, as I experience more intensely the power of the dangerous memory of human suffering, doubt as to the possibility of reconciliation also rises." [14]

This, of course, is why I am raising questions about pedagogies of the oppressed, but let us pursue the possibilities for a bit. Another advocate of a pedagogy of the oppressed is Ivan Illich. His analysis concentrates, as does the present one, on the helplessness of poverty. "The poor," he says, "have always been socially powerless. The increasing reliance on institutional care adds a new dimension to their helplessness: psychological impotence, the inability to fend for themselves." For Illich the institutionalization of values is a prime evil that produces effects very like the ones we have already named: "Physical pollution, social polarization, and psychological impotence: three dimensions in a process of global degradation and modernized misery." [15] These three dimensions are aspects of physical pain, separation, and helplessness. Because Illich's purpose is to criticize the role of modern institutions in creating these miseries, however, he does not treat the full range of either the inducing evils or their evil effects. He too moves too far away from the well-intentioned oppressor in his diagnosis and his prescription for change. As lovely as his vision is, it rings of impracticality. We must discover how to work with all people of moderate goodwill who have a natural interest in their own well-being.

The first effort to deinstitutionalize values, Illich says, should target schools, since they are more vulnerable than other institutions to such an attack. He claims that "the disestablishment of schools will inevitably happen—and it will happen surprisingly fast. It cannot be retarded very much longer, and it is hardly necessary to promote it vigorously, for this is being done now. What is worthwhile is to try to orient it in a hopeful direction, for it could take place in either of two ways." [16]

He goes on to describe the possibilities in a "brave new world dominated by well-intentioned administrators of programmed instruction" or, more to his liking, a decertification of learning—a process of giving access to all forms of learning to all those who wish to participate in them. Today his plea for decertification sounds hopelessly naive. We have lived through the dreams of "greening" and the age of Aquarius, and we have seen how a threatened culture can tighten the reins of control. Moreover, we have learned that many people prosper, feel more comfortable, and become more loyal in such an atmosphere. Many women respond to feminism in exactly the same way. A truly liberating pedagogy must work with, not against, the so-called oppressor.

At one level both Illich and Freire recognize that the acts of love that constitute both liberation and teaching must consider all people. Illich speaks of educational webs that will transform living into "learning, sharing, and caring," and he writes eloquently on the "priceless character" of the master-disciple relation.[17] In this discussion he agrees with Aquinas that such teaching is an act of love and mercy. But here we come up against a long tradition of harsh interpretation of what constitutes love and mercy. Many prosecutors of witches considered themselves loving and merciful because they were saving immortal souls at the mere cost of pain to mortal bodies. Many, many ordinary parents and teachers do things in the name of love and mercy that others of us find questionable.

I am not accusing either Illich or Freire of advocating violence, meanness, or carelessness. But both walk somewhat too close to the edge of self-righteousness in pressing their cause. Illich speaks frankly of "a new elite" in the construction of Epimethean man:

> The suspicion that something is structurally wrong with the vision of *homo faber* is common to a growing minority in capitalist, Communist, and "underdeveloped" countries alike. The suspicion is the shared characteristic of a new elite. To it belong people of all classes, incomes, faiths, and civilizations. They have become wary of the myths of a ma-

jority: of scientific utopias, of ideological diabolism, and of the expectation of the distribution of goods and services with some degree of equality.

. . . Yet whereas the Promethean majority of would-be spacemen still evades the structural issue, the emergent minority is critical of the scientific *deus ex machina,* the ideological panacea, and the hunt for devils and witches.[18]

But why a "new elite"? We are unlikely to escape the hunt for devils and witches by branding the majority of persons living in "developed" nations "Promethean men." Here again we encounter the twin traditional temptations: first, to set up two warring forces—one good and wise, the other bad and foolish—and, second, to insist that people need to be saved. Freire wants the oppressed to become the saviors (liberators) of both themselves and the oppressors; Illich wants Epimetheans to save themselves and set the Prometheans free from the ideological rock to which they have tied themselves.

Clearly I am not arguing that there are no natural or cultural categories into which human beings can be divided. Nor am I arguing that different groups have no special contributions to make to the general welfare. I am arguing simply that women and men, acting at long last on the logic of women's experience, have a great deal to learn and to contribute to the betterment of all life. But I do not want to claim that women will be or can be the saviors of humankind, and I do not want to negate the great achievements of Promethean man. Rather, the contribution I have in mind invites the kind of partnership people need to work out their problems cooperatively.

A PEDAGOGY FOR THE OPPRESSOR

Women are in a peculiarly advantageous position to plan and implement a pedagogy for the oppressor. First, they constitute an oppressed group—at least in Freire's language, whereby, "any situation in which 'A' objectively exploits 'B' or hinders his pursuit of self-affirmation as a responsible person is one of oppression."[19] Thus they should have both the understanding of suffering and the longing for freedom that Freire mentions. Second, because many women have not been and are not now economically oppressed in the way that some ethnic subgroups have been, some are at least formally educated in the ways of the oppressor; they can use his language, political machinery, and disciplines if they choose to do so to increase their own power. Third, and most important for present purposes, women's experience can yield genuine insights on a "power that springs from weakness" and can contribute to our understanding of human acts of love; thus it can be used to develop a pedagogy of the oppressor that may transform oppressors into less harmful companions on an earth that all people must share.

What are the components of such a pedagogy, and how exactly does feminine experience suggest them and fill them out? One component is mediation. Women have for centuries lived with both oppressors and oppressed in their own families. They have learned to please those who have exploited them and hindered their self-affirmation. They have learned to interpret father to children and children to father. They have learned that human beings thought evil by the world at large nevertheless have lovable qualities. In all this learning skills develop and can surely be maintained and extended into public life. The lesson women can teach the goodwilled oppressor is how to submit to mediation—when to mediate and why. In political life mediation is used to settle cases and to effect compromises. It is instrumental and rule governed. But from a feminine perspective mediation is a task of the loving peacemaker. It is not primarily judgmental, but rather aims at restoring a loving balance. Its objective is not simply to settle a case but to interpret A to B and B to A in such a way that reconciliation will result.

Precisely because women have had little power, they have had to consider what they might feasibly accomplish. Fact-finding and binding rulings based on a summary of facts have not been within women's usual powers. Instead, women have had to ask: What attitude will I take toward the contending parties? How can I help them understand each other? What does each want most? How close can we come to a solution that will be mutually satisfactory? And if such a solution is impossible, how can I keep the reactions of both parties nonviolent? In an important sense these questions imply acts of love as Freire envisions them, but they address oppressed as well as oppressor. The questions express love for both and do not foreclose the possibility of dialogue with the oppressor.

There *is* a power in this weakness—a power arising from the recognition of being unable to pronounce an arbitrary judgment that must be obeyed. In the absence of such power one must persuade, plead, appeal to sympathies, interpret, reword, and above all attribute the best possible motive consonant with reality to both parties in the dispute. By standing as a bridge between two warring parties, a woman (or feminine mediator) may bring out the best in each. Being vulnerable, she is in a sense at their mercy. Recognizing her position and persisting, she displays a trust in them that is hard to violate. In her presence, at least, hostilities may cease. It is this spirit of mediation that we must develop, and it is a spirit best conveyed by those who love and understand both sides. In male politics it is a spirit approximated only when the threat from outside is so great that those inside must forsake a narrow partisanship for a new, broader, one. In female politics it derives from love for the contenders themselves and not for some overriding principle that both represent.

Clearly mediation of this sort is both process and product in a pedagogy of the oppressor. It directs the oppressor to connect with and consider the projects of the other. But what should be the core content of a pedagogy aimed at reducing or eliminating poverty? One answer, perhaps, is moderation. People should learn that the extremes of great wealth and poverty are disgusting.

An analogy may be useful here. Our society regards both obesity and anorexia as eating disorders. We now place tremendous emphasis on fitness, on maintaining optimal levels of weight. Problems at the lower end of the scale are complex but have surely been aggravated by a pervasive (and perverse) ideal of ultraslimness. For anorexics self-worth seems entirely bound up in body image, and autonomy is reduced to control over one's eating. They lose the normal, healthy celebratory function of eating and sharing food. Indeed, our society may ignore this function at every level of thinking on weight and fitness, where the temptation is to concentrate on calories, nutritional status, breathing capacity, muscle tone, heart rate, and other physiological matters. In spite of all this single-minded attention to appearance and fitness, however, we seldom hear fears that humankind would become too much alike—that all interesting variations would disappear—if everyone were healthy, slim, and trim.

When we consider material wealth we find both similarities and differences in our attitudes. We often look on poverty as disgusting and view the people suffering it as though they had a disorder of some kind. But we rarely compare great wealth with gluttony; wealth does not revolt us. Further, when wealth-sharing schemes are suggested as political measures, a great fear of mediocrity and uniformity arises.

We are afraid that everyone will be condemned to a dull and colorless existence and that an entirely gray and uninteresting landscape will be peopled by interchangeable human automatons. But why should this be the case? Is wealth the only thing that differentiates us from one another?

Just as a sick ideal of thinness has contributed to ailments like anorexia, so might a sick ideal of success lead to a constant striving for more and more wealth. Further, this particular ideal is supported by myth (for example, Horatio Alger), history, education, politics—by attitudes in nearly every component of our culture. It is never enough in any part of our society to be doing well; we must always strive to be *best*. We only approach the threshold of disgust when it becomes public knowledge that an enormously wealthy person continues the pursuit of wealth with obvious cruelty, utter ruthlessness, or such avarice that no human being can stand him or her. The pursuit of wealth remains not only a cultural ideal but almost a compulsory one. Persons who reject it have to explain themselves, and only a few explanations are acceptable—for example, taking a religious vow of poverty.

Our culture has little interest in the middle range of phenomena. We are intrigued by the extremes—the big winner and the born loser. Even in education, while we supposedly pitch our instruction to the median, our great concern lies with the talented and the handicapped. In these areas expertise develops. We fail to study seriously the merits of moderation. Yet a mystique has grown up around middle-class family life, and television shows, movies, stories, and theme parks such as Disneyland all idealize this way of living. The present danger is that we will overlook the real beauty and solidity depicted in this ideal as we realistically challenge the romanticism that surrounds it. The task now is to encourage moderation when the possibilities for immoderation proliferate.

Deliberate moderation, as opposed to the accident of landing in the middle class while working one's way upward, is not a virtue in which we are instructed. We learn at best how to make the most of it. The management of wealth is rarely taught, and when it is, instruction focuses on conservation and increase, not on leveling off and sharing. But education for moderation is possible. We should encourage students to think about decent levels of material well-being in much the same way that we should think about physical fitness. When our weight creeps up to the high point of a five- or ten-pound limit, we cut back; we discipline ourselves to stay within a healthy and happy range. Similarly, when our wealth creeps up, we should ask ourselves how to use it to empower others, improve the community, extend our usefulness, or simply celebrate our joy of life. We ought consciously to draw lines—appropriate to our needs and circumstances—that represent the upper limits of healthy gains in wealth.

In this way of thinking we do not use the philanthropy associated with enormous wealth as an excuse for pursuing it, because we recognize that the processes of accruing such wealth and giving from its interest both contribute to the helplessness and psychic pain of those who must depend on it. There are other ways to support art, build museums, and establish universities than to depend on the gifts of enormously wealthy patrons, and little by little we must formulate, express, and internalize this message. Enormous wealth is disgusting; it is unnecessary; it is unhealthy.

None of this requires us to hate the wealthy or to find them evil in themselves. This is the great mistake of traditional thinking—to get at the sin through the sinner. Rather, we must begin to view the inordinately wealthy as unhealthy, as people who have succumbed to an addiction, and we must help each other avoid the temptation of success measured in purely financial terms. Wealth is not in itself evil. The evil is the psychic pain inflicted on those deprived, the separation between people who have and those who need, between those who can give and those who must receive, and the helplessness induced in those who are powerless.

Recognizing what makes great wealth a contribution to evil suggests how the experience of women can help teach moderation. First, of course, there is the experience of sharing—of feeding and clothing one's own children and taking responsibility for the feeding and clothing of others. Descriptions of such sharing abound. In *Eleni,* Nicholas Gage describes his heroic mother's habit of sharing—how it reflected the Greek village culture in which the family lived and how it persisted in Eleni even through the horrors and deprivation of guerrilla warfare. In relatively secure times the whole community shared events such as weddings:

> The cooking began a week before the wedding, and on Wednesday the women of the neighborhood prepared the dough for the six huge wedding breads. On Thursday, the breads were brought to the Gatzoyiannis

house, fat and round as millstones, and Olga, using two spoons, "embroidered" the tops of each one with crosses and lovers' knots, wild roses and doves, studding the patterns with Jordan almonds for fertility.[20]

In such accounts we observe women sharing in preparing food, transmitting family and village customs, teaching children, beautifying house and countryside, providing each new family with the necessities and simple treasures to start a new household. But Eleni's sharing went beyond anything demanded by ritual and custom. She continued to share what she could even when starvation threatened and suspicion had torn the village into frightened factions. One day when she had set out to take some beans to a neighbor who had once shown her kindness, a woman named Tassina stopped to tell her that anyone seen accepting a gift from her—even so small a gift as beans—would be politically endangered. Eleni's response was characteristic: " 'Thank God you told me,' Eleni said sadly. 'I didn't mean to do her harm. Here, you take the beans for your children.' " The political situation was so dangerous that Tassina, in spite of her great need for food, hesitated to take beans from Eleni, who was under the severe scrutiny of the guerrillas. Ashamed of her own fear and ingratitude, Tassina nevertheless suggested that Eleni pass by and throw the bag into her yard. Eleni did so, and Tassina "picked it up with a mixture of relief and guilt and never spoke to Eleni again." [21]

We cannot blame Tassina for her ungracious behavior in the face of real danger and the sick fear it produces. We may consider her weak, but she is not guilty of moral evil. But those who deliberately induced the pervasive fear of pain, separation, and helplessness are guilty of moral evil. The people in this village could have withstood the pain of poverty (they were never securely prosperous) if they had been allowed to face it together in their traditional ways. A wide range of human virtue, vice, and weakness would have been manifested then—as always, everywhere—but the emergency would probably have called forth more courage and sharing than cowardice and hoarding. The guerrillas separated people, put them in fear of each other, precisely to prevent their drawing on each other's generosity and courage and to ensure dependence on the leaders of the cause.

In Gage's detailed historical account we find the best and the worst of human behavior in both women and men. Virtue in each has its characteristic form. Because history has concentrated on the experience of men, we are more familiar with the warrior model of courage than with that of domestic virtue. Yet we see clearly in the life of Eleni the story of women's courage in the face of violence and hostility, their compassion and sharing while tired, hungry, and hurt, their devotion to children even when their own lives are at risk. Through it all runs the sound of laughter, of singing, of the irrepressible urge to celebrate life when an occasion arises.

We touched on this universal feminine story earlier in Alice Walker's account of her mother's life in the South during the depression. It was a white *woman* who inflicted psychic pain on Walker's mother and threatened her family with the physical pain of hunger, but the virtues that redeemed the situation were also peculiarly feminine. Another story of sharing and endurance is that of Gladys Milton. A black nurse and midwife working long hours, Gladys has always had time to perform volunteer services—even while raising a large family of her own: "Her days off are often jammed with volunteer work, taking blood pressures or visiting shut-ins. 'I like to do things for people. It's my friends who make me tick, always have. I love people and I care what they think of me. I'd feel awful if someone didn't like me.' " [22] Some take such a statement as proof that women lack the detachment necessary to think deeply about moral issues. But Gladys does not mean that she would do anything, even morally questionable acts, to get people to like her. Her life is a testimony to goodness far beyond the ordinary call of duty. Gladys uses the response of others to judge whether she is effective in her efforts to care. Her approach is perhaps the essence of an ethic of care. [23] It is not enough to act according to principle and thus achieve a sense of personal rightness or moral goodness; the response of the other must demonstrate that the caring has been received. [24]

The stories of these women suggest that evil is overcome not by a form of violent overthrow but rather by a steady refusal to participate in it. In another sense, of course, the story of evil is as much the story of Tassina's fear and weakness and the white woman's vindictiveness to Walker's mother as it is of Eleni's courage, Aunt Mandy's generosity, and Gladys Milton's enormous energy and beautiful altruism. The courage, generosity, and resourcefulness help us see the real face of evil, which reveals itself not in disobedience or alienation from an angry and possessive god or in sexual abandon or in love of earth over heaven or in a lack of intelligence or in laziness, but rather in the careless or willful infliction of pain, separation, or helplessness.

The pedagogy of the oppressor must include at least lessons in mediation, moderation, and sharing. We must provide far more opportunities for students of all ages to plead each other's cases, to stand between opposing parties in appreciative efforts to bring people together in common understanding. We also need opportunities to learn moderation and to embrace it as an ideal. We must relearn sharing—not as a special privilege of those who have and therefore may be further blessed for their generosity, but as a way of life that sustains everyone in mutual giving and receiving. Those who share even when they have little feel like whole and valued human beings.

In recent years some have expressed concern about women's role in social reform and moral education. Many feminists fear that women will continue to sacrifice their own opportunities for success in efforts to pass on the altruistic elements of a culture that values talk of altruism over its enactment. Unfortunately the message of selflessness that organized religion delivers has too often been accepted by women and ignored (except in theory) by men. In *Habits of the Heart* Alexis de Tocqueville is quoted on the subject of women and moderation in America:

> [Religion] is often powerless to restrain men in the midst of innumerable temptations which fortune offers. It cannot moderate their eagerness to enrich themselves, which everything contributes to arouse, but it reigns supreme in the souls of their women, and it is women who shape mores. Certainly of all the countries in the world America is the one in which the marriage tie is most respected and where the highest and truest conception of conjugal happiness has been conceived.[25]

This passage is loaded with insights, half-truths, and allusions to myth. Religion has for the most part been powerless to restrain men from the pursuit of riches, and I have previously contended that this attempt has been typically halfhearted and insincere. The observation that its message reigns supreme in women may be a faulty attribution of causality. In reality Judaism, Christianity, and Islam may include messages of moderation and charity because women would not have devoted themselves to religions that lacked these elements. Further, as Alice Walker comments on the Southern black sharecropper's dedication to a religion that oppressed him in its deliberate attempts at pacification, women too have used their religions as an antidote to bitterness. (I would not credit women with what Walker calls a "transformation," because there is no women's church; there *is* a black church—perhaps a genuine transformation.)

Tocqueville's assertions that women shape mores and that marriage ties in America are, conceptually at least, the acme of conjugal happiness are both, perhaps, mythic statements. They illustrate beliefs that hold people together in common faiths and common myths. Both are questionable. But the ideas they suggest are important. Women are now in a position to exercise some power in shaping mores, and women can indeed use the strength they have learned in weakness to empower. Further, the myth of conjugal happiness can be extended to the joys of relatedness in general, and the celebrations of ordinary life so characteristic of the best family living can help reeducate people on what it means to succeed in life. But to accomplish these goals requires a high level of critical thinking combined with a resolute commitment to transform our education into a pedagogy for the transformation of the oppressor.

WOMEN AND POVERTY

It would be a mistake to leave this discussion of the pain of poverty without noting the poverty that women experience as a direct result of the caregiving that I have so far extolled. In *Women Take Care*, Tish Sommers and Laurie Shields document a grim story of the "consequences of caregiving in today's society." Three-fourths or more of those who care for disabled adults at home are women, and of these about one-third are poor. The poverty of these caregivers is a consequence of social policy that requires them to use up all their financial resources before any public help becomes available. As Sommers and Shields forcefully put it, "*Women are being assigned the social role of providing compassion and care, without being given any of the resources to do it.*" [26]

Women's assignment to the role of caregiver is not new, of course. It was a standard expectation for the angel in the house. But people— even severely handicapped people—are living longer and in smaller nuclear groups. The task of caregiving can go on for years with little respite for the caregiver, who is often no longer young or in good health. When the physical and emotional strains of continuous caregiving are aggravated by financial hardship, caregivers face disaster. All the "isms" men fight in the name of overcoming evil pale beside the enormous cultural evil we are discussing here—the exploitation and oppression of women forced to perform tasks that bring them neither compensation nor recognition. "Compassion," write Sommers and Shields, "must take the center stage in social policy because the only real solutions to the problems of the caregiver are social." [27]

Solutions must be social, but this does not mean that they can be found in the traditional detached ways, nor should they embody detachment in their content. The answer cannot be merely for "all of us" to pay higher taxes to support enormous expenditures for "professional care." Such a solution risks financial and emotional waste. As Kari Waerness, whose work we looked at earlier, recommends, we need to see caring as rational and to explore ways to maintain the *caring* in public efforts to give care. This involves not only the allocation of funds but sweeping changes in our attitudes toward caregiving and caregivers. The most difficult problems of cultural evil are illustrated vividly here. First, any society takes a long time just to see and name its cultural evils, and second, because of the patterns of social interaction ingrained in the society, solutions are likely to perpetuate the very evils that underlie the one under attack. Thus if we see the evil of undeserved poverty and respond merely by increasing funds for caregiving, we leave untouched the basic evil that disregards separation and helplessness and undervalues the sharing and celebration of connection that have been so important in women's lives.

The problem of induced poverty crosses racial and ethnic lines, but language difficulties and racism often exacerbate it.

> Marian is a Black woman in her early 50s who cares for her mother while working full-time. She describes her experience trying to get some assistance: I don't ask for help. Once I did, and they gave me such a runaround at the county. "Call back after lunch" and "If you are working, you should be able to take care of these matters yourself." Finally when they did send a woman out, she was so disrespectful she left my mother in tears. I don't need that kind of help. [28]

Sometimes the contributing cultural evil is a form of sexism. Lesbian caregivers may find that professional health care personnel ignore them. "A lesbian caregiver may have great difficulty even getting information about her lover's condition from health care professionals." [29] Situations of this sort illustrate the great and really evil power of patriarchy—its power to separate and make helpless. That power does not decrease, I should emphasize, when it becomes implicit rather than explicit, for then it simply shifts its locus of control—it finds a new fulcrum.

Clearly education must play a substantial role in uprooting cultural evil. As we have seen, the solutions likely to emerge in an ailing culture often ratify evil. That is why pedagogies of the oppressor are essential. Freire is right on this much: an oppressor *as oppressor* cannot find a solution to the problems of the oppressed.

SUMMARY

Here we have considered the helplessness that often accompanies poverty. The evil of poverty lies in its evil effects: the physical pains of deprivation, the psychic pains of separation and helplessness. Human beings have traditionally been ambivalent toward poverty—extolling it when saints freely choose it and suspecting it when it happens to people against their will. In the latter case we often assume that the poor are poor in will, spirit, and intelligence as well as in financial condition.

Pedagogies of the oppressed are in many ways attractive, and we should heed the basic message of empowerment. But even these powerful pedagogies reflect the traditional views of good and evil in that they divide the world into oppressed and oppressor and counsel that one group must act as "savior" to the other as well as to themselves. These poignant and potentially powerful pedagogies enervate themselves by ignoring the potential positive role of a well-intentioned and reeducated oppressor.

It is necessary, then, to suggest a pedagogy of the oppressor, one that involves *mediation* as a key element in its process and *moderation* as a cornerstone in its content. Because women's experience has been rich in opportunities to mediate—that is, to engage in a process of explaining one side to another with the aim of reconciliation—I suggested drawing on this experience to create a pedagogy to reeducate the oppressor. Similarly, because women are aware of the contingency of their own economic condition, because they have so often been dependent on others for their economic welfare, their experience may be valuable in constructing the content of such a pedagogy.

Finally, a solution to the exploitation of women as caregivers must build on the experience of women in sharing and caring. It cannot relieve their induced poverty and psychic pain simply by removing the physical tasks of caregiving. This is a trap that feminists as well as other social meliorists are likely to fall into. We are simply not going to make the world better by making it possible for women to live like traditional men—that is, to escape the vocation of caregiving—for then *no one* will live with the assurance of compassion and the security of devoted love.

7

War

Most modern cultures acknowledge war as a great evil. From the perspective of this volume it is surely an enormous evil, one that causes excruciating pain, separation, and helplessness. Yet war and warriors have long been glorified. Seth Schein remarks, "The earliest poetry extant in several major Indo-European language families—poetry which presumably reflects earlier, originally oral traditions—includes stories of the exploits of warrior-heroes who fight both for the benefit of their people and for their own glory." [1] This early poetry describes men caught up in wars instigated by gods; they fight and suffer heroically, but they do not cause wars, and efforts to prevent or stop wars entail propitiating the gods—not understanding each other.

War is not only an enormous evil; it is a huge topic. Volumes of history, religious and legal criticism, biography, and fiction focus on it. Oddly, however, as Richard Wasserstrom points out, philosophers have paid little attention to war. [2] When philosophers do analyze questions of war they usually concentrate on problems of conducting it, not of preventing it. My purpose in discussing it here—in a fashion that must inevitably be incomplete—is to address the second set of problems by applying the methods developed in earlier chapters.

We begin by looking at the traditional attitudes toward war that we must set aside. We then look at war as a phenomenon and ask, What can we do to prevent it? It seems unlikely that political methods will prevent war as long as people continue to think of one another as enemies. We must face the evil in ourselves instead of locating and trying to overcome it in other humans or in gods to be appeased. The notion that the prevention of war must begin somewhere other than in politics is not new. John Dewey clearly took such a stand, and so did Jane Addams. Dewey is quoted as saying: "The only way to make headway in the international community is to start with the nonpolitical aspects of society—conversation, food, technical meetings, congresses and so on—and end up with politics. But certainly don't start with politics!"[3]

Many of the remedies for war—balance of power, mutually assured destruction (deterrence), graduated reciprocation in tension reduction (GRIT), tit for tat—do start with politics in the sense that they attack the problem of international conflict and war directly.[4] Dewey's approach differed, and so does the one I will take. I will explore a pedagogy of the oppressor further.

GLORY AND HORROR

Perhaps no one has written more eloquently on the virtues of the warrior and the horrors of war than William James. In both *The Varieties of Religious Experience* and "The Moral Equivalent of War" James extols the virtues and energy that accompany just war but deplores its destruction and horror. Recognizing the great attractions of war and the romantic role it plays in our national histories, James advises us to search for "the moral equivalent of war: something heroic that will speak to men as universally as war does, and yet will be as compatible with their spiritual selves as war has proved itself incompatible."[5]

Although anyone opposed to war will find much to applaud in James's essays, there are worrisome points as well. He writes:

> History is a bath of blood. The *Iliad* is one long recital of how Diomedes and Ajax, Sarpedon and Hector *killed*. No detail of the wounds they made is spared us, and the Greek mind fed upon the story. Greek history is a panorama of jingoism and imperialism—war for war's sake, all the citizens being warriors. It is horrible reading, because of the irrationality of it all—save for the purpose of making "history"—and the history is that of the utter ruin of a civilization in intellectual respects perhaps the highest the earth has ever seen.[6]

The worrisome point here is that James, like so many other writers, does not take seriously the challenge that Greek behavior throws out to Greek intellect. How can a civilization so highly rated "in intellectual respects" be also governed by irrationality? Rather than simply deploring such a contradictory state of affairs, we might do better to question some of the basic assumptions of Greek intellectual life. Earlier chapters contested both the association of women and nature and the denigration of bodies and menial tasks. We might extend the challenge to the Greek philosophical ideal of the contemplative life. To live a life of contemplation—the appropriate life for those at the top of the natural human hierarchy—men needed a mass of inferior beings to serve them. The Greeks, of course, saw and affirmed the necessity. Indeed, they rationalized the system elegantly. Women and slaves would achieve the greatest happiness, they reasoned, by exhibiting the virtues prescribed for them by their masters. This is not a small point. Whenever individuals or groups posit for themselves an ideal life, they should—according to the standpoint of women at least—ask themselves an ethical question about what this ideal means for the lives of other human beings. The absence of this question in Greek thought makes it a dangerous body of work on which to model our moral life.[7] We can lodge the same complaint against Kantian ethics.

A second point that concerns us in James's analysis is his unquestioning acceptance of the hard virtues of men at war. He pokes fun at "reflective apologists" for war, saying that they suppose war to be the only way to keep a check on "a world of clerks and teachers, of co-education and zo-ophily, of 'consumer's leagues' and 'associated charities,' of industrialism unlimited, and feminism unabashed." But he follows this statement immediately with one that grants the apologists' central point. "Militarism," he says, "is the great preserver of our ideals of hardihood, and human life with no use for hardihood would be contemptible. Without risks or prizes for the darer, history would be insipid indeed; and there is a type of military character which every one feels that the race should never cease to breed, for every one is sensitive to its superiority."[8]

What we require at this point is a careful analysis of the virtues of hardihood, not a quick leap to an alternative outlet for them.[9] In searching for the moral equivalent of war, James fails to consider that there may be no equivalent, moral or otherwise, for certain military virtues and certain features of war. In *The Varieties of Religious Experience* James contrasts ascetic saintliness with militaristic hardihood. His method is interesting. First, he describes the "pathetic futilities" and egotism of monastic asceticism, and he concludes that men have good reasons for rejecting it. Second, he explores the possibility of a "renovated and revised ascetic discipline." Here he observes that many would suggest military life as an attractive alternative (an equivalent hardihood), and he admits that war is "congruous with human nature," whereas asceticism is not. But then he notes the irrationality and horror of war and concludes that we must surely reject it and perhaps consider voluntary poverty as an alternative mode of hardiness.[10]

James's argument has at least two important weaknesses. First, as I have already pointed out, he does not tease apart the virtues that military life supposedly requires and engenders, and so we do not have an opportunity to evaluate them and explore alternative outlets for those we wish to cultivate. He asks us to take a model of hardihood whole. Second, his desire to avoid "effeminacy" badly constrains his argument. When he considers war as an alternative to asceticism he says, "But when we ask ourselves whether this wholesale organization of irrationality and crime be our only bulwark against effeminacy, we stand aghast at the thought and think more kindly of ascetic religion."[11]

He again reveals the common fear of being like a woman in his discussion of poverty as a virtue. He asks, "Does not the worship of material luxury and wealth, which constitute so large a portion of the 'spirit' of our age, make somewhat for effeminacy and unmanliness?" James sees the violence, greed, and "prevalent fear of poverty," which he regards as the "worst moral disease from which our civilization suffers," but he does not seem to see that the traditional view of masculinity—one that defines itself in opposition to femininity—may be a substantial cause of this moral disease.[12]

It is in part understandable that James should extol poverty in his conclusion. He was, after all, writing a chapter on saintliness. But his discussion reminds us sharply of a major flaw in many traditional accounts: an incessant emphasis on the agon, or contest. Men must always strive to be best at what they do, often with little or no regard for what such striving means to those around them. The warrior must kill enemies, and he becomes famous by killing more than his fellows kill. The saint must be poorer, suffer more, than those around him. We recounted in chapter 2 the lengths to which saints have gone in their attempts to mortify the flesh. It should be no wonder, then, that men are attracted to the opposite extremes as well, especially to the acquisition of great wealth. To reach the extremes by choice, whether of war or pacifism, of poverty or wealth, requires striving, and striving for extremes has been a mark of manhood.

Few have recognized the hard, patient, loving work of carers (women or men) as an alternative to striving. It is not in the tradition of the Greek agon but rather in the tradition of service and relation. The test of such devotion is not in winning contests—defeating others—but in enhancing the quality of relations and of other personal lives. Men of the agon are willing to admire Mother Teresa but not teachers, child care workers, nurses, and social workers. One must strive for and attain the heights to be worthy—or, of course, one might die in the attempt, and such sacrifice also wins much admiration.

To admire freely chosen poverty rather than to despise enormous wealth is a way of avoiding the problem. It distracts us from the tough problem solving needed, and at the same time it maintains the attitude responsible for the problem. So too an overemphasis on total nonviolence and complete pacifism distracts us from the discussion of feasible alternatives to war and sustains our worship of heroes. When we identify and glorify heroes of nonviolence we suggest that we do not expect nonviolent behavior of the masses even though we exhort them to strive toward it. We pay too little attention here to the phenomenon of enantiodromia that Jung analyzed so well; that is, we fail to realize that strenuous striving may induce a dangerous flow of energy to the opposite pole and cause a burst of activity from the "shadow side." Nothing in what I have said so far or in what follows constitutes a total condemnation of striving. I am not, for example, suggesting that we uncritically adopt an Eastern view that requires detachment along with nonstriving. Rather, we want to remain connected to the world and even to its suffering. Eventually we will want to find a reasonable attitude that will help us understand and control striving.

Being like a woman has for too long been associated with a feeble sort of existence devoid of genuine striving. To be sure, such a life may involve hard work, but hard work must not be confused with striving. Striving means moving toward something, trying to excel, intending to win. A woman knows that she can never win the battle against dust, that she will have to feed family members again and again (and that no meals are likely to go down in history), that she must tend the garden every year, and that she cannot overcome most of its enemies but must treat them with the sort of moderation that encourages harmony. This is a totally different way of looking at life, and we want to see what can be said of war when we take this perspective.

Before taking the perspective of caregivers (those responsible for the life-sustaining and -enhancing activities we have discussed), we might simply *look at* war. War is destruction, pain, separation, gore, and savagery as well as strength, courage, and heroism. The association of destruction with strength and virtue is part of the Greek tradition:

> *Aristeia* is a word used in later Greek for "excellence" or "prowess," including, in particular, the excellence or prowess of a Homeric warrior when he is on a victorious rampage, irresistibly sweeping all before him, killing whomever of the enemy he can catch or whoever stands against him. . . . [*Aristeuo*] is used by Glaukos when he tells Diomedes (6.207–9; cf. 11.783) that his father sent him to Troy and told him "always to be best and bravest and to surpass all others, / and not to disgrace the line of my fathers, who were / much the best." . . . In Greek of all periods, the adjective *aristos*, "best," is the superlative of *agathos*, "good," but in the *Iliad*, whose world is a world of war, "good" and "best" mean "good [or best] in battle." [13]

But if we are not one of those in control of the victorious rampage, we are likely to feel something different. Reaction to the intensive bombing of Hamburg during World War II was "terror . . . terror . . . terror . . . pure, naked, bloody terror." [14] Often this is the reaction of those in battle as well, since soldiers in modern warfare cannot overcome the enemy by sheer physical strength and courage, and the story of pure terror that embattled men experienced even in earlier days goes unsung in heroic ballads. When we return to a closer look at war it will be through the perspective of those who are not enchanted by the individualistic or tribal conception of striving. First we need to elaborate on the relational perspective we have been developing since chapter 4.

RELATIONAL ETHICS

In one sense all ethical systems are relational; that is, all ethical theories say something about how moral agents should relate to external entities. Usually, however, an ethics lays out the relation between moral agents and certain principles. The object of this relation is sometimes to guide people in their actual human relations, but often the objective becomes a narrow guide toward an ideal life for the individual. An ethic of principles usually prohibits actively harming innocent others, but it rarely forces the individual to consider the role of others in supporting his or her ideal life. In contrast, relational ethics concentrates on the moral health and vigor of relations, not of individuals. It recognizes that decisions about how to act and evaluations of morality must take into account the relations in which moral agents live and find their identities. Daniel Maguire comments:

> What is moral for one person may be immoral for another because of the diversity of circumstances. The moral quality of behavior depends on circumstances and how those circumstances relate to one another. This, however, does not open the door to the mush of a complete relativism. What it does do is make the art-science of ethics a permanently questing process. It also makes ethics humble and firm in its resistance to the human penchant for unfurling false absolutes.[15]

A relation, in the perspective I adopted in *Caring* and will maintain here, is any pairing or connection of individuals characterized by some affective awareness in each.[16] It is an encounter or series of encounters in which the involved parties feel something toward each other. Relations may involve love or hate, anger or sorrow, admiration or envy; or, of course, they may reveal mixed affects—one party feeling, say, love and the other revulsion. I am most interested in the caring relation, but I am also interested in how we develop other kinds of relations and what we might do, in particular, to discourage the making of rivals and enemies.

A relational ethic differs dramatically from traditional individualistic ethics. First, ethical agents adopting this perspective do not judge their own acts solely by their conformity to rule or principle, nor do they judge them only by the likely production of preassessed nonmoral goods such as happiness. A consideration of both principles and utilities may influence the thinking of such ethical agents, but neither can be decisive. What we must also consider is the relation, not only what happens physically to others involved in the relation but what they feel and how they respond to the acts under consideration. In traditional ethics it would seem odd to include the response of the other in judging our own ethical acts; moral agents are instructed to consult a set of principles and select one that is relevant and binding on all agents who find themselves in similar situations. By remaining in proper connection to principle, we behave appropriately toward other entities in the situation. This is a familiar pattern in ethics of justice. In relational ethics, however, the response of another is one important criterion by which we judge the morality of our acts.[17]

A relational ethic springs from and depends on natural caring. In situations where we act on behalf of the other because we want to do so, we are acting in accord with natural caring. Maternal caregiving usually arises from and exemplifies natural caring, and I have used it as a prototype of caring. I do not mean, of course, that all other cases of caring must imitate the mother-child relationship in either intimacy or intensity, but that what we discover in an examination of this dyad is the basic structure of caring and its source in biological life.

The first member of the dyad (the one caring, or the carer) responds to the needs, wants, and initiations of the second. Her mode of response is characterized by *engrossment* (nonselective attention or total presence to the other for the duration of the caring interval) and *displacement of motivation* (her motive energy flows in the direction of the other's needs and projects).[18] She feels with the other and acts in his or her behalf. The second member (the cared for) contributes to the relation by recognizing and responding to the caring. A mature relationship is mutual; that is, the two parties may exchange places, each acting alternately as carer and cared for. But the contributions of the carer (whichever party that may be) and the cared for remain theoretically distinct. It is clear from this brief description of the caring relation why an ethic of caring is often characterized in terms of responsibility and response.

But ethical caring differs from natural caring, and this distinction brings us to a second great difference between relational ethics and traditional ethics. In traditional ethics the moral or ethical point of view is somehow higher or more admirable than natural caring. From the relational perspective, however, ethical caring develops as we reflect on our experience of caring and being cared for and commit ourselves to respond to others with an attitude of caring. There are times when the plight of another triggers in us both the empathic "I must" characteristic of the caring response and a self-regarding "I do not want to." In these moments we must draw on our memories of caring and being cared for and remember what has occurred in our own best moments. We use these memories to sustain or to summon the empathic feeling—the "I must"—that activates a caring response to the other.

> Recognizing that ethical caring requires an effort that is not needed in natural caring does not commit us to a position that elevates ethical caring over natural caring. Kant has identified the ethical with that which is done out of duty and not out of love, and that distinction in

itself seems right. But an ethic built on caring strives to maintain the caring attitude and is thus dependent upon, and not superior to, natural caring. The source of ethical behavior is, then, twin sentiments—one that feels directly for the other and one that feels for and with that best self, who may accept and sustain the initial feeling rather than reject it.[19]

This "best self" is a relational entity, something akin to what Richard Rorty calls a "network,"[20] but it is not based solely on actual social relations; it is also based on potential relations. When we take a caring attitude toward ethical life, we respond directly, or indirectly in imagination, to concrete others. We test our actions not against a principle of universalizability, but rather against the response of a genuine other; that is, we do not believe that an ethical act on our part binds all humankind to act in the same fashion in like situations. Rather, the morality of our act depends heavily on the sort of relation we are in, and our faithful use of natural caring is an ideal that guides us. Although the response of one particular other may serve as a guide to ethical action, it cannot always be decisive. We also test the proposed action in the imagination against the potential responses of others who may be affected by what we do and even against responses this particular other might make at a different stage of his or her life or in a different mood.

We see, then, that the requirement to respond does not squeeze a continuous string of yeses from us. Sometimes we must say no, but even then we are still guided by the response of the other. We need not refuse self-righteously or shortly. Rather, we explain, elaborate, persuade, offer alternatives. We seek the understanding of the other; we want the other to see that our response really is in his or her best interest or, occasionally, in the best interest of some other—even ourselves. Another reason to persist in the dialogue, of course, is to be sure that our decision *is* in the best interest of those we have considered; that is, we talk to increase the range of actual and imagined responses and to make the imagined responses more accurate and realistic. We use the relation to inform our ethical thinking, and we use our ethical thinking to strengthen the relation.

I mentioned earlier that a relational ethic—one that has the caring relation at its heart as an ideal—may be characteristically feminine. Such a statement may be taken as a claim that women adopt this moral orientation more often than men. This is an interesting empirical question, but it is not one that we will pursue here, and the coming argument does not depend on it. What is necessary to the elaboration of relational ethics is a careful analysis of both the logic and the psychology of relations.[21] A phenomenological examination of feminine experience may well provide insight into both, as we observed in chapter 4, because women have for centuries found "caring occasions" to be central in their lives.[22] It may indeed be the case that a relational perspective has been overlooked—even despised when considered—precisely because of its association with subordinate creatures (women) compelled to maintain caring relations to survive. We have already considered that possibility and will not explore it further here.

The questions that women have had to pose and answer in their relational experience are important for all people to consider: How should I behave to maintain appreciation or respect, if not love? How can I get disagreeing parties to put aside their differences so that we can have a pleasant meal (or visit, outing, meeting)? How can I, without using violence, protect my children from violence? How should I treat others so that they will not hurt me or those I love? These ordinary questions lead to questions at a higher level of abstraction: What causes or predisposes people to hate? to care? Why do we so easily hate those whom authorities tell us are our enemies? How can we remain in caring relations with those who seem clearly to be doing wrong? They lead also to the development of practical skills: attending to how people feel, to how feelings are manipulated for personal or group interests, to diplomatic ways in which to explore perceived offenses, to nonviolent methods of correcting offenders.

Traditional ethical systems ignore many of the questions so important to women. When they address these questions, they formulate rules of reciprocity designed to prevent inequities and ensure justice but pay little attention to the constellation of feelings and inclinations that predispose people to ignore or override the rules. Naturally our educational system embodies the same mixture of implicit will to dominate and well-intended insensitivity, and so the logic and psychology of relations do not figure in the content we present or in the methods we use or in the structures within which we operate. Thus, perhaps without intending to do so, educators perpetuate a system that creates strangers, rivals, and enemies. It makes sense, then, to continue our discussion of appropriate pedagogies for the oppressor.

CREATING RIVALS

Schools have long been prime sites for rivalries. In *A Separate Peace*, John Knowles describes schoolboy rivalry turned deadly. His protagonist, Gene, is consumed by the need to surpass his best friend, Phineas (Finny). Finny is a superb natural athlete but an indifferent student. He seems also to be indifferent to winning—wanting only to turn in better and better performances—but Gene convinces himself that Finny is as competitive as he himself is, that Finny really wants to defeat him. "We were even after all, even in enmity," Gene argues to himself. "The deadly rivalry was on both sides after all." What is the effect of this perceived enmity? Gene remembers:

> I became quite a student after that. I had always been a good one, although I wasn't really interested and excited by learning itself, the way that Douglass was. Now I became not only just good but exceptional, with Chet Douglass my only rival in sight. But I began to see that Chet was weakened by the very genuineness of his interest in learning. He got carried away by things; for example, he was so fascinated by the tilting planes of solid geometry that he did almost as badly in trigonometry as I did myself. When we read *Candide* it opened up a new way of looking at the world to Chet, and he continued hungrily reading Voltaire. . . . He was vulnerable there, because to me they were all pretty much alike . . . and I worked indiscriminately on all of them.[23]

We could argue, as James and others have, that people are naturally competitive and that schools inevitably reflect the rivalry in natural communities. We could argue further that competition motivates learning. By his own account Gene became "quite a student" once he entered into deadly rivalry. But not all societies are competitive, nor are all individuals—a fact Gene learned too late to prevent tragedy. Further, education need not support and encourage all natural traits and indeed has long been charged with the task of controlling and modifying many traits thought to be both natural and undesirable. Thus the competition seen in schools is not merely a mirror image of natural phenomena that the culture has not yet mastered; it is calculated preparation for a competitive way of life.

Schools force students to work by themselves or sometimes in well-defined teams or groups, and competition flourishes in both settings. Even "cooperative" small groups often compete with one another; the locus of competition shifts from individual to group.[24] Most observers hold that competition provides powerful motivation for learning the subject matter at hand, but it seems that students learn a good deal more than the subject matter in these settings, and indeed they certainly embrace the way of life thus learned more passionately than the mathematics or grammar that is the instructional goal.

An ideology of individualism supports the competitive, adversarial way of life, and this individualism is pervasive; it appears in our politics, sports, religion, and ethics. Paul Tillich, for example, writes of the "courage to be as an individual" and the "courage to be as a part." [25] In both forms of courage, however, we find lines drawn tightly around entities that are sharply defined by their differences from other enclosed entities. The individualism of the group is revealed in Tillich's discussion of the risks incurred when being a part is carried to extremes. The main risk is fanaticism. As Tillich describes it, the courage to be as a part is not the fundamental recognition of relatedness that forms the core of relational ethics, but rather the courage to commit oneself to a cause or set of beliefs in which one joins others for strength and companionship. The group is an extension of the self and as such must be defended and kept whole. This is a legacy of an old, old tradition, as we have seen. In this kind of setting, individuals relate to each other through the group, and separation from the group may change the relation of two individuals from friendship to enmity. What seems at first glance to be a dichotomy—individual or part—turns out to be a single creation with two faces. This is, by the way, an important reason for remaining wary of a romantic return to Greek ethics. Even though there is a strong sense of community in Aristotle's ethics, it is not grounded in the relatedness of encounter. Rather it is grounded in a view of community acting as an individual, and it is marred by exclusivity.

Tillich's analysis nevertheless captures a familiar part of human experience. It describes the male experience that has long been synonymous with Western culture, but it fails even to recognize the experience of women. The argument would be, of course, that the experience described is universal and that there is no more need to consider the special experience of women than there is to examine that of, say, an ethnic group or an occupational group. But this is an enormous mistake. First, it may indeed be necessary to analyze the experience of ethnic and occupational groups to construct an accurate picture of the universal (or, alternatively, to decide that such a picture is impossible to create). Second, the experience of women—so far as one can generalize it—is as likely a candidate for human universality as that of men. Where men take the warrior model as universal, for example, women might propose the mother model. As James said, "War is a school of strenuous life and heroism; and, being in the line of aboriginal instinct, is the only school that as yet is universally available." [26] But motherhood too is in the line of aboriginal instinct and is, from the perspective of women, universally accessible. The male model depends on an individualistic ontology, the female on a relational one.

I have been talking about the pervasive individualism that supports the warrior model (even when, as with the Greeks, it masquerades as a community model), adversarial relations, and competition, and I have contrasted it with the relational orientation of women. I can summarize the reasons for treating the topic as follows: First, it is important to recognize that the adversarial/competitive model is deeply entrenched in our customs, beliefs, and institutions, and we cannot transform it easily, if at all. Second, relational thinking is a promising theoretical line to develop in the interest of attempting that transformation. Feminine thinking, articulated as relational thinking, may be attractive to men as well as women in an age when the warrior model threatens to destroy us all.

What can schools do to counterbalance the structures and processes that create rivals? We already include *All Quiet on the Western Front* and *A Separate Peace* in our standard curriculum. But we rarely connect the tragic events of these stories to the structures of society and schooling. We blame them instead on human nature—on something both heroic and tragic that we cannot and, as James pointed out, do not wish to give up. In *A Separate Peace* Gene comes closer in his assessment when he says, "Wars were made instead by something ignorant in the human heart." [27] The remark is doubly enlightening; it locates the problem in ignorance—not the usual ignorance in the head, but rather ignorance in the *human heart*. This gives us a clue that our entrenched ignorance will not be overcome by mere knowledge but only by transformed affect and experience.

The possibilities for transformed experience are as numerous as the examples of structures and practices that support rivalry. I will consider one example here to show not only what we might do from a relational perspective, but also how difficult it will be to accomplish anything close to a transformation. Suppose we recommend as part of our pedagogy of the oppressor that all students engage in some sort of community service in addition to their regular academic studies. The purposes of such service are at least to induce a felt understanding of human interdependence, an appreciation of the value of sharing, and the need to empower each other rather than best each other. Many schools are now considering such a recommendation, and a few—more private than public—have actually instituted the practice. Further, at least one recent major study recommends that such service become a standard expectation in schools. I too have suggested that all students should engage in "apprenticeships in caring." [28]

What will be the status of such a practice if we initiate it? It seems clear that caring as a requirement will not have the status of, say, algebra in our schools. From the relational perspective, we would not want to treat it like algebra; that is, we would not want to grade it and use it as a vehicle to induce a fresh round of rivalry for honors and privileged access. But then we must consider it either extracurricular (and thus not required) or an ungraded requirement—as physical education is in a few schools. If we treat it as the latter, dare we ask students to engage in it regularly, every year, or must we define it as a one- or two-semester course? "But it is *not* a course," the relational thinker wants to insist. It is not part of the little racetrack; it is a way of life that challenges the whole structure into which we are placing it. If we must restrict ourselves to currently available alternatives, caring apprenticeships will inevitably have a lower status than traditional subjects, or, worse, they will be warped to the standard mode.

Individualist thinkers may respond that this is nonsense. Public service, they may say, is noble and should indeed be part of the educational experience of all students. Further, we should praise such work as a worthy aspiration, urge our brightest and best to dedicate at least part of their lives to it, and honor people who do so devotedly along with our other champions and heroes. Take note of the language: worthy aspiration, brightest and best, honor, champions and heroes. The ignorance of the human heart emerges here in all its glorious poverty. Now we are tempted to uphold the structures of oppression to give ourselves opportunities to do good. Jean-Paul Sartre saw this possibility clearly and spoke of good intentions so clouded that the intended good would "be turned into radical evil." Paulo Freire said simply, "The oppressors use their 'humanitarianism' to preserve a profitable situation." And Martin Buber pointed out the nonmutuality of helper and helped in the example of a man coming to another for help: "The essential difference between your role . . . and his is obvious. He comes for help to you. You don't come for help to him. And not only this, but you are *able,* more or less, to help him. He can do different things to you, but not to help you." The implicit aim of much individualist helping is to maintain the honorable and profitable position of the helper.[29]

Our preference would be, of course, that people engage in caring occasions because they recognize their mutual dependence and relatedness. Caring for others is both love giving and love seeking. A loving mother does not command her children to love her, nor does she set out to earn their love in the sense that love can be something owed to her. But she does seek their love and that of her mate if she has one. It is healthy too for teachers to want their students to like them as well as each other. The regard expressed in loving, liking, and caring is a sign that the relation is fertile—that it can nourish its members. Behavior that is both love giving and love seeking asks something of the other and thus in an important sense empowers him or her. It is not a gift that lays a debt on the receiver but an expression of regard and vulnerability. What the giver hopes for is genuine response in the receiver—more confident growth, more open communication, more joy in companionship, more serenity in trouble and stress.

All this means, I think, that teachers must find ways to be with their students: to talk with them (and not at them) about their own lives and about great intellectual ideas, to solve problems with them rather than merely setting the problems, to share cultural delights with them without testing the joy out of the shared event. Teachers can discourage rivalry by reducing the artificial separation between teacher and student, student and student. There are, of course, natural separations that we need to maintain to keep relations genuine. As Martin Buber points out, the teacher-student relation is marked by reciprocity, but it is not a mutual relation. The teacher bears the authority of expertise and the burden of seeing things through both expert and novice eyes; the teacher sets the student free to pursue his or her learning.[30] But grades, honors, competitions, summative evaluations, rankings, and the authority of hierarchical position all introduce artificial separations that cripple caring relations and maintain the human heart in ignorance.

In closing this section I want to make clear that I am not saying that all rivalries and all strivings are dangerous and evil. I am saying that they are suspect, that we must explore their creation and their effects more fully than we have and share what we learn with our students. It may be that some rivalry can be stimulating and conducted in the spirit of fun, but too much of contemporary rivalry is— as Gene's was toward Finny—fatally in earnest, and we have not taken seriously enough the task of teaching our students the difference.

MAKING ENEMIES

It is a small but terrible step from rivalry to enmity. We may admire and love our rivals, but we find it easier to hate enemies if we can attribute evil motives to them. My major theme here involves our use of educational content to produce people who easily attribute evil to enemies and goodness to friends and allies. We somehow maintain an ignorance of the human heart through our profound lack of understanding of how such relations are formed and enhanced and our unwillingness to examine them or even to consider them worth examining. We avoid real moral debate like the plague and yet pride ourselves on being a nation devoted to justice, human rights, mercy, and honest dealing. Suppose we really dedicated ourselves to such qualities. What might we teach that we do not teach now?

I will build my argument around an example that is almost never considered in secondary school social studies, even though the topic under which it might fall is part of the curriculum. The situation here is very like our inclusion of *A Separate Peace* in the curriculum together with a steadfast refusal to question the structures that lead to rivalry, betrayal, and tragedy. We look for alternatives, as James did, before getting to the bottom of things.

Contemporary texts discuss war crimes, but students do not often debate them or explore and logically apply the rules for judging them. The crimes reported in texts are horrible, but students come to associate these acts with vicious enemies, and often the students believe that "our side" fights only to prevent and to avenge such horrors. Even when texts admit that an act of our own is questionable—the nuclear bombing of Hiroshima and Nagasaki, for example—they usually provide a humane reason to maintain the attitude that we are different, that we put a higher value on life than those others. We do not encourage students to dig out the roots of human tragedy.

Two prominent cases, both part of World War II, might be especially valuable for students to consider: Winston Churchill's decision to bomb population centers in Germany and the punitive action of the United States against Japanese military leaders. I suggest the Churchill case here because the terror bombing of German cities established a precedent that seemed to justify Truman's decision to use nuclear weapons on Japan.[31] Further, the Truman decision is at least debated in schools, whereas the Churchill one is rarely mentioned.

We now know that Churchill not only decided in 1942 to maintain the policy of bombing German cities even though the entrance of the Soviet Union and the United States into the war "rendered other possibilities open," but actually encouraged an escalation of civilian bombing. "So the raids continued," Michael Walzer notes, "culminating in the spring of 1945—when the war was virtually won—in a savage attack on the city of Dresden in which something like 100,000 people were killed."[32] Applying the rules to which we ourselves subscribed prior to World War II (and which we never formally rejected), the deliberate killing of civilians was unlawful. In the absence of clearly defined necessity or what Churchill in 1939 called a "supreme emergency" such killing was clearly culpable, and Churchill knew it. But Churchill was one of our heroes, one of us, and he was never charged with a crime. We do not easily look for evil within ourselves.

It is not my purpose to judge and convict Winston Churchill in retrospect, but rather to explore the events surrounding his decisions and our acceptance of them to uncover what students should learn about friendly and adversarial relations. Churchill knew—or thought he knew—what was required to induce and maintain a fighting spirit. He announced to his people that the civilian bombings of Germany were making its "people taste and gulp each month a sharper dose of the miseries they have showered upon mankind." He assumed that his own people wanted revenge. But interestingly, an opinion poll taken in 1941 showed that the strongest support for such bombing came from parts of England that had not experienced bombing themselves; less than half the respondents in central London favored it.[33] This response shows, I suspect, that central Londoners were still able to reconstruct in imagination a relation with German civilians; the dominant affect was one they themselves had experienced—terror—and they were not eager to visit terror on other innocents. It also shows how the careful and articulate severing of ordinary relations can stir otherwise neighborly people into savagery. Under ordinary conditions mothers would have felt sympathy for other mothers, children, and the elderly, all of whom were victims of civilian bombing. But in the absence of a strong affect that might have allowed them to feel with their German counterparts, a segment of the British population was willing to accept Churchill's identification of German civilians with the Nazis.

We were not prepared in the 1940s to seek moral alternatives, in part because we were in a perceived crisis and in part because we did not understand the psychology of relations, nor did we have much practice in tracing the logic of our actions in connection with our values. We had learned to compartmentalize logic and values. We still teach this way, and the custom harms our students. Further, both the methods and the content selected in our schools support the harmful effects. Students need to know how their moral values can be twisted and how even just causes can be unjustly prosecuted. One key to this learning is a careful cultivation and analysis of affects typical of various kinds of relations.

In addition to knowing how to manipulate relations—to produce the affective results he wanted by associating all Germans with Nazis, for example—Churchill was also aware of the need to project an image of moral goodness for his own people. Most Britons considered World War II a just war because they fought against supreme evil, and it was vital that those fighting against fascism continue to believe that their countries lived the values they were asked to defend. It was clear after the terror bombing of Dresden that such acts were incompatible with the image Western democracies wished to present. The result of this realization was that Churchill separated himself from the head of Bomber Command, Arthur Harris. Harris and his men were never honored as were the leaders and men of Fighter Command, and Churchill successfully diverted attention from his own role in supporting Harris. Walzer comments: "Churchill's success in dissociating himself from the policy of terrorism is not of great importance; there is always a remedy for that in retrospective criticism. What is important is that his dissociation was part of a national dissociation—a deliberate policy that has moral significance and value." [34]

But Churchill's success is important in analyzing the national phenomenon. By not honoring Harris, Churchill effectively separated him from relations with his countrymen. There was no condemnation, which might easily have extended to Churchill himself. Neither was there praise. The severing of relation—"this is not I, not we"—allowed people to forget that they and their leaders had been party to acts contrary to their own voiced values.

I am not suggesting that we reconstruct the classroom as a place in which students systematically learn to have sympathy only for the other side and to seek out relentlessly wrongs committed by their own nation. That approach builds on the harmful foundation already laid—the notion that we must choose sides and that our side (whichever it is) must be right and good while the other is wrong and evil. We saw this phenomenon again and again in the debates over Vietnam. Rather, I am suggesting that a pedagogy of the oppressor must illuminate the ways in which we use separation and helplessness to inflict pain on those we judge to be evil.

We do tend to project evil onto others. Using World War II as a continuing example, we might consider the case of Japan's General Yamashita. Yamashita was executed as a war criminal because troops officially—but not tactically—under his command committed atrocities. The troops he actually controlled did not, according to Walzer's account, commit crimes.[35] Further, the very success of U.S. campaigns in cutting Japanese communications made it impossible for General Yamashita to control the troops for whose actions he was ultimately condemned. It is hard to avoid the conclusion that we based our decision on victory and vengeance and rationalized it to reflect our theoretical worship of justice. Sometimes we sever a connection when we fear the taint of evil; at other times we exploit a break in normal patterns of relation to project evil onto the unknown and separated other. In both cases a profound lack of understanding of relation permits terrible acts to be repeated and prepares each generation anew to behave as accomplices in acts they will also be taught to disavow.

The harm to students that I have discussed so far does not derive directly from the teacher-student relation. Rather, it begins at the level that constructs the setting for teaching and learning. But what can teachers do to counteract structures, content, and methods all apparently designed to create strangers, rivals, and enemies?

First, it seems clear that prospective teachers need to study human relations and not just the psychology of learning. They need help in observing and analyzing those events and structures that separate people and create adversarial relations. They need opportunities to discuss such relations in some depth: Are adversarial relations always bad? If we understand them and the powerful affects they generate, can we learn to modify them so that rivalries can serve good ends? These are, of course, just sample questions; the possible list is long.

Second, in their study of human relations teachers especially need to know something about the techniques used to create various kinds of relations: projection, techniques of association and dissociation, omission, rhetoric, compartmentalization, and the use of oaths and passwords, to name a few. I do not mean to suggest that teachers should learn these techniques to use them on their students—even for good ends—but rather that they should be prepared to help their students understand these techniques and thus become more able to resist manipulation.

Third, teachers need to understand and appreciate the tragic sense of life. The study of history and political science should not be a search for heroes and villains; neither should it be a frank attempt to inculcate uncritical patriotism. All of us need to recognize the tragedy in human existence and to understand that we are not immune to committing evil. This is difficult material for teachers to convey, and if they are to convey it successfully they need to have well-established trusting relations with their students. A teacher who is loved and trusted can talk about the moral failings of Churchill and U.S. tribunals without inducing a sense of betrayal in students. Further, he or she can help students apply the lessons to their own lives.

In the rest of this section I want to concentrate on one area that is of paramount importance for teacher-student relations: how our moral behavior depends in practice on the moral worth we assign to others. As early as kindergarten and first grade, for example, teachers associate all sorts of good traits with good readers, and many studies have documented that teachers often treat good and poor readers differently; they talk to them differently and offer them different opportunities. At every level of schooling teachers refer to bright students as their "good kids." "With my good kids," they say, "I do . . ." and they go on to explain how lessons progress in classes populated by academically bright students. The tendency to conflate academic prowess and

moral goodness is pernicious. It leads us to neglect the moral education of bright students and both the moral and academic education of
slower students.

Students too need to understand how their moral judgments of others affect their own moral behavior. From their earliest school days,
for example, children are taught that lying is wrong, that "honesty is
the best policy." But we rarely discuss with them the relational conditions that determine how the familiar standard applies. Must we, for
example, tell the truth to our enemies? The answer seems obvious: of
course not. Enemies, as Sissela Bok points out, are often liars—or
thought to be liars—and therefore do not deserve, on one account, to
be told the truth.[36] Further, they are likely to use the truth to harm us,
and so we are justified in lying to them in a crisis to defeat them and
protect ourselves. Bok rejects both these familiar justifications in their
simple and global form, urging more stringent criteria of judgment,
but in the end she finds that each captures a nucleus of truth about
human relations. While people are actively our enemies, most of us
would not dream of telling them the truth. It is only when we seek an
end to hostilities that truth telling again becomes an expectation, and
if the enemy does not meet our expectation hostilities are likely to
resume or even escalate.

When we think of people as enemies it is easy to put them outside
the moral community, to devalue their moral worth. This is what
Churchill did so effectively. He made the enemy-other supremely evil,
and thus acts that would normally be abhorrent to Churchill's moral
community became acceptable in the cause of overthrowing evil. This
is an old and sad story with which our children should become thoroughly familiar.

Students need to understand the logical chain that Bok describes so
well: labeling people as enemies leads us to devalue their moral worth,
and this devaluation permits us to treat them in ways that would be
unthinkable if they were part of our moral community. But there is
another direction from which we should examine this chain, and it is
perhaps even more relevant to the lives of young people. Sometimes
when we have wronged another we find it hard to accept the moral
status of our acts. Is it possible that we ourselves could have done a
really rotten thing? When we cannot come to grips with the evil in
here, we often seek justification for our acts. What better than to find
that "he deserved it"? Thus a morally unacceptable act on our part

leads to a moral devaluation of the victim and ultimately to the creation of an enemy.

This is an area in which teachers really can help students lead better and happier lives. They can do it by modeling the better way (admitting mistakes and ill-tempered acts), by discussing examples as they become available, and by encouraging students to reflect on their habits of relating. Besides making a difference in the personal lives of students, we might come to a point as a nation where an enlightened citizenry would not praise its leaders for branding a whole people "an evil empire." Like Gene, Knowles's tragic antihero, our students might overcome some ignorance of the human heart. Gene saw at last that his best friend and enemy, Finny, was unique among his school friends: "All of them, all except Phineas, constructed at infinite cost to themselves these Maginot Lines against this enemy they thought they saw across the frontier, this enemy who never attacked that way—if he ever attacked at all; if he was indeed the enemy." [37]

RELATEDNESS AND STRIVING

The primary meaning of *striving* is "to struggle in opposition" or "to contend." It is this sort of striving that I have labeled suspect. Such striving inevitably produces separation, a mark of evil. When we first discussed separation, however, we saw that it is not always an evil, and so we must inquire more deeply into the nature of the separation that accompanies striving.

The story of Gene and Finny describes two sorts of striving. Finny's striving illustrates a second meaning of the word, "to devote serious energy or effort." He strove to surpass his previous performance. Even in this form of striving we must monitor the intensity of effort. When we devote "serious energy" to an undertaking, just *how* serious can it be and remain healthy? Activities and projects that we really enjoy probably retain an aspect of playfulness. That was certainly the case with Finny. We devote great energy to such activities, but we have no opponent.

In one variation of opponentless striving, however, we create an opponent within. When we pursue projects that challenge some strong inclination in ourselves, we create a formidable opponent in our own shadow side. This is the form of striving that Jung diagnosed so brilliantly. If a man evaluates one of his own inclinations as evil and devotes all his energy to overcoming it—that is, if he focuses his effort in the opposite direction—he may experience enantiodromia. Then there is an explosion of activity, sometimes only in the imagination, from the shadow side. As we develop a morality of evil and a psychology to accompany it, we have to find ways to accept the shadow side. I do not mean that we have to approve of it, although the shadow is sometimes worthy of approval, but that we have to recognize it as belonging to ourselves.

The two forms of striving are clearly related. The form that originally has no external opponent can be dangerous in generating such opponents. It is easy to forget that the real opponent is our own shadow, and when we do so we externalize evil and create enemies. The situation becomes dreadfully dangerous when the people who project evil onto others also have both the power to attack them and a belief system that supports such action. Gene's projection of competitive evil onto Finny triggered retaliatory action, which in turn led him to justify his own behavior. A rationale was not hard to construct as long as he placed the evil in Finny and not in himself.

The first form of striving involves struggle with an external opponent and raises the question whether we should regard the separation that results as evil. There is no doubt that separation is evil when it brings psychic pain without compensating joy. But in chapter 4 we saw that separation is not always evil. When adult children leave home, for example, the pain of separation is balanced by pride and anticipation in both parents and child. When a desperately unhappy couple separate, the cessation of marital warfare outweighs the pain of separation. If there is evil here, it has occurred in the events that led to separation, not in the separation itself. Thus separation is linked to evil in a variety of ways: to separate persons deliberately can be evil in itself when it causes psychic pain directly, and it can also be evil because of what follows. Churchill's separation of the German people from the moral community made it possible to destroy them by firebombing. Such an act would ordinarily be unthinkable for a people who consider themselves moral.

Besides acts that are intended to separate, there are attitudes and bodies of thought that contribute to evil by encouraging a neglect of human relations. Indeed, the neglect of relation might be named as the great moral evil that correlates with separation. Here, as we have seen, the religious tradition has ratified evil by distracting us from each other and leading us to believe that our salvation rests in our relation only to God. This account supposes that war is either the direct result of our aggressive human nature or just punishment for our sins.

Keith Nelson and Spencer Olin remark:

> The idea that a human is a dependent creature, vulnerable to baser instincts and hardly a step above the rest of the animal world is a concept that has been present in our culture a long time, going back in one of its versions at least as far as early Christian doctrines of original sin. . . . Augustine developed a heavily deterministic theory which explained conflict as either (1) arising from "human passion" and unregulated desire, or (2) occurring in obedience to the will of God in order to "rebuke, or humble, or crush the pride of man."[38]

In this view human beings are the cause of war, but they are not really responsible for it; that is, this view does not encourage us to study the full range of human relatedness. Instead of developing a morality of evil, then, it leads us over and over again to find evil "out there" and to destroy it. Further, the Christian church has too often urged people to battle the "evil" passions in themselves, focusing attention on personal morality rather than on the morality of relations. As we have seen, it also leads to pitched battles with the shadow.

From what I have said so far it is clear that striving—one of the virtues long identified with James's hardihood—needs analysis and reevaluation. It is not a pure virtue. In its primary form it has an association with the excellence of the warrior, and the warrior's activity finds both its source and its fulfillment in separation. From the perspective of women such striving is evil or near-evil. It is near-evil when playful striving—in games, for example—begins to get serious, when the players can no longer take pleasure in their opponents' victories. It is evil when the only purpose is to best the competition and not, for some good reason, to turn in a better performance or to turn out a better product.

The second form of striving is often evil too because it separates us from ourselves and can lead either to self-righteousness or self-contempt, neither of which bodes well for our neighbors. A better relation with the shadow entails a wary recognition and some playfulness: "I know you are there," we might say to our shadow selves, "and you may as well come along. That way I can keep an eye on you."

Striving often appears to be antithetical to relatedness. We hear stories of strivers who have no time for people because they are totally engrossed in their work. What we mean is that such persons do not enter into or contribute to *caring* relations. They are, however, inevitably in some sort of relation, and the longing to be in a relation characterized by positive feelings may indeed lead to a distorted evaluation of the actual relation.

This phenomenon accounts for the love and admiration warriors often come to have for one another. Hugh Duncan also considers war a concerted effort to overcome external evil and thus to relieve ourselves of guilt: "At the same time as we wound and kill our enemy in the field and slaughter his women and children in their homes, our love for each other deepens. We become comrades in arms, our hatred of each other is being purged in the sufferings of our enemy."[39] Sometimes the love of warriors even extends to the enemy warrior, especially in person-to-person combat. It is as though wounding and killing the evil opponent reconciles the warrior with himself. Now that he has overcome the evil the warrior can feel the love and admiration that he really directs to himself. Similarly, a viciously competitive businessman may begin to love and admire his most ruthless competitors. Because his longing for positive relation is so great, he finds it, but at the terrible cost of supposing that the common activity in which it is found is itself a worthy enterprise. James saw this aspect of the problem clearly but did not probe deeply into either the nature of the particular virtues involved or the neglect of relation that produces such horrible distortions.

Some hold that women do not construct distorted relations, and there is considerable evidence that this view is to some degree true. Nancy Chodorow argues that women retain a sense of relatedness because they can find their gender identity without separating from their primary caretakers, mothers.[40] In contrast, male gender identity requires separation, since small boys must seek their identities in the absent ones, fathers.

John Fowles also claims that women have a clearer sense of what constitutes a genuine relationship. In *The Magus* the spokesperson, Conchis, says:

> I should like you also to reflect that its events could have taken place only in a world where man considers himself superior to woman. In what the Americans call "a man's world." That is, a world governed by brute force, humorless arrogance, illusory prestige, and primeval stu-

pidity. . . . Men love war because it allows them to look serious. Because they imagine it is the one thing that stops women laughing at them. In it they can reduce women to the status of objects. That is the great distinction between the sexes. Men see objects, women see the relationship between objects. Whether the objects need each other, love each other, match each other. It is an extra dimension of feeling we men are without and one that makes war abhorrent to all real women—and absurd. I will tell you what war is. War is a psychosis caused by an inability to see relationships. Our relationship with our fellow men. Our relationship with our economic and historical situation. And above all our relationship to nothingness. To death.[41]

I too have been arguing that the logic of women's experience should lead to an emphasis on relatedness as a basis for moral thinking and action. But there are pathologies in women's experience too. Women, whose maternal thinking should find war a contradiction to the maternal project,[42] often support war vigorously. Jean Elshtain presents vivid evidence of women's enthusiastic participation in war efforts. Writing of women in Sparta as well as women in the U.S. Civil War, she says:

> The woman of republican militancy is no mere victim of events; rather, she is empowered in and through the discourse of armed civic virtue to become an *author* of deeds—deeds of sacrifice, of nobility in and through suffering, of courage in the face of adversity, of firmness in *her,* and not just her polity's "right." Just as the soldier is prepared to de-realize himself as a civilized being ("Thou shalt not kill") to preserve the civic mother that gave birth to his civility in the first instance, the mother/wife of the soldier is prepared to sever herself from the most potent imperative under which she ordinarily labors: "Thou shalt protect the bodies of thy children."[43]

Women too want to belong. They have internalized a large part of what men have taught them about being a good woman. An important virtue of the good woman, pointed up dramatically and unfortunately in the writings of Jung's followers, is her generous support of her man's conception of honor. A good woman in this view does not undermine her man's sense of honor and duty. Her virtues *complement* his. It may be, as Fowles says, that war is "abhorrent to all real women," but women have been taught to prefer the memories of dead men to the presence of dishonored ones. Further, an abhorrence of war should not be a test of real womanhood (for what then is the corresponding test for "real manhood"?); it should be a mark of rational personhood.

Women's acceptance of war does not seem to emerge from an evaluation of striving as a virtue. Rather, it arises from the desire to remain in a positive relation with those who worship striving. Women do not seem so much interested in overcoming opponents as they are in supporting their own combatants. But this support too is a pathological distortion of relation, and the prescription has to be reeducation.

SUMMARY

We have looked at the neglect of relation that causes separation and that is instrumental in creating rivals and making enemies. Some of the neglect we can trace to a faulty or incomplete analysis of virtues such as James's unconditional acceptance of "hardihood." Examining *striving*, for example, we found signs of evil as well as good. Another factor is the dominance of individualism. Even in Tillich's "courage to be as a part," we saw merely another aspect of the self-enclosed individual, this time disguised as a group. A third force in our neglect of human relations has been religion. The notion that salvation rests in our relation to God and not in our relation to other human beings has often led to a devaluation of persons and a tendency to place those with whom we differ outside the moral community. Finally, we identified a powerful fourth factor—the fear of being like a woman.

These four large factors in the neglect of relation have contributed to the creation of social structures that maintain our neglect. We attempted to extend the pedagogy of the oppressor into the field of caring. Here we saw how difficult it will be to introduce the practice of caring into schools without corrupting it. The machinery already in place produces a product that differs essentially from caring.

We elaborated on our earlier discussion of women's relational orientation in a somewhat more formal analysis of relational ethics. This form of ethics puts primary emphasis on the relation of natural caring, and it develops ethical caring as a means to restore shaky relations to that preferred state. A relational ethic prescribes attention to the relational situations in which we find ourselves, and it makes significant use of imagined relations and situations in testing its decisions.

In chapter 5 we considered pain as a form of natural evil. In chapter

6 we explored a form of cultural evil—poverty. Now we have looked at another form of cultural evil, war, and we have suggested that a large moral evil—the neglect of relation—lies at its root. In each of these discussions we have made recommendations for revised forms of education, forms cleansed of the disabling fear of being like a woman.

8

Terrorism, Torture, and Psychological Abuse

So far we have looked at natural evil and cultural evil, both of which reveal forms of moral evil supporting them. Now we will look at practices that are ultimately evil—those that deliberately cause pain, separation, and helplessness and build on these states for their own ends. Who performs such acts? What is their purpose and genesis?

WOULD WE EVER TORTURE?

Many believe that a distinguishing feature of civilized societies, as opposed to primitive or uncivilized ones, is their unwillingness to engage in torture.[1] No one seriously believes that modern democracies do not use terrorism and torture, but we all know that these societies condemn the routine use of such acts and that those who commit torture do so without official sanction. When a nation is pressed hard—as Britain was in World War II—it may respond with acts of terror, such as the firebombing of civilians, that its people find reprehensible. When the acts happen, some form of disavowal follows that maintains the people's image of themselves as a civilized society.

In these cases—and perhaps in most cases of violence—the enemy has what H. D. Duncan calls a "ritual role" to play. Through this role playing and being overcome "evil is redeemed." Right from the start I have denied the possibility of redeeming evil, but we have not finished with the ways in which people have tried to do it. Duncan comments that "the psychoanalytic grouping of guilt, anality, and sadism is translatable in this way to the highest levels of human striving and to the age-old problem of good and evil."[2]

If we understand that much evil results from the desire to destroy filth, expunge defilement, and overcome evil, might we then be free of the inclination to harm one another? This is a hard but essential question. I will experiment by asking it of myself and by suggesting that each reader try a similar thought experiment.

Would I ever torture another human being? Would I, that is, ever deliberately inflict physical pain on a person who is helpless to prevent my doing so? One properly shudders at the thought. Suppose, however, that one of my daughters was in captivity somewhere and that she would surely die within the hour if I could not find her. I have before me a man who knows where she is, and he is at my mercy. Would I torture him? Of course I would. There are many things I would not do to him because of aesthetic sensibility and because I would get no pleasure from his pain, but I feel quite sure that I would inflict the cleanest and meanest pain I could contrive to save my child.

From one point of view this confession underscores Kant's advice that if we wish to be moral we must detach ourselves from emotion. Would I torture to save a child other than my own? Yes, I probably would. Would I torture to save one who, for whatever reason, was incapable of the human response described in chapter 5? Probably not. This is not hopelessly unprincipled thinking but part of the quest for a realistic morality, one that encompasses a morality of evil. We can ignore how we feel only if we are willing to risk unspeakable horrors.

So I return to the captive before me. Is there a possibility that he does not know where my child is? For me this is a crucial question. In the usual form of these dilemmas we know only what the fictional moral agent knows at the time in question, and this agent is always oddly forbidden to seek more information. If the man before me does not know or may not know, then I would hesitate to torture him. Why? People who do not know the answer for which they are undergoing pain are helpless psychically as well as physically. They literally cannot help themselves. Those who can help themselves by answering are in an important sense still fully human beings. To inflict pain on one who is truly helpless is irredeemably evil. Therefore I cannot inflict pain on the loved ones of the culprit who does know, for I cannot torture the helpless. In the case where my captive actually has the information I need to save a life, he has separated himself from the moral relation in which we would normally meet. In the case where he serves as a means only, I separate him to justify my infliction of pain. Then I have given way to evil, and nothing can redeem my act.

What if I cannot be sure whether my captive has the information I need? I can imagine choking, kicking, beating, and threatening him in desperation. I can imagine crying and pleading. I can imagine his crying and pleading that he does not know. The least evil of us would have to give way regardless of the outcome. Traditionally, however, we have not regarded the one who gives way as "least evil" but only as weak. The fear of being like a woman arises again to prevent us from falling into each other's arms in tears of compassion.

Perhaps most of us would torture under the circumstances I have described. That we would do so, or might do so, does not, of course, justify our choosing to do so, but I will put this important question off for a bit. Are there other conditions that would lead people who normally abhor the practice to commit torture?

In 1963 Stanley Milgram published his now famous obedience experiments.[3] Under the pretext of conducting learning experiments, Milgram and his assistants instructed their subjects to administer apparently painful electric shocks to learner-victims who were actually collaborators in the experiment. A surprising number of people continued to administer shocks even when their victims screamed in pain and begged to be let out and instruments reported the shock to be at a dangerous level. All that most subjects needed to keep going was an authoritative "You must continue" from the scientist in the white coat. The results demonstrated with frightening clarity that many decent, ordinarily compassionate people will torture other human beings if strong authorities tell them that there is justification for doing so.

People torture others not only out of desperation or obedience to authority. They also torture simply to gain knowledge. Consider Milgram's description of what happened to his subjects:

In a large number of cases the degree of tension reached extremes that are rarely seen in sociopsychological laboratory studies. Subjects were observed to sweat, tremble, stutter, bite their lips, groan, and dig their fingernails into their flesh. . . . On one occasion we observed a seizure so violently convulsive that it was necessary to call a halt to the experiment.

After the maximum shocks had been delivered . . . many subjects heaved sighs of relief, mopped their brows, rubbed their fingers over their eyes, or nervously fumbled cigarettes. . . .

At one point he [a subject] pushed his fist into his forehead and muttered: "Oh God, let's stop it." And yet he continued to respond to every word of the experimenter, and obeyed to the end.

I observed a mature and initially poised businessman enter the laboratory smiling and confident. Within 20 minutes he was reduced to a twitching, stuttering wreck, who was rapidly approaching a point of nervous collapse.[4]

Milgram's subjects *thought* they were causing pain. Professor Milgram *knew* he was causing pain, and yet he continued. His justification was the search for knowledge. Since the Milgram experiments controversy has continued over both his conclusions and the ethicality of his methods.[5] Although many social scientists defend Milgram's methods because "so much was learned" from the experiments, the vigor of opposition led to controls that now protect human subjects from such treatment.

From the perspective developed here Milgram and his assistants clearly participated in evil acts, acts that inflicted pain, induced feelings of helplessness, and increased the separation of one set of human beings from another. The justification they offer is familiar: there was no intention to cause pain; pain just happened to accompany the effort. Further, some argue that the subjects suffered minimally. They did not die, after all, nor did they leave with gaping wounds or missing parts; even their psychological discomfort was temporary, and they learned something important about themselves.

But all these rationales miss the point. If we know that it is wrong to inflict pain on others, how can we deliberately do so to find out what we already know—that given apparent justification people will do dreadful things to one another? The question is not *whether* people will do such things but when we will use the knowledge we have had before our eyes for centuries to help each other not do these things. When we reflect on what the Hebrews did to the Midianites, what the Athenians did to the citizens of Melos, what God allowed Satan to do to Job, what the witch hunters did to accused witches, what the Nazis did to Jews, what the British and Americans did to German civilians—when we reflect on the continuous performance of horror shows that constitutes history, why do we need an experiment to prove that ordinary people will do horrible things?

Theoretical controversy centers on what Arthur Miller calls the "normality thesis" versus the "pathology thesis."[6] Are the people who commit horrors "normal" or "pathological"? Certainly most such people are normal in the important sense that they look, act, and live just like everyone else in ordinary conditions. Just as certainly they harbor some pathology in the sense that under suitable conditions they exhibit traits that the societies in which they live condemn. When we reach a conclusion of this sort, it is logically necessary to recast the question. We might do better to ask: What is this pathology of normality? What is wrong with the vast majority of us? The answer I have been suggesting all along is that we do not understand or accept our own disposition toward evil and that we lack a morality of evil. It is normal (in both the "ordinary" and "healthy" senses of the word) to incline toward evil; it is pathological to ignore or deny this inclination. By analogy, all of us are susceptible to the streptococcus, but some of us are allergic to it and get dreadful sicknesses such as nephritis or rheumatic fever instead of the usual sore throat or earache. Similarly, there is a continuum of susceptibility to the evil within, but no one is immune. Evil is neither entirely out-there nor entirely in-here; it is an interactive phenomenon that requires acceptance, understanding, and steady control rather than great attempts to overcome it once and for all.

So far we have seen that ordinary, good people—*we*—might commit torture in desperate situations (to save our child or our nation), to obey authorities thought to be legitimate, or, like Milgram, to gain knowledge. Our torture might be bloody or dry, physical or psychological, permanently damaging or temporary, but it always carries the signs of evil and involves either the intention to inflict pain or a willingness to accept pain as a known effect of our actions.

Sometimes we engage in forms of psychic torture by withdrawing from those who address us, and this form of torture induces elaborate justifications. Consider the story Simon Wiesenthal tells in *The Sunflower*:

> A young Jew is taken from a death camp to a makeshift army hospital. He is led to the bedside of a Nazi soldier whose head is completely swathed in bandages. The dying Nazi blindly extends his hand toward the Jew, and in a cracked whisper begins to speak. The Jew listens silently while the Nazi confesses to having participated in the burning alive of an entire village of Jews. The soldier, terrified of dying with this burden of guilt, begs absolution from the Jew. Having listened to the Nazi's story for several hours—torn between horror and compassion for the dying man—the Jew finally walks out of the room without speaking.[7]

Haunted by the experience, the Jew, Wiesenthal, asks a symposium of listeners to decide whether his silence was "right or wrong." Then he asks each of us to "mentally change places" with him and ask,

"What would I have done?" Both questions, while tremendously challenging and interesting, are fundamentally unhelpful if our purpose is to face and control the evil in ourselves. The quest should not be for judgment and vindication but for understanding and moral improvement.

The questions should be something like these: What should I wish I could have done? If my best self had been able to respond, what would I have done? These questions allow us to see what stands in the way of our best selves and thus to sympathize with Wiesenthal while seeing at the same time that he was not—could not have been—his best self. They also encourage us to enter the situation itself and not flee to the language of abstraction.

Here before us lies a young man who has committed a terrible crime—a horror. He is full of remorse, and he is suffering dreadful pain, both physical and spiritual. Wiesenthal is horrified and moved. He says to himself, "He sought my pity, but had he any right to pity?" Herein lie the roots of our ratification of evil. Wiesenthal felt pain, rage, and despair. Suffering from monstrous evil, he did not expect to live much longer. We could excuse him for almost any reaction. But his reaction is not one of blind feeling. He *thinks*, and his thoughts reflect the long tradition that has subjected us to so much pain.

He asks whether the young man has any *right* to pity, and he asks whether he himself has the right or authority to forgive. What can he mean by a "right to pity"? This question, prompted by Aristotle, is still with us. A better approach is to note that one *feels* pity in such a situation, and the appropriate response is one of compassion. Wiesenthal and a surprising number of his respondents saw the young Nazi not as one particular suffering and repentant evildoer but as a symbol. Roger Ikor, for example, says:

> The SS man represented the entire SS, the entire Nazi system, the whole of Germany, and even beyond Germany, the whole of man's evil forces. Wiesenthal for his part was not just Wiesenthal but the entire deportation, and beyond this, the bulk of the Nazi victims. Man to man, I think Wiesenthal would have forgiven in the face of so obviously sincere a repentance; one which was sanctioned, as it were, by the criminal's sufferings. He could not do so because of what he represented and what the person he was dealing with represented.[8]

Seeing each other and ourselves as symbols is, of course, part of what sustains our capacity to inflict suffering. Like Augustine, we want to balance the evil in the world with an equal heap of suffering. To what end? More suffering.

Some respondents, while properly refusing to judge Wiesenthal, suggest that they would have forgiven the dying man or at least that they hope they would have done so. Several of these writers express religious views. The inadequacy and unsuitability of such forgiveness are obvious. First, ritual forgiveness is always inadequate. Given in obedience to God, it serves the giver, not the suffering penitent. We forgive, that is, so that we ourselves will stand well with God. Advancing the opinion that Wiesenthal should have forgiven Karl, Edward Flannery says, "It is a cardinal principle of the Judaeo-Christian ethic that those who sincerely repent should be granted forgiveness." [9] This makes it a duty for those of whom forgiveness is asked to forgive; the commandment centers on the relation of person to God, not of person to person. Forgiving or worrying over whether we should have forgiven makes us feel connected to God and gives us evidence of what Friedrich Torberg, another respondent, calls an intact morality. "It is in this intact morality," he says, "that we are superior to the others, to the murderers and to those who held their peace about the murders when they were committed and are still holding their peace today." [10] This superiority is, as we have seen, a fragile thing, and it becomes more fragile as we lean more heavily on it.

I refer to Simon's possible forgiveness of Karl as a "ritual forgiveness" because there was no real relation between the two men. They were symbols to each other, and because they were symbols Simon had no right to forgive. He felt that he had *no right* to represent all the dead Jews whom Nazis had murdered. But perhaps more important, Simon felt that the God who had given the commandment to forgive had absented himself from the world—that he had abandoned the scene like an absentee landlord. To whom, then, could he connect by granting forgiveness? Thus we can see that ritual forgiveness involves the evil of separation. We separate ourselves from the human other, forgive him to connect ourselves to God, and allow ourselves to stand as symbols—superior symbols—to the other. Ritual forgiveness is therefore inadequate and unsuitable.

There is another sense in which forgiveness would have been inappropriate. Karl was not really asking forgiveness. True, he said he needed to talk to a Jew and "beg forgiveness from him," but that way of putting the matter reflected the ritual education we all undergo.

When we sin, we must ask forgiveness. But intuitively Karl knew that ritual forgiveness was an empty gesture in the face of real horror and terror. He knew also that ritual forgiveness was readily available through a priest. What did he want? What lay beneath the ill-phrased plea?

I think Karl wanted assurance from someone least likely to deceive him that he was still human. He needed to know that beneath the bandages that made him unrecognizable and despite the terrible crime in which he had participated, there was still something of the "good boy" his mother had dutifully sent to Sunday school. He needed a response that was not phony, not loaded with the language of mystification that had destroyed his better self. He was twenty-one, badly miseducated—as I have suggested we all are—and dying in physical and spiritual agony. He needed a genuine human response. If Simon had said, "Oh, God! I could strangle you! How could you do such a thing? Those people—they could have been my family. In another time and place, they could have been yours. How could you kill helpless people? Children? Mothers who had dreams for their children as yours did for you? Why, why, why?" the two men would have been in relation—not yet, or perhaps ever, in a positive relation, but in a human-to-human encounter in which each felt something for the specific other. Then gradually each might have seen the full horror of their situation. They both might have seen that the possibility of perpetrating unspeakable crimes lay in Simon as well as in Karl and that the possibility and thus the responsibility to resist lay also in both. At bottom the evil separation induced by patriarchal schemes run amok in Nazism had cut Karl loose from his parents, and their silence (another form of separation) had made the task of mystification easy. In this task of separation his church colluded a priori, because it was prepared to absolve, to cut loose, its members from any sin they might commit except rejection of the father-God.

Simon's heritage also served him poorly. As we have seen, it includes its own horrors and injustices. But worse, that heritage—like scholasticism—maintains an endless dialogue of distraction, of wrangling over abstractions, of making distinctions, of separating, separating, separating. Simon, a good and sensitive human being, suffered for years supposedly because he walked out on a dying boy without "forgiving" him. In truth he suffered because he walked out on a suffering part of himself—a hated, feared, and half-pitied part of himself. The years of agonizing turned into intellectual gymnastics, a continuous search through a flawed heritage for an answer to the question, Was I right or wrong? And still at the end of it Simon thinks that "the crux of the matter is . . . the question of forgiveness."[11] The real question is whether we will receive the hand that extends toward us in supplication or friendship, whether we will respond to the anguish in eyes that address us, whether we will see that evil is ratified resoundingly in the relentless cultural press for separation.

Both Christian and Jewish traditions have worshiped the Absolute—the One totally cut off or separate, the One who stands completely outside of and unmoved by his creation. As Catherine Keller recently pointed out, this religious tradition has permeated our culture. Separatist thinking dominates politics, psychology, fiction, and ethics. Further,

> separation and sexism have functioned together as the most fundamental self-shaping assumptions of our culture. That any subject, human or non-human, is what it is only in clear division from everything else; that men, by nature and by right, exercise the primary prerogatives of civilization: these two presuppositions collaborate like two eyes to sustain a single worldview.[12]

In extremis, however, and in the less strongly gendered periods of life—infancy and old age—another eye opens. Maudie, Cyprian, and Pearl Buck's father (Andrew, the "fighting angel") all sensed the falseness of the separatist worldview, but none of them fully trusted what he or she was now seeing. For Cyprian and Andrew full acceptance would have required a painful rejection of large parts of their lifework. A change in worldview is not like a change of clothes. Karl, the dying SS man, saw clearly where his separatist worldview had brought him and longed to restore himself in human relation. He had neither adequate language nor sufficient practice to understand and express his need. Neither did Simon, and so he and most of his respondents allowed themselves to be distracted again, to be cut off—"absolved"—in their longing for attachment to the Absolute.

In closing this section we should return to the question of justification that I raised earlier and deferred. Having confessed that I might torture one who was in a position to save my child from pain or death by disclosing her whereabouts, I must now ask whether I would be *justified* in doing so. From a practical perspective I could argue that I am not only justified but obligated to save my child. If the facts of the case are clear—this man has abducted my innocent child, intends her death, and knows where she is—justice is on my side. Further, he can save himself by speaking; he is not helpless. But suppose he believes with all his heart in the cause for which he committed the crime. Suppose I know that he is willing to die for this cause. I may still be able to get him to talk if I am sufficiently cruel. Would I proceed to the necessary extremes? I do not know, and my lack of clear knowledge on this decision must become part of a morality of evil. (If I *did* know, this knowledge would also be important in constructing such a morality.) *Should* I proceed? This is the question of justification. The answer is probably no, but the question does not help much in guiding ethical life. If I find a justification in this situation, I may well find justification in other situations—as Churchill did for bombing civilian centers. It may be better to explore the question for insight, to recognize how contrived are the situations for which we can give clear answers, and to face the tragedy of our human condition: we *will* often act out of passion, and it is best to put our efforts into preventing situations in which we are likely to act against our moral scruples. We are not immune to committing evil, and we cannot even be sure, faced with a choice among evils, that we have chosen the least of them.

THE GODLIKENESS OF TORTURE

People—even *we*—torture to save loved ones or great causes, to gain knowledge, and to defend justice and righteousness. Many would object, however, that the cases I have discussed so far (with the exception of the unknown pain inflicted on the man who could save my child by speaking) are not cases of real torture. They are not sufficiently horrible, and the torturers are not sufficiently evil. There are, of course, gradations in moral evil. We cannot call Simon Wiesenthal an evil man for walking out on Karl without a word. Yet he intentionally contributed to a basic condition of evil, separation. This grade of evil threatens us daily.

But history resounds with cases of the sort that most of us think of when we hear the word *torture*. In the earlier discussion of the witch craze we saw that torture was an official government strategy to obtain confessions in most European countries. Although England boasted of an accusatorial system and did not include torture as a legal procedure in its common law, English royalty licensed torture, and two horrible devices were employed in the Tower of London. Given the long association of women with evil, we should not be surprised that both received feminine labels. One, named the Duke of Exeter's Daughter, was the rack. The other—the Scavenger's Daughter—is described as follows:

> This was a device that crushed the body until the blood spurted out of the nostrils and the tips of the fingers instead of, like the rack, stretching it "until the bones and joints were almost plucked asunder." The use of both the Scavenger's Daughter and the rack became more and more common under the Tudors, and by the latter part of the reign of Elizabeth I, the rack, it was said, "seldom stood idle in the Tower."[13]

Another form of torture, the *peine forte et dure,* was used until 1726 to coerce those who refused to enter a plea to an indictment. A man who accepted this form of death could at least pass on his earthly goods to relations, whereas a guilty plea or verdict allowed the crown to confiscate his entire estate. It was the rule to warn a prisoner three times that recalcitrance would result in the *peine forte et dure.* Then came the dread words, that the prisoner

> shall be remanded to the place from whence he came, and put in some low dark room: he shall lie without any litter or anything under him, and that one arm shall be drawn to one quarter of the room with a cord, and the other to another, and that his feet shall be used in the same manner, and that as many weights shall be laid on him as he can bear and more. That he shall have three morsels of barley bread a day, and that he shall have the water next the prison, so that it be not current, and that he shall not eat the same day upon which he drinks, nor drink the same day upon which he eats; and he shall so continue until he die.[14]

In this sentence, cruelty is deliberately pronounced, and it is justified not by the crime for which the condemned man was arrested but by his defiance of the royal will. Gods and kings have often killed and tortured and considered it their right to do so. The Jungians, as we have seen, commented on the sacred power of killing as it is revealed in myths, and *The Iliad* repeatedly describes the complicity of men and gods in inflicting horrible wounds and destruction.

What is new, arising only in modern times, is the association of agony with pleasure. Philippe Ariès points out that the joining of love and death that became such a popular theme in the art of the nineteenth century has its roots in the late fifteenth century and that we can observe a rise in sadism from the sixteenth to the nineteenth centuries. To demonstrate his point he contrasts early (fifteenth-century, or at least prebaroque) paintings and writings of the same scenes with later ones. The earlier scenes depict torture dispassionately; in the later ones every detail seems designed to increase the horror, to reveal the sadistic pleasure and power of the torturers, to arouse something like sexual excitement in the onlooker. Ariès quotes Rousset's comments on a description of the torture of Saint Lawrence (Spain, 1603): "The torturers are busy preparing the gridiron, lighting the fire, tearing off the saint's clothes, stripping his flayed body, and throwing him on the coals. The tyrant, with bloodshot eyes, grinning face, and foaming mouth, howls with sadistic joy as servants fan the flames." [15]

What can account for the sick combination of pain, horror, power, and ecstasy? And why did it arise in a period of intellectual awakening? The Enlightenment brought about an actual reduction in the use of torture as a legally approved method, and from the mid-eighteenth century to the present day more and more states have joined the humane circle that condemns torture. In spite of that important change, the Enlightenment is marred by the rise of sadism. This is also the period in which philosophical theodicy became a central interest. Thinkers were beginning to question whether there was a God at all and, if there was, whether that God could be described in his relation to evil as earlier theodicists had laid down. The theodicies described in chapter 1 as Augustinian and Irenaean drew on the words and teachings of the early church fathers. But they differed dramatically in context. As Kenneth Surin puts it, "Pre–seventeenth century Christian thinkers were certainly not unaware of the conceptual difficulties that these antinomies generated; but, unlike their post–seventeenth century counterparts, they did not regard these problems as constituting *any* sort of ground for jettisoning their faith." Surin asks why this should be the case and notes Alasdair MacIntyre's answer. The conceptual incoherences in Christianity were, MacIntyre suggests, "taken to be tolerable (and treated as apparent and not real) because the concepts were part of a set of concepts which were indispensable to the forms of description used in social and intellectual life." [16]

As Klaits counseled with respect to the witch craze, no simple answer can explain such dramatic changes in worldview. But we can explore several factors as historically verified and logically implicated. First, the rights of rulers went largely unchallenged in earlier days except by those who intended to displace them, and their reasons for rebellion were rarely concerns with justice. Rather, ruler-candidates already carried some mark, some similarity to the stereotypical ruler. Augustine's theodicy did not really try to figure God out. It accepted him as revealed in the world and laid the blame for evil on human beings who clearly needed conversion to the will of God the ruler. God's love as Augustine described it was a love of justice, harmony, and order, and it was not open to challenge or inspection. From early Greek days through the Middle Ages gods and rulers behaved in ways that were unsurprising to human beings—idiosyncrasy was their prerogative. Obedience and propitiation were the choice of wise and fearful human beings.

As the idea of God's personal love came to the fore in Christian thinking, a need grew to reconcile this love with the reality of evil. Further, advancements in scientific thinking began to suggest natural causes for many of the phenomena previously attributed to God. If God were not directly responsible for tides, planetary motion, deformities, and the like, then what was his nature? God must be studied rationally along with a whole universe of phenomena, and given the heady powers of rational thinking, he *could* be so studied. One possibility, of course, was to give up the idea of gods entirely, and another was to reclaim the earlier notion of a panoply of deities competing for power and favoring various human beings idiosyncratically. The latter possibility was simply incompatible with the new age of rational thought, and the former seems to have been incompatible with the psychic yearning of humanity. As Jung said, "God is a psychic reality." Thus in an age of burgeoning intellect God had nevertheless to be retained and, more than that, had to be explained and made consistent.

Tillich has described the pre-Reformation period as an age characterized by the anxiety of guilt and the fear of condemnation. Like Klaits, he points to a constellation of sociological factors responsible for the pervasive feeling of guilt: the growing economic disparity between an emerging middle class and the poor, conflict with the church, whose authority was still heeded and feared, and the tendency toward absolutism in rulers. This last seems a natural consequence of challenge. Any institution under attack—verbal or physical—is likely to tighten control and find more elaborate rationales for its existence. This strategy reached its acme with respect to human rulers in the doctrine of the divine right of kings and, with respect to God, in the philosophical theodicies.

An age that emphasized the personal love of God also emphasized his wrath; that is, great concern arose about the relations of the individual to God. It was no longer sufficient to participate in the comforting rituals of the church. One had to demonstrate that one belonged by expressing orthodox beliefs, by avoiding the contamination of witches and heretics, and—in the new Protestantism—by prospering and doing good works. Good works were no longer a means of placating or pleasing God, however, but were now thought to be a sign that one was graced by God. This belief no doubt provided a convenient rationalization for those who might otherwise have felt some guilt about the suffering of the poor. The poor became not just poor in material goods but poor in spirit as well.

It seems likely that in this period, as in any period of guilt, there was much repression and projection. An important aspect of God that theodicy continually repressed was the possibility of his irrationality and cruelty. Evidence in favor of this possibility was everywhere, but, as we saw earlier, people could not come to grips with the idea of an unloving God. If the suspicion that God is not all-good is repressed, it is predictable that those who would imitate God might manifest the great cruelty they deny in God. They would have to redefine love in harsh terms. Absolute control, cruelty, and torture would be signs of power and godlikeness; they would be evils in everyday life (in, for example, English common law) but good when exercised by legitimate authority.

It is not surprising that torture and sexuality became conflated in such an age. The knowledge that torture is a fundamental evil was repressed. The knowledge that the God of monotheism might be cruel and unjust was repressed. We might say that both became bits of forbidden knowledge. At the same time the bawdiness of the Middle Ages was under attack; there was a new and heavy emphasis on personal morality. The result was a thoroughly sexual interest in causing pain and in suffering itself. To be godlike was to be loving, cruel, powerful, dominant, and knowledgeable.

The religious undertones of sadism and necrophilia are clear in the work of the Marquis de Sade. Ariès quotes de Sade's description of the grand duke of Tuscany's gallery, from which an anatomy room could be observed: "A bizarre idea had been executed in this room: a sepulcher filled with cadavers in which one could observe all the different stages of decomposition from the moment of death until the total destruction of individuality. This grim work of art was made of wax that was colored so naturally that nature herself could not have been more expressive or more real." [17] We can explain such interest as the result of brooding on what God does to—or allows to happen to—his creatures. The church represses a horror of decomposition, preserving Jesus and Mary from that fate, but insists that it is the just end of all sinners. De Sade wanted to rub humankind's face in the fate it had accepted as decreed by a good and loving God. Here is what it looks like, says de Sade. Glory in it!

Many writers recognize the divinity in the marquis's rejection of the Christian God. Georges Bataille opens his study of de Sade's work with a quotation from Swinburne full of such allusions:

> In the midst of this rowdy imperial epic we see a blasted head flashing, a massive chest crossed by lightning, the phallus-man, an august and cynical profile grimacing like a ghastly and sublime Titan; we feel a thrill of the infinite in the accursed pages, the breath of a tempestuous ideal vibrating on these burnt lips. Come nearer and you will hear the arteries of the universal soul, veins swollen with divine blood palpitating in this muddy and bleeding carcass. This cloaca is impregnated with azure, there is a god-like element in these latrines. Close your ear to the rattle of bayonets and the bark of cannon; turn your eye from this moving tide of war, of victories or defeats; then you will see a huge ghost bursting out against the shadows; you will see the vast and sinister figure of the Marquis de Sade appear above a whole epoch sewn with stars. [18]

In an important sense the disgusting acts and horrors de Sade endlessly describes are designed to reveal one of the greater evils—the persistent mystification that leaves us helpless to live in authenticity. Bataille says of one of de Sade's works: "This book is the only one in which the mind of man is shown as *it really is*. The language of *Les Cent Vingt Journées de Sodome* is that of a universe which degrades gradually and systematically, which tortures and destroys the totality of the beings which it presents." [19] A clear consciousness sees the possibilities of a supremely evil being or of impersonal nature creating and destroying. Most clearly, however, it sees the utter depths of depravity within the reach of minds continually flogged by contradictions. Believe your fairy tales, fabricate your elaborate rationalizations, repress what you know to be true, de Sade suggests, and eventually the monster will burst forth, and that monster will be you in the image of God.

Most of us recoil from the excesses in which de Sade reveled, and few of us can imagine ourselves actually engaging in such horrors. The question is, Why not? It may well be that most of us are held back more by the aesthetics of horror than by tender feelings for our victims. As Bataille writes, "The amputated fingers, the eyes, the torn finger nails, the tortures of which moral horror intensifies the pain, the mother induced, by cunning and terror, to murder her son, the cries, the blood and the stench, everything contributes to our nausea."[20] We just do not have the stomach for it. We are paralyzed by direct knowledge and nausea.

Bombs and bullets are popular with us, however, and yet they certainly amputate fingers, blow out eyes, rip fingernails, rupture bowels, truncate sexual organs, and cause all the rest of de Sade's horrors. The only thing missing is the eye-to-eye contact between torturer and victim. We are spared the nausea that might save us. Some would say, of course, that the greater difference lies in intention. Soldiers who drop bombs on enemies do not intend to torture them; they do not deliberately inflict pain for pain's sake, and they do not howl with glee as their enemies writhe. But neither, it turns out, do most torturers.[21] People, real people, rarely choose evil (Sartre would say that we never can because such a choice involves a logical contradiction),[22] but we do evil in the name of some overriding good—usually, paradoxically, the conquest of evil.

Albert Bandura also notes that it is easier to commit horrors at a distance.[23] People can detach themselves from both consequences and intentions when they cannot hear the victim's pleas directly. Bandura explains that cognitive restructuring puts a positive value on acts that would normally be considered immoral, a phenomenon I discussed in the chapter on war. There can be no doubt that cognitive restructuring occurs. The question is what prompts and supports it, and the answer has to include the pervasive acceptance of the traditional view of evil that is under critique here. If evil were directly associated with pain, separation, and helplessness, we would see immediately that the following constitute great moral evils:

1. Inflicting pain (unless it can be *demonstrated* that doing so will or is at least likely to spare the victim greater pain in the future)
2. a. Inducing the pain of separation
   b. Neglecting relation so that the pain of separation follows or those separated are thereby dehumanized

3. a. Deliberately or carelessly causing helplessness

   b. Creating elaborate systems of mystification that contribute to the fear of helplessness or to its actual maintenance

Nothing can change this assessment. No justification can transform these evils into goods. From the perspective of women—whose task has been to preserve the lives of children, to maintain homes that provide physical and psychic comfort, and to care for the helpless—it is irrational to attempt to justify such deeds. One who does so must be so overcome by fear that he or she cannot think logically. That fear is often aggravated by the belief that ordinary human life is somehow radically separate from the life of the soul. Even Unamuno, that "man of flesh and blood" who should have known better, insisted that we must somehow infinitely treasure the human soul over the human life:

> And it happens that the less a man believes in the soul—that is to say in his conscious immortality, personal and concrete—the more he will exaggerate the worth of this poor transitory life. This is the source from which springs all that effeminate, sentimental ebullition against war. True, a man ought not to wish to die, but the death to be renounced is the death of the soul.[24]

For those who care directly for others, one's soul dies as soon as it detaches from the concrete persons who stretch out their hands in need or friendship. It begins to die when we turn toward a god (master, authority) who demands cruelty and away from those who want to be cared for. The fear that often sustains men in their wars and tortures is the fear of being like a woman—of confessing dependence on other human beings, of being moved to tears over the pain of another, of saying directly: "Please don't hurt me! What is it you want?" In suggesting this response I mean to shock the reader into reflecting on our attitudes toward men and women and the reactions we evaluate as appropriate for each. But more than that I want to recommend seriously that we guide our responses to perceived evil by policies of connection. Instead of separating ourselves from those whose actions we condemn, we should saturate them with our presence. Nations ill at ease with one another should exchange citizens in all walks of life, and conversations should increase, not cease.

A soft answer, one that appeals to the best in an other, does not, however, always turn away wrath, and I do not recommend a thoroughgoing pacificism. Too often that sort of program actually induces violence in others who are infuriated by the righteous superiority of those they injure. We need to follow a course of steady negotiation, of staying with. We require a dignified human, womanly, attitude—an attitude that seeks to prevent harm, to preserve relation rather than to elevate itself. This last is important, for whenever human beings become engrossed in their own virtue they misdirect attention to their own perfection and miss opportunities for genuine resistance and reconciliation. We need not, indeed should not, give an oppressor all he demands (no one should simply have given Czechoslovakia to Hitler, for example), but we must press for public conversation. As soon as we label the other evil, we commit ourselves to battle or abject submission, and we thereby strengthen the tendency to evil. If, in contrast, we can give a little with much warning and watching, with public counteroffers of cooperation, many destructive leaders and regimes would pass away under the disillusionment of their own people. Instead we strengthen unworthy leaders by recognizing their power, taking it seriously by reacting with violence. And then, of course, we must insist that our action is necessary, our cause just, and the end worth all the misery.

Such a course of action is the godlike warrior's. It construes evil as disobedience, disloyalty, weakness, and possession by powers in opposition to God, and it seeks to preserve the soul by living a life that should be shunned in heaven. Many contemporary Christians are helping to promote the new view discussed here.[25] Whether they represent, as some say, a return to the genuine message of Jesus or an enlightenment of Christians who now recognize the dynamic nature of their faith seems to me unimportant. That a good and gentle God provides a new image of good and gentle people concerned with each other's well-being here on earth is an insight of tremendous importance.

PSYCHOLOGICAL ABUSE

Women have suffered psychological abuse for centuries. The fundamental form of this abuse, as Simone de Beauvoir brilliantly describes it, is man's identification of woman as "other," the ready-to-hand object for his subjectness.[26] Hazel Barnes elaborates on Beauvoir's description:

To the overt political oppression that men were able to impose by virtue of their physical strength and by male-established laws supposedly based on the needs of the species, Beauvoir adds the psychological damage that turned women into self-oppressors. The obvious corollary of Sartre's pronouncement, "Man makes himself" is that a woman (comparably with a man) makes herself both as an individual and as a woman. This is the thrust of the central thesis of *The Second Sex:* "One is not born but becomes a woman."[27]

Those comments draw attention to the descriptions of women we discussed earlier. To some degree we can choose whether to accept descriptions of ourselves as the devil's gateway or the angel in the house, but it is a mistake to suppose either that our freedom is huge or that we can define ourselves in simple opposition to those descriptions, and that was a main point in the earlier defense of domestic life. We usually escape oppression not by separating ourselves entirely from the oppressor, but rather by transforming the oppressor into someone with whom we can coexist. Therefore women—and the oppressed in general—must contribute to their own transformation. Barnes continues her elaboration of Beauvoir's view:

Beauvoir argues that woman, viewed by men as a hybrid, midway between the human which man is and the natural world which he is not, becomes essentially the Other—the Other which man loves, hates, needs, resists, despises. The myth of Woman, Beauvoir shows, flexibly accommodates her as angel, demon, evil flesh, redemptive spirit, life force and mortal death—man's other half but the half which in some mysterious way he himself is not. Women have internalized this myth, trying to model themselves after whatever particular version of it males in their immediate society demanded.[28]

The upshot of all this is that women, like men, cannot ignore or simply discard the package of expectations that their culture has created for them. They must sort through the expectations carefully, re-evaluating and choosing. Values and ways of life become more attractive as the people embracing them articulate their positions with some joy and without exclusionary language or strategies. If there are elements of fulfillment and happiness in women's traditional activities, then women should describe and defend them and should urge men to consider participating in them. Further, if the male descriptions of woman are, as so many writers have suggested, projections of a loved and hated "other half," then incorporation and acceptance of this other half is a human developmental task—not just a male one.

Women do not automatically possess all these qualities; indeed, a major thesis of feminism is that such a claim is false and, given the contradictory qualities described, is logically invalid. The question for all of us is which qualities to affirm and which to regret but understand and accept as part of a morality of evil.

Men too have suffered psychological abuse from societies that have created uniform expectations for them, and this fact is often overlooked. William James's surprisingly unreflective acceptance of the general virtues of "manliness" reflects this abuse. Further, some writers have posited biological factors as determinants of man's nature as well as woman's. From Charles Darwin to E. O. Wilson theorists have attributed warfare to man's natural aggression and the noble traits thought to be a genetic product of the trials of combat.[29] Sherwood Washburn and C. S. Lancaster go so far as to say, "Men enjoy hunting and killing, and these activities are continued as sports even when they are no longer economically necessary," and, "War has been far too important in human history for it to be other than pleasurable for the males involved."[30] Attitudes such as these force every young man into activities and displays of feeling that might be contrary to the vision of self that he longs to develop. If he cannot or will not fight, he must find some other way to prove that he is manly—for example, by becoming a priest or engaging in a profession from which women are excluded by virtue of some perceived weakness. It is hard indeed simply to reject the model. We can thus identify a cultural form of evil in the pervasive mystification that induces helplessness in both women and men.

Besides the universal psychological abuse that every society holds ready to ensure conformity, there is the abuse that individuals visit on one another. Psychiatrists see all sorts of psychological abuse. M. Scott Peck, the Christian psychiatrist whose views on evil I mentioned earlier, describes "people of the lie," those who are so steeped in destructive ways that they do not wish to be delivered from them.[31] They are, from his perspective, literally seized by the powers of evil. Except in extraordinary moments (when there is hope for their recovery), they deny problems in themselves. They do evil in the name of good.

Peck describes parents who totally control their children in the name of preparing them for autonomous futures, wives who dominate their husbands and despise them for their weakness, parents who give their children destructive "gifts"—gifts the children do not want and that effectively pass along messages of hate rather than love. In many of these accounts Peck shows great insight into the ways people inflict pain in the name of good. Over and over again we hear stories of people who have no real feeling for those close to them, who make decisions on the basis of abstract rules or for their own convenience without regard for the needs and wants of those they "love." They make these decisions from a perspective of righteousness; that is, the doer of great harm acts in the name of good.

In many of the cases Peck describes, the best solution for a victim of destructive control would be physical separation. This sort of separation need not be evil (that is, harmful). It need not involve psychic separation. Indeed, physical separation from a controlling, destructive, and seemingly powerful individual may only be possible through psychic connection. One must understand what the other wants and seeks. With such understanding a victim can pity the oppressor as a weak, fearful, and pathetic creature and at the same time find the strength to reject his or her constant demands.

For all its insights, however, Peck's is a frightening perspective on evil. Without intending to do so, he perpetuates many of the myths that contribute to universal psychological abuse. He admits, for example, that "many readers are likely to be concerned" about his use of masculine pronouns for God. He says that he appreciates this concern. He says that he supports the women's movement and "action that is reasonable" in combating sexist language. But then he makes everything worse by saying:

> God is not neuter. He is exploding with life and love—even sexuality of a sort. So "It" is not appropriate. Certainly I consider God androgynous. He is as gentle and tender and maternal as any woman could ever be. Nonetheless, culturally determined though it may be, I subjectively experience His reality as more masculine than feminine. While He nurtures us, He also desires to penetrate us, and while we more often than not flee from His love like a reluctant virgin, He chases after us with a vigor in the hunt that we most typically associate with males.[32]

These images are so dreadful that one hardly knows how to respond. Why is God not neuter? It would be far easier to accept the natural evil of the world if there were no person-God supposedly watching over us. To consider the he-God "androgynous" is a monumental denigration of women. What do women contribute to the conception of either humanity or deity? Peck tosses out a few qualities that we see in mothers but that reach their pinnacle in the he-God. Like so many patriarchal writers, Peck takes the only consistently observable human tendency to tenderness and altruism and makes it a property of the invisible he-God. This is psychological abuse of the first degree. To compound this horrific description with a metaphor of God as panting rapist is to demonstrate how right deconstructionists are on their major point: language often drives us and speaks the culture through us. Peck, I am sure, had no intention of revealing so thoroughly the true nature of the god that has so dominated and infected human lives.

In contrast to his use of *he* for God, Peck uses *it* for Satan. Why? "While I know Satan to be lustful to penetrate us, I have not in the least experienced this desire as sexual or creative—only hateful and destructive. It is hard to determine the sex of a snake." [33] How can we respond to that? If "to penetrate" is the defining characteristic of male sexuality and Satan has this desire, how can "it" not be male? Peck answers that the desire is not creative, and his response can mean only that a *creative* sexual desire is masculine. Once again we find the ancient association of the male with all that is causal and effective, and again we see the noxious move to associate snake and evil. Peck simply cannot accept a blend of good and evil in his deities. The male deity must be perfect, encompassing all goods—even those observably female. Evil, although personified, is "it," and there is no role whatever for "she" at the cosmic level. One wonders whether this form of psychological abuse will ever end. Peck's much-praised book on evil thus contributes to the ongoing ratification of evil.

SUMMARY

In discussing torture, we saw that it is both normal and pathological; that is, that tendencies to inflict pain are in all of us and that different agents in the environment trigger the illness in different human beings. Some of us would inflict pain to save the lives of loved ones, some to gain knowledge, and some to remain faithful to great causes or unshakable beliefs. Whenever we actually inflict pain we separate ourselves from the victims. If possible, we avoid their eyes, and we shudder at the thought of human beings who can commit atrocities face to face. The belief that justifies us in inflicting pain parallels the belief in the male God who inflicts or allows pain to accomplish his ends.

We saw too how a good man can perpetuate evil when he perceives another as a symbol and not as an individual. In the tale of *The Sunflower*, we saw both the original storyteller and the commentators deny the longing for relation.

In discussing the rise of sadism during the Enlightenment, we saw what might be called the logical conclusion of theodicy. Cruel acts must be good. The capacity for cruelty is godlike and the acts pleasurable.

Finally, the discussion of psychological abuse centered on the organized potential for abuse at the heart of feminine and masculine models. We saw just how pervasive this potential is in the brief examination of M. Scott Peck's analysis of the mental illnesses that lead to psychological abuse. Although the work contains useful insights, the language of possession, of power, and of he-God goodness overwhelms the female reader and illustrates vividly the cultural abuse that well-intentioned men continue to inflict on women.

9

Educating for a Morality of Evil

The purpose of this last chapter is to bring together the recommendations of the preceding chapters and to direct them toward education. The main task of the book has been to examine evil from women's perspective. To do so it has been necessary to analyze traditional views of evil, to consider our culture's expectations for women and for men, and to explore what we might call the logic of women's experience. What have we learned in our long history as the second sex? What positions are logically compatible with the view from our experiential standpoint?

Early on I rejected the notion held long ago by Socrates and recently by Hannah Arendt that evil is simply the absence of knowledge or good.[1] Evil is a real presence, and moral evil is often the result of trying to do something either genuinely thought to be good or rationalized layer on layer in gross bad faith. Evil is thus intimately bound up in disputes over good. Nor do I believe that evil is necessarily ugly or that people cannot think on that which is ugly. De Sade showed us vividly how untrue these notions are. Although Sartre was technically right when he said that we cannot sustain a choice to do evil for its own sake (we do evil mainly in opposition to some perceived evil and therefore choose something we rationalize as right or good), this only points up the power of mystification and repression. We cannot think for long on our own evil motives, so we think about obedience, the knowledge to be gained, the cause to be won, and the safety of our lives, and we evaluate all these as good. But this slippery bit of thinking comes into question when we regard evil as relational and positively real. When we acknowledge that pain, separation, and helplessness are the basic states of consciousness associated with evil and that moral evil consists in inducing, sustaining, or failing to relieve these conditions, we can no longer ignore that we *do* think on and intend evil when we perform such acts. Just as disease is real and not just an illusion or absence of health, evil is real, and to control it we need to understand it and accept that the tendency toward it dwells in all of us.

If we believe this, a primary purpose of education should be to reduce pain, separation, and helplessness by encouraging people to explore the nature of evil and commit themselves to continue the search for understanding. Further, faced with the temptation or apparent need to do something evil, appropriately educated people should ask themselves: Is there a different way to accomplish my goal? Is the goal *itself* evil or tainted with evil? What good am I trying to achieve? Thinking this way should govern our political and social relations as well as our personal lives. Because such thinking requires analytical skill, all students need practice in considering their lives philosophically. And because we should not reduce such consideration to a purely contemplative state divorced from action, philosophy *becomes* largely as John Dewey advised—philosophy of education, that is, philosophy of life. An important purpose of education should be to combat mystification. This chapter explores topics of special importance to educators: curriculum and instruction, relational virtues, and the possibility of spirituality.

CURRICULUM AND INSTRUCTION

Literacy on evil comes to mind as a reasonable aim to guide the selection and presentation of content. A few days ago in a graduate class on curriculum theory a student drew our attention to the current campus debate on courses in Western culture. His theme was the "bleaching of history," and he circulated several beautifully illustrated books that pictured the great figures of Greek and biblical history as Nordic types. Although he was a humanities major, this young man had come to believe that Western culture has so demeaned people of color and women that we should abandon it as an educational requirement. A substantial number of people have already pressed for curricular changes that would introduce courses in non-Western cultures and include female writers and writers of color. Many—but by no means all of us—agree that this is a move in the right direction.

The arguments that have led to change have largely followed the liberal tradition. They argue from conceptions of equality. When we examine the situation from the perspective adopted throughout this book, another sort of argument begins to develop, and a different solution emerges. It takes account of—even though it ultimately rejects—the rationale many scholars offer to retain required courses in Western culture. Even though this culture and the works chosen to represent it are filled with arrogance, cruelty, gross injustice, and distorted arguments for Western male dominance, this *is* our heritage. This is the thinking that has controlled our troubled rise to high culture and technology. We teach it, they argue, not only to admire its intellectual grandeur but to critique it, to understand and grow beyond it.

This strikes me as a powerful argument if it is honest. But people who make it—if they have learned the lessons supposedly taught by their beloved material—should know that the very requirement of this material honors it. It is not enough for the enlightened professor, usually white and male, to hold forth on the errors and injustices revealed in the works we study with such reverence. At the least the critical perspectives of those injured should be included and attended to with material written and spoken in their own voices. If we require students to read Aristotle, Augustine, and Aquinas, then we should require them as well to read Mary Daly, James Baldwin, Susan Moller Okin, and other critics where their works are directly relevant. We would not dream of requiring our students to read old works of science riddled with errors. In the rare cases when we do so because of some allegedly great literary value, we make sure that other material in the curriculum corrects the errors. In the case of the great works in humanities, it is not simply a matter of error; it is a matter of *evil* enshrined in a culture that does not really want to forsake it.

In earlier sections I referred to the glories and horrors of *The Iliad* and *The Odyssey.* Should all students read these books? I think the books should be available—present in the curriculum—for those who are led to or choose to study them, but students should study them with attention to details that traditional instruction has regularly overlooked. Penelope is often used as a model of the faithful and passive wife (totally unproductive—weaving and tearing out, weaving and tearing out, day after day), and Telemachus is interpreted developmentally. Many interpretations portray Telemachus as a compassionate figure who begs his father to spare Medon and Phemiosa, but part of his growing up involves his ability to assert total control over the women in his household, including his mother, who is lost in admiration for his newly acquired manliness. In contrast to the mercy he encourages for Medon and Phemiosa, his treatment of the slave women—whose only apparent crime was succumbing to the romantic overtures of the wooers—exceeds in cruelty the demands of his father. Odysseus had ordered him to have the twelve unfaithful women clean up the great hall that was littered with the bodies and blood of the slain wooers. After their cleaning, he wanted the women taken outside and slain with swords. But Telemachus in the full fire of manhood says, "God forbid that I should take these women's lives by a clean death, these that have poured dishonor on my head and on my mother, and have lain with the wooers." (I should note that these same women may have "lain with" Odysseus in the past, given that such use of women was common among Homeric princes.) Homer proceeds to describe Telemachus's action in graphic terms:

> With that word he tied the cable of a dark-prowed ship to a great pillar and flung it round the vaulted room, and fastened it aloft, that none might touch the ground with her feet. And even as when thrushes, long of wing, or doves fall into a net that is set in a thicket, as they seek to their roosting-place, and a loathly bed harbors them, even so the women held their heads all in a row, and about all their necks nooses were cast, that they might die by the most pitiful death. And they writhed with their feet for a small space, but for no long while.[2]

What we should impress on students is not only the cruelty of Telemachus—in the next passage he and his fellows cut off the nostrils, hands, feet, and ears of Melanthius and throw his "vitals" to the dogs—but the pattern of his development. He grows in direct opposition to all that is feminine and exhibits a large part of his manhood in his control of women. The women he murders are not even named, and they behave passively—like caught thrushes or doves—even in the face of death.

When we treat material of this sort in the classroom, we should address the great themes of torture, cruelty, and misogyny in some depth. Students should not leave with the idea that people no longer do such dreadful things to one another. The results of Hiroshima, for example, were a sanitized form of torture. No one played bold Telemachus stringing up meek women or tearing the guts out of a shamed enemy. But people were nevertheless gutted and burned and strangled, and many suffered for years, not simply "for no long while." Nor did misogyny end with Telemachus and his hero father. Curriculum makers should begin to assemble appropriate materials for following up on *these* themes and not just on the traditional themes of the warrior's courage, the wife's faithfulness, the son's obedience and "growth," the hero's triumph, and the alleged victory of good over evil. (The dreadful scenes just described include many references to vengeful acts as righteous, as defeats of evil.) If we are concerned, as we continually say we are, with the development of our children, then we must carefully consider the development of Telemachus and ask whether that is the pattern we wish to perpetuate. We may answer that we should indeed admire and encourage *part* of the pattern. In trying to redress an imbalance and reject obvious tendencies to evil, I do not mean to throw out everything associated with a model that contains both admirable and despicable qualities.

It is not possible in one short chapter to describe fully the sort of education that is compatible with a morality of evil. I will undertake that task in a separate work. But clearly that education would require changes not only within the subjects now taught but also in the constellation of topics now addressed as "subjects." Jane Roland Martin cautions that we should "not delude ourselves that education can be created anew." [3] She is thoroughly familiar with the discouraging literature on schooling and change. In our theoretical work, however, we *should* create education anew. We can then use the vision we create to guide the actual changes we find feasible. Without such a vision we have no way to order our priorities or to seize opportunities when they present themselves. Similarly, I have argued throughout this book that without a morality of evil we lack the questions needed to prevent us from continuing to ratify evil.

Martin, who also wants the school curriculum to include the activities and interests of women, argues for a dramatic change in subjects and also for changes in the ways we teach traditional subjects. She recommends that "caring, concern, and connection" be made goals of education:

> I do not mean by this that we should fill up school time with courses in the 3 Cs of caring, concern, and connection. In an education that gives Sophie, Sarah, and the reproductive processes of society their due, Compassion 101a need no more be listed in a school's offering than Objectivity 101a is now. Just as the general curricular goals of rationality and individual autonomy derive from the productive processes of society, so too the reproductive processes yield general goals. [4]

The difficulty here is even greater than Martin admits. The notion of objectivity is peculiarly compatible with courses, teacher dominance, grading, and hierarchical structures of school organization. That is why Objectivity 101a is not needed. Even if schools added courses in caring, concern, and connection to the curriculum (and we can imagine at least one such course being added as a sop to feminist academics), this move would not accomplish our purpose. Indeed, it might vitiate the sort of program I envision. Converting a way of being in the world to a set of courses is more likely to destroy the way of being than to transform the curriculum, which by its structure belongs to the world of male dominance. Objectivity 101a would remain in the implicit curriculum.

With this realization we face a hard point that Catherine Mac-Kinnon makes repeatedly: sex and gender are not mere differences; gender is a hierarchy marked by male dominance.[5] The structures of this dominance pervade our entire society, and they do not depend on the active malevolence of individual men. On the contrary, individual men of goodwill are as much caught in their tentacles as are women. In such a society—one in which the separation and helplessness of women has defined the ego strength and identity of men—it will not be easy to make changes that signify an upward evaluation of women's ways and experience. Madeleine Grumet vividly describes the ways in which the school curriculum is a masculine project. In the early years of schooling, for example, children learn in semiformal ways reminiscent of the mother's way; they learn to live together in play, song, dance, art, and story. But from third or fourth grade on, the curriculum becomes discrete—separated into well-defined subjects—and the children learn "to master the language, the rules, the games and the names of the father."[6]

Schooling has not remained recalcitrant because of a lack of critics. Critics have always been plentiful. Most of them want only to strengthen the existing structures. Some want to reform schools along Marxist or neo-Marxist lines.[7] Some want to deschool and, as we saw, even believe that schools will collapse under the weight of their own corruption.[8] A few see the need for teacher-student relations to become more genuinely collaborative and for teaching to become an act of empowerment. Maxine Greene, for example, concludes a call for critical pedagogy by saying, "In 'the shadow of silent majorities,' then, as teachers learning along with those we try to provoke to learn, we may be able to inspire hitherto unheard voices. We may be able to empower people to rediscover their own memories and articulate them in the presence of others, whose space they can share. Such a project demands the capacity to unveil and disclose." [9]

"To unveil and disclose" is the first essential task, and the second is to subvert the structures of dominance by challenging standard grading practices, administrative hierarchies, and whatever practices clearly support relations of dominance / submission. Some things we can do. We can change the content of standard subjects (such as the themes in literature), augment the subjects themselves, and guide our modes of instruction by our desire to educate people who will commit evil infrequently and with great regret. I have already described the influence of competitive processes in our schools as largely pernicious—as ways of creating rivals and making enemies. Cooperative processes can certainly be substituted for at least some competitive ones. We can also replace some authoritarian practices with more genuinely participatory ones.

But I must emphasize again that we cannot fully describe education in terms of subjects and instruction. Something else, a fuller experience, is essential. Marxist thinkers like Antonio Gramsci recommend, for example, that education dedicate itself to producing working-class intellectuals.[10] How can this project succeed? Surely not by turning working-class children into nonlaboring intellectuals who will then speak in abstractions about the dignity of labor! It can succeed only by incorporating into education itself real work—both physical and intellectual—that will be at least partly planned, executed, evaluated, and revised by students and teachers working together. A working-class intellectual is one, or ought to be one, who works and thinks and theorizes. The long-range goal would be to have a society of worker-thinkers and no classes. Similarly, if we want people to internalize the logic of feminine experience with respect to good and evil, we have to provide children with opportunities to engage in the activities that have induced this logic in women. It is not simply a matter of talking about tasks, but of doing them. It is a way of living and relating.

Now, of course, the full power of an entrenched patriarchy is likely to descend on us. How can schools accomplish all this, some will ask, when they cannot accomplish the tasks now assigned to them? I cannot answer that question satisfactorily here, but the first part of the answer has to be simply that the schools are now largely engaged in irrelevant tasks that are meaningless to many students. The schools are not providing education for fully human *being*. Rather, they are trying desperately to perform tasks necessary to sustain the pain of separation and helplessness. Students could learn everything worthwhile that the schools now teach more easily and rapidly in a situation that also provides opportunities to work and to live together.

In this short section on curriculum and instruction I have suggested four sorts of changes to consider: changes within the subjects of the standard curriculum (such as themes in literature and history), the augmentation of the standard curriculum with new subjects that attend to the traditional concerns of women, changes in instructional patterns, and a total reorganization of the patterns of schooling. Realistically the first and third are to some degree feasible and desirable. The second might be distorted and used to maintain the subordination of women. The last is next to impossible, and yet it must be our goal.

RELATIONAL VIRTUES

Now I want to say more about the transformation of relation that can be accomplished through the two kinds of changes that seem feasible, and I want to show how this transformation can lead in the direction of revolutionary change. Again there are tasks for both philosophers and educators.

We discussed the relational thinking of women in several chapters—in connection with the assessment and alleviation of pain, with poverty, with war, and with the distortions of thinking that sometimes accompany our deliberations on justice and rights. This thinking arises out of experience that has both positive and negative aspects. Women have for centuries been defined in relation—Dan's wife, Johnny's mother, Bill's daughter—and the health and stability of relations have been matters of survival for us. As this old pattern changes and women begin to define themselves in the public world, there is a real danger that we will lose the strengths of relational thinking. This is why educators must provide the kinds of experience that may promote relational thinking and philosophers must explore the underpinnings of relational thinking in relational ontologies.

An ethic of caring is based on a relational ontology; that is, it takes as a basic assumption that all human beings—not just women—are defined in relation. It is not just that *I* as a preformed continuous individual enter *into* relations; rather, the *I* of which we speak *so* easily is itself a relational entity. *I* really am defined by the set of relations into which my physical self has been thrown. This is not to adopt a total determinism, because *relation* involves affective response in each of the emerging entities, and this response is at least partly under the control of the present occupants of the relation. We cannot escape our relational condition, but we can reflect on it, evaluate it, move it in a direction we find good. We are neither totally free and separate in our affective and volitional lives, as many existentialists would have us believe, nor totally determined by the physical conditions of our past.

Caring is not an individual virtue, although certain virtues may help sustain it. Rather, caring is a relational state or quality, and it requires distinctive contributions from carer and cared for. A relation may deteriorate either because no one takes *care*—that is, attends to the messages and needs of the other—or because there is no response from the cared for. When either party rivets attention on himself or herself, for example, as the self-sacrificial and virtuous carer, a pathological condition arises. A child may be smothered, for example, by a woman who "lives" for her children; such a woman sees only her contribution to the relation. In general, pathologies of caring, whether public or private, manifest themselves in actual helplessness or feelings of helplessness in those "cared for."

Relational virtues are of two kinds: virtues that belong to the relation itself and individual virtues that enhance relations. Caring, friendship, companionship, and empathy are of the first kind, although they are not discrete. The task of philosophers with respect to this class of relational virtues is to describe the contributions of each member of the relation, the conditions under which the relation develops positively or negatively, and the place of such virtues with respect to individual virtues and vices. The task of educators is to encourage the actual growth of relational virtues, to explore relational themes in literature and history, and to establish learning conditions that permit people to contribute to their own relational growth.

Closely related to relational virtues are relational tasks. Teaching, parenting, advising, mediating, and helping are all relational tasks. Their success depends not only on the goodwill, sensitivity, and skills of the more powerful member of the relation, but also on the goodwill, skills, and responsiveness of the less powerful member. It is ridiculous to study any of these relational tasks by focusing only on the teacher, parent, adviser, mediator, or helper. Research that radically separates teacher and student into treatments and outcomes inadvertently ratifies the evils of separation and helplessness. It supposes that something the teacher-as-treatment does causes a particular effect in a class of students. Even in studies that acknowledge an interaction between what the teacher does and what particular students are capable of doing, we find the same defect. There is no way to account for the obvious fact that teaching-learning is relational, not just interactive. A student may do better, achieve more, out of love for his or her teacher (or out of hate), out of rivalry with another student (or as a result of helping another student), or out of understanding a concept (or catching on to the awful truth that understanding is irrelevant). Clearly, achieving a slightly higher grade on some test may be something to rejoice over, something to deplore, or something to safely ignore. It tells us nothing about the student's likely contribution to good or evil in the world.

The second class of relational virtues is the set of individual virtues that contributes to the quality of relations. Schools have always attended to the so-called virtues of character. Early in this century the Character Development League published *Character Lessons in American Biography,* a guide to character education for use in "public schools and home instruction." It extolled, grade by grade, the traits of obedience, honesty, truthfulness, unselfishness, sympathy, consecration to duty, usefulness, industry, perseverance, patience, self-respect, purity, self-control, fortitude, courage, heroism, contentment, ambition, temperance, courtesy, comradeship, amiability, kindness to animals, justice, habits, fidelity, determination, imagination, hopefulness, patriotism, and character—the last established by the practice of the preceding "principles of morality." [11] I have taken the trouble to reproduce the entire list because it illustrates vividly the task we need to undertake. Almost every trait on the list needs analysis from the relational perspective. *Character Lessons* introduces fidelity, for example, as "an essential in crystallizing habits"—as a virtue students should cultivate in connection to principles, not in connection to persons and relations. These meanings are not, of course, entirely separate. One may cultivate a habit faithfully out of genuine concern for others, but the focus of such fidelity is still oneself and one's status with respect to a principle. The point is that almost every virtue has a dark side that we must examine in the context of relation.

Not only should schools teach the relational nature of virtue thematically and directly, but they should also approach conflicts and disputes relationally. In studying past and present conflicts, such as those between the Israelis and the Palestinians, the Sandinistas and the contras, and Iran and Iraq, a relational perspective should be enlightening. Students need not take sides or decide who is right. Their task should be to study the problem with questions of reconciliation as a guide. How can these people come together to live in peace? Students are not, of course, in a position to effect the policies they might create in response to such a question, but both their present learning and their future attitudes may be deeply affected as a result.

Some may object that a study plan of this sort induces a lack of commitment. After all, is not one side usually more right than the other? Should we not commit ourselves to standing by those nations and groups that share our principles? The answer to this objection is to stop thinking in terms of a zero-sum game, in terms of either / or. We should stand by both parties. We should stand sympathetically between the apparently evil and the apparently good and work toward reconciliation. The naive temptation, as we have seen, is to attribute good qualities to our allies and monstrous ones to our opponents. We see this inclination regularly even at the highest levels of government. But an opposite danger also arises. During the Vietnam War many intellectuals rejected the naive temptation. They saw clearly that the United States was supporting a repressive regime and that their own government was committing shameful deeds. This realization led some to suppose that the other side must be right. (Someone must be right, and if our side is wrong, then . . .)

Thinking in oppositional terms supports partisanship and reduces the likelihood of reconciliation. Further, it makes the development of beneficent patriotism very difficult. Intelligent students are often disillusioned and make the mistake noted above, namely, that their own government is totally wrong. Those exposed to little inquiry and critical thinking embrace a simplistic version of chauvinistic patriotism. Careful study from a relational perspective should reveal both strengths and weaknesses in the nation's past activities and present policies. There are things of which American citizens can be proud.

That more people want to enter the United States than to leave it is something to be proud of. We can be proud also of our unfortified borders. The economic hegemony that reduces the need for border fortification should be a matter of far less pride. The point is that identifying and analyzing faults in ourselves or in our friends should not lead to abandonment and betrayal but to a deeper appreciation of how hard it is to avoid evil and a greater sense of affiliation with those we might otherwise label enemies.

In the relational study of conflict the parties should be allowed as nearly as possible to speak in their own voices. Textbooks generally reduce the discussion of conflict to an abstract recital of "facts." Sometimes they attempt to present a balanced picture, but the passion of genuine conflict dissolves in the bland language of an impartial recorder. The relational perspective demands restoration of the aggrieved voices. We should hear the hate, fear, terror, cruelty, and all the excesses that accompany conflict in their most eloquent expressions. When we *live* with warring parties, we often find it hard to take sides. What we want to do is to stop the suffering, to explain each side to the other, to mediate. For women "to mediate" does not mean to decide who is right and what the loser should pay to the winner; it means to bring together, to reconcile. We do not expect all the good deeds to be on one side and all the monstrous ones on the other.

Adopting a relational approach is in itself a form of deep commitment. It signifies that we care enough about each other to learn more about human relations. Clearly it will also identify new models of relations and individual behavior for special attention and emulation. Moderation in the pursuit of wealth would, for example, become an admirable trait. Some time ago the nightly news reported a survey of the "heroes" teachers selected to present to their students. Several teachers selected Lee Iacocca. Why? Because, they said, his success proves that a person can make it in this country by striving. A far better model from the relational perspective would be Atticus Finch, the small-town lawyer and wonderful father in *To Kill a Mockingbird*.[12] In Atticus (so addressed even by his children) we find a model of steady integrity, of fidelity to persons—both to his children and to the innocent black man he was assigned to defend—of reasonable contentment with ordinary life and its achievable dignity. Atticus did not admire great wealth. Great personal wealth can no longer be a criterion of health and success; pursuing it must be seen as a sign of sickness in the individual and in the society that encourages such pursuit.

Educational efforts to encourage moderation are essential. States can redistribute wealth by force and adopt ideologies to justify the redistribution. But unless people understand and admire moderation as a relational virtue, their longing to contend, surpass, and prove themselves superior to others will result in behavior very like the pursuit of wealth. Power or fame may substitute for wealth. Before people can safely emerge from oppression they must have models of moderation, and so the education of such models must be part of the pedagogy of both oppressors and oppressed.

Moderation as I have described it does not entail mediocrity. Just as Finny in *A Separate Peace* found joy in surpassing his own previous performances, so most of us can strive for higher levels of performance in many things we do so long as the effort does not destroy others or lead to a debilitating neglect of relation. We must understand and choose moderation. We might then experience a tremendous sense of freedom, well-being, and renewed interest in the wonders of everyday life.

A relational approach suggests the careful study of relational virtues—both those that belong to relations and those individual virtues that contribute to positive relations. It also suggests the meticulous analysis of virtues, traits, and ways of life such as *striving*. We should pick apart each item of the long list in *Character Lessons* to locate the evil that so often accompanies individual virtue. Educators should commit themselves to this analysis and to the study of themes and counterthemes that arise as a result. Instructional arrangements should reflect this commitment by establishing conditions in which positive relations may flourish.

THE POSSIBILITY OF SPIRITUALITY

I have taken a critical attitude toward traditional religion throughout this book. This attitude does not mean that I believe—with Freud—that people must be liberated from religion. Rather, I believe that the subject needs demystification. As we have seen, some theologians and philosophers of religion have worked and are working on projects that might remove much nonsense at the level of theoretical doctrine. But unless they work on the education of ordinary people and the doctrine preached from ordinary pulpits, mystification will remain. We must discuss religion critically, much as we discuss "problems of American democracy." Although schools do not often perform at the critical level we would like in PAD courses, at least the topics are present in the curriculum. Religion, in contrast, is usually entirely absent from public school offerings.

Some people want prayer and Bible reading in the schools without critical discussion. Such activities are clearly out of the question if our goal is demystification. Many others oppose any form of religious discussion in schools out of an avowed fear of indoctrination. I suspect a deeper fear lurks behind the one spoken. There is an understandable fear that religion will look foolish unclothed by critical eyes. So it might. Critical thought should challenge many, many practices and beliefs scattered throughout the major religions. Should not students be aware of and reflect critically on magic rituals that change wine into blood, prayers that thank God for making the one praying a man and not a woman, rules that condemn unrepentant women to hell for having abortions, practices that exclude persons of certain classes or gender from some rituals, elaborate hierarchies of divine and semi-divine persons, doctrines that establish an elite, a chosen, or an elect, and the pervasive notion that God is male? We talk about a liberal education—one that frees its participants—but we avoid discussing the topics that might actually free us. If helplessness is evil, then mystification is a great moral evil and the failure to reduce it is also a moral evil.

To avoid indoctrination the major religions should be presented in the words of their own spokespersons, in words appropriate to the level of instruction. The idea is to share beliefs and practices respectfully, to question, to wonder. Children so challenged should go home with lots of questions, and parents in turn may have questions for their religious leaders. They may even begin to wonder why priests and ministers *preach* instead of teaching in the open, critical way they admire in real teachers. It will not do to say that such discussion destroys the traditional respect we have had for free religious determination. There is nothing respectful about a conspiracy of silence. To the contrary, honest and interested questions are a genuine mark of respect, and any religious position that rejects dialogue deserves to look foolish.

It follows that free critical discussion should be the approach to creationism. Why go on fussing over whether secular humanism is a religion? Let the voices speak, and let it be clear who is speaking and with what social backing. It is true that students may become bewildered. They may come to a point where they say, "I don't know what to think anymore." That is the time when real study makes sense, when the spirit hungers for knowledge. The teacher's job, then, is not to give an answer but to direct the inquiry in a defensible fashion.

This discussion brings us back to the earlier material on curriculum. When we consider those things that matter most deeply to human beings—the meaning of life, the possibility of gods, birth and parenting, sexuality, death, good and evil, love, happiness—we may well wonder how the standard set of subjects became our curriculum. The usual answer is that people can study all these important matters at home and in religious institutions and that schools are specially organized to teach those subjects that cannot easily be taught in other settings. But one wonders whether the real reason might not be different. Perhaps the great topics of life are not used to organize the curriculum because it is not in the interests of those in power to encourage free critical inquiry on such important questions. In rebuttal we could argue that the curriculum was once so organized (roughly) and that religious indoctrination was the result. This historical warning is no reason to reject reform, but it is an important reminder that no plan designed to seek something better—to reduce evil—is entirely free of the potential for evil.

God is a psychic reality, Jung said, and in this assessment he seems closer to the truth than was Freud. Human beings long for God "as the hart panteth after the water brook." The quest is neither juvenile nor primitive. There is, after all, the fact of the universe, the fact of our existence, the fact, as Unamuno pointed out, of our longing after life, and life, and more life. But it should be clear that we cannot really know the form or nature of God any more than we can answer the questions: What came before time? What was there before something?

It is just whimsy or personal longing to consider God male or female. Scott Peck (and many men) feel God as male. To me, when that longing for holy communication arises, God is clearly female. As I hold a new infant, or dive through a marvelous ocean wave, or spot one of my grown children at the airport, or feel the warmth of the sun on my back as I garden, or listen to a gentle snore from my sleeping husband, I speak thanks to someone like Ceres—a deity who loved her child as I would like to be loved. It is, as I said, a bit of whimsy at one level and at another an expression of wonder and longing.

It is also a mode of learning, for Ceres was not perfect. Was she right or wrong to let the earth go to ruin over her personal grief? From the perspective of women's experience this is not the question to ask. Surely her reaction was problematic. What can I learn from it? So far as She is *my* god, then She contains my aspirations and my faults as well. I, like Her, may love my own children too fiercely and so may neglect others who need my care. When I see this, however, I also see that the many others who have been created in Her image (or who have shared in creating Her) have the same aspirations and faults. They too love their children fiercely. This realization induces prudence. To preserve the lives of my own children I must maintain positive relations with others who have the same project.

As I leave the mystical mode, I can drop the name Ceres and the capital letters on *she* and *her* and *god*. What a wrenching loss it is to do so! But after all I do not want to spend my intellectual and spiritual life describing Ceres, justifying her in the face of evil's reality, or trying to convert others to her worship. I do not want to build a relation with her that can be used to dominate others. Instead, I may use this spiritual longing to connect myself to real human beings in whom spirit is manifest and to learn more about good and evil in myself and in them.

Education has—at least in modern times—been guided by optimism and notions of progress (notions that are, I think, peculiarly masculine). Perhaps we should now consider an education guided by a tragic sense of life, a view that cannot claim to overcome evil (any more than we can overcome dust) but claims only to live sensitively with as little of it as possible. Even as I write this, I realize that the expression "tragic sense of life" will not quite work. It has been used to describe experience that is essentially male, and it points to the male hero who strives courageously with or against a deity—a god good or evil but often aloof or absent. The sense of sadness is right, but the response is wrong. It includes the notion Ricoeur endorsed: "Man enters into the ethical world through fear and not through love." [13] We cannot deny that fear inspires some ethical thinking, but so does love. The desire to be like a loving parent is a powerful impetus toward ethical life, and so is the desire to remain in loving relation. A woman's view has to find new language or at least to modify language as it seeks expression. It should not be articulated as mere opposition, but rather as a positive program for human living. From this perspective, in agreement with those who adopt a tragic sense of life, life is at bottom sad. All the more reason for us to give and take what joy we can from each other.

Notes

INTRODUCTION

1. Carl G. Jung, *Answer to Job*, trans. R. F. C. Hull (Princeton: Princeton University Press, Bollingen Series, 1973), sections 696, 742.

2. For a discussion of standpoint epistemologies, see Sandra Harding, *The Science Question in Feminism* (Ithaca and London: Cornell University Press, 1986).

3. Coventry Patmore, *The Angel in the House,* (New York: E. P. Dutton, 1876). On Hegel, see the discussion in Jean Bethke Elshtain, *Women and War* (New York: Basic Books, 1987).

CHAPTER ONE

1. Rosemary Radford Ruether, *Sexism and God-Talk* (Boston: Beacon Press, 1983), p. 160.

2. Ibid., p. 13.

3. "The Problem of Evil," *Encyclopedia of Philosophy,* ed. Paul Edwards (London: Collier Macmillan; New York: Macmillan and Free Press, 1967), 3:136.

4. Jean-Paul Sartre, *What Is Literature?* trans. Bernard Frechtman (New York: Philosophical Library, 1949), p. 217.

5. Ibid., p. 219.

6. See the extensive discussion in Martha C. Nussbaum, *The Fragility of Goodness* (Cambridge: Cambridge University Press, 1986).

7. Paul Ricoeur, *The Symbolism of Evil*, trans. Emerson Buchanan (Boston: Beacon Press, 1969), pp. 5, 161–174.

8. Marie-Louise von Franz, *Shadow and Evil in Fairy Tales* (Dallas: Spring, 1983), p. 146.

9. See Eli Sagan, *Freud, Women, and Morality* (New York: Basic Books, 1988).

10. Ricoeur, *Symbolism of Evil*, part 1.

11. Ibid., pp. 25–26.

12. See M. Esther Harding, *Woman's Mysteries* (New York: Harper Colophon Books, 1976), pp. 55–63.

13. Ibid., p. 58.

14. Ibid., p. 36.

15. Ibid., p. 81.

16. Ibid., p. 81.

17. Sagan also makes the connection between love in early life and morality in *Freud, Women, and Morality*.

18. Ricoeur, *Symbolism of Evil*, p. 214.

19. Martin Gardner, *The Whys of a Philosophical Scrivener* (New York: Quill, 1983), p. 249. The list of horrors are among those Gardner selected.

20. Merlin Stone, *When God Was a Woman* (New York: Dial Press, 1976), p. 171.

21. Von Franz, *Shadow and Evil*, p. 37.

22. Algernon Charles Swinburne, "Atalanta in Calydon," in *Swinburne's Poems*, ed. Richard Henry Stoddard (New York: Thomas Crowell, 1884), pp. 24, 25.

23. Ibid., p. 25.

24. Von Franz, *Shadow and Evil*, pp. 163–167.

25. Ibid., pp. 167, 163.

26. See Carl G. Jung, *Answer to Job*, trans. R. F. C. Hull (Princeton: Princeton University Press, Bollingen Series, 1973).

27. Gardner, *Philosophical Scrivener*, p. 251.

28. See the essays in Paula M. Cooey, Sharon A. Farmer, and Mary Ellen Ross, eds., *Embodied Love* (San Francisco: Harper & Row, 1987).

29. Ricoeur, *Symbolism of Evil*, p. 315.

30. My thanks to Hazel Barnes for bringing this trilemma to my attention.

31. John Hick, *Evil and the God of Love* (London: Macmillan, 1966), p. 81.

32. G. W. Leibniz, *Theodicy*, trans. E. M. Huggard (New Haven: Yale University Press, 1952), para. 225.

33. See ibid., para. 237.

34. Hick, *Evil and the God of Love*, p. 95.

35. Ricoeur, *Symbolism of Evil*, p. 239.

36. Ronald Schiller, "How Religious Are We?" *Reader's Digest*, May 1986, pp. 102–104.

37. Mary Midgley, *Wickedness* (London: Routledge & Kegan Paul, 1984), p. 6.

38. Hick, *Evil and the God of Love*, p. 400.

39. See Immanuel Kant, *Religion Within the Limits of Pure Reason Alone*, trans. Theodore M. Greene and Hoyt H. Hudson (New York: Harper Torchbooks, 1960).

40. Augustine, *On Free Will*, in *Augustine: Earlier Writings*, ed. John H. S. Burleigh (London: S. C. M. Press; Philadelphia: Westminster Press, 1953), 3.9.26.

41. See Hick, *Evil and the God of Love*, pp. 91–93.

42. Augustine, *On Free Will* 3.23 and 3.15.42–43.

43. Arthur Schopenhauer, "On the Suffering of the World," in *Studies in Pessimism*, selected and trans. by T. Bailey Saunders (1893; London: Swan Sonnenschein, 1976), p. 22.

44. Ricoeur, *Symbolism of Evil*, p. 273.

45. Immanuel Kant, *The Metaphysics of Morals*, part 2, *The Doctrine of Virtue*, trans. Mary J. Gregor (New York: Harper & Row, 1964), pp. 44–45.

46. C. S. Lewis, *A Grief Observed* (Toronto: Bantam Books, 1976), p. 50.

47. C. S. Lewis, *The Problem of Pain* (New York: Macmillan, 1962), p. 144. Lewis quotes Romans 8:18.

48. C. G. Jung raises this question in *Answer to Job*, p. 16.

49. See also Alfred North Whitehead, *Process and Reality* (Cambridge: Cambridge University Press, 1929); Charles Hartshorne, *The Logic of Perfection* (La Salle, Ill.: Open Court, 1962).

50. See Jung, *Answer to Job*.

51. These categories appear regularly in philosophical-religious writing. The last category, "redemptive," is sometimes called "vicarious." See David Little, "Human Suffering in a Comparative Perspective" (Paper presented at the conference Perspectives on Human Suffering, University of Colorado, Boulder, November 1985).

52. Hick, *Evil and the God of Love*, p. 45.

53. Jeffrey Burton Russell, *Satan: The Early Christian Tradition* (Ithaca and London: Cornell University Press, 1981), pp. 165–166.

54. Ibid., p. 165.

55. For a fascinating discussion of this myth, see Ricoeur, *Symbolism of Evil*, part 2, chap. 4.

56. M. Scott Peck, *People of the Lie* (New York: Simon & Schuster, 1983), pp. 37–38.

57. Hal Lindsey, *Satan Is Alive and Well on Planet Earth* (Grand Rapids, Mich.: Zondervan, 1972), pp. 40, 42.

58. Ricoeur, *Symbolism of Evil*, p. 300.

59. Russell, *Satan*, p. 207.

60. Ibid., p. 25.

61. See Elisabeth Schussler Fiorenza, *In Memory of Her: A Feminist Theological Reconstruction of Christian Origins* (New York: Crossroad, 1983); see also Fiorenza, "Discipleship and Patriarchy: Early Christian Ethos and Christian Ethics in a Feminist Theological Perspective," in *Women's Consciousness, Women's Conscience*, ed. Barbara Hilkert Andolsen, Christine E. Gudorf, and Mary D. Pellauer (Minneapolis: Winston Press, 1985), pp. 143–160.

62. In a discussion of the Cathars, Russell lists four possible positions that might logically be taken on the problem of evil. See Jeffrey Burton Russell, *Lucifer: The Devil in the Middle Ages* (Ithaca and London: Cornell University Press, 1984), p. 187.

63. See, for example, Frederick Sontag, *The God of Evil* (New York: Harper & Row, 1970).

64. William Barrett, *Irrational Man* (Garden City, N.Y.: Doubleday Anchor, 1962), pp. 189–190.

65. Ibid., p. 190.

66. Nietzsche, *Beyond Good and Evil*, trans. R. J. Hollingdale (Harmondsworth, Eng.: Penguin Books, 1973), p. 70.

67. Ernest Becker, *The Structure of Evil* (New York: George Braziller, 1968), pp. 375, 17, 18.

68. See ibid., pp. 259–262.

69. Ernest Becker, *Escape from Evil* (New York: Free Press, 1975).

70. Lance Morrow, "Africa," *Time*, February 23, 1987.

71. Russell, *Satan*, p. 222.

72. Jung, *Answer to Job*, sections 696, 742 (pp. 434, 457).

CHAPTER TWO

1. The verse by J. K. Stephen, a disreputable kinsman of Virginia Woolf, appeared in *Granta*, then the Cambridge University literary magazine, in 1891. Nannerl Keohane passed it to me as "one man's perspective on women and evil."

2. Mary Daly, *Beyond God the Father* (Boston: Beacon Press, 1974), p. 47.

3. M. Esther Harding, *Woman's Mysteries* (New York: Harper Colophon Books, 1976), pp. 59–60.

4. Daly, *Beyond God the Father,* p. 76.

5. Ibid., p. 66.

6. Eleanor Commo McLaughlin, "Equality of Souls, Inequality of Sexes: Woman in Medieval Theology," in *Religion and Sexism,* ed. Rosemary Radford Ruether (New York: Simon & Schuster, 1974), pp. 229–230. McLaughlin points out in a footnote that women's sexual parts were known as "turpitudo feminarum" (p. 263 n. 56). She cites Josef G. Ziegler, *Die Ehelehre der Ponitentialsummen von 1200–1350* (Regensburg, 1956), p. 181.

7. Harding, *Woman's Mysteries,* p. 62.

8. Ibid., pp. 62, 63, 131.

9. See Merlin Stone, *When God Was a Woman* (New York: Dial Press, 1976), pp. 180–197. There is some controversy on these matters; the history of goddess worship and its suppression in no way implies a "golden age of matriarchy." So far as I can judge, Stone does not commit this error, but the debate is lively. See Charlene Spretnak, ed., *The Politics of Women's Spirituality* (Garden City, N.Y.: Anchor Books, 1982), pp. 531–573.

10. Jean-Paul Sartre, *Being and Nothingness,* trans. Hazel E. Barnes (New York: Washington Square Press, 1956). For a full discussion on holes and slime, see Margery L. Collins and Christine Pierce, "Holes and Slime: Sexism in Sartre's Psychoanalysis," *Philosophical Forum* 5 (1975): 112–127.

11. Collins and Pierce, "Holes and Slime," p. 118.

12. Christine Pierce, "Philosophy," *Signs* 1 (1975): 496. Pierce credits Mary Daly with the observation on dangling.

13. Mary Daly, *Pure Lust* (Boston: Beacon Press, 1984), p. 58.

14. See Marina Warner, *Alone of All Her Sex* (New York: Alfred A. Knopf, 1976), chap. 6.

15. See Jane Dempsey Douglass, "Women and the Continental Reformation," in *Religion and Sexism,* ed. Ruether, pp. 292–318.

16. Pearl S. Buck, *The Exile* (New York: Triangle Books, 1936), pp. 134–135.

17. Ibid., p. 309.

18. Ibid., p. 251.

19. See the discussion in Larry Blum, Marcia Homiak, Judy Housman, and Naomi Scheman, "Altruism and Women's Oppression," *Philosophical Forum* 5 (1975): 222–247.

20. Judith Hauptman, "Images of Women in the Talmud," in *Religion and Sexism,* ed. Ruether, p. 198.

21. See William Faulkner, *The Unvanquished* (New York: Random House, 1938). Pam Grossman gave me this example in an unpublished paper entitled "Characters Who Care" (Stanford University, December 1983).

22. Daly, *Pure Lust,* p. 16. Daly says later in the book that estimates range from an unlikely low of 300,000 to several million.

23. Joseph Klaits, *Servants of Satan* (Bloomington: Indiana University Press, 1985), p. 1. As statistical sources Klaits cites E. William Monter, *Witchcraft in France and Switzerland: The Borderlands in the Reformation* (Ithaca: Cornell University Press, 1976); and Hugh V. MacLachlan and J. K. Swales,

"Lord Hale, Witches and Rape," *British Journal of Law and Society* 5 (1978): 251–261.

24. Barbara Ehrenreich and Deirdre English, *Witches, Midwives and Nurses* (Old Westbury, N.Y.: Feminist Press, 1973), pp. 7–8. Klaits also discusses the frequent accusation of midwives as witches; see *Servants of Satan,* pp. 94–103.

25. McLaughlin, "Equality of Souls," pp. 253–254.

26. Daly, *Beyond God the Father,* p. 63. Margaret Murray also claims that wiping out female religion was the purpose of the witch hunts. See Murray, *The Witch Cult in Western Europe* (Oxford: Clarendon Press, 1921). Although her methods have apparently been discredited, Klaits suggests that her conclusions might nonetheless be true.

27. Klaits, *Servants of Satan,* p. 51.

28. Ibid., pp. 6–7.

29. See Bram Dijkstra, *Idols of Perversity* (New York and Oxford: Oxford University Press, 1986).

30. Philippe Ariès, *The Hour of Our Death* (New York: Alfred A. Knopf, 1981), p. 372.

31. See Klaits, *Servants of Satan,* p. 152.

32. Harding, *Woman's Mysteries,* p. 109.

33. Ibid., pp. 16–17.

34. Marie-Louise von Franz, *Shadow and Evil in Fairy Tales* (Dallas: Spring, 1983), p. 211.

35. Ibid., p. 215.

36. Ibid., p. 195.

37. See Nel Noddings, *Caring: A Feminine Approach to Ethics and Moral Education* (Berkeley and Los Angeles: University of California Press, 1984).

38. Simone Weil, *Gravity and Grace,* trans. Arthur Wills (New York: G. P. Putnam's Sons, 1952), p. 120.

39. Jakob Sprenger and Heinrich Kramer, *Malleus Maleficarum,* trans. Montague Summers (London: Pushkin Press, 1928).

40. Tertullian, *De cultu feminarum* 1.1. Translations of this passage vary. This one is from Rosemary Radford Ruether, "Misogynism and Virginal Feminism in the Fathers of the Church," in *Religion and Sexism,* ed. Ruether, p. 157. The translation in Warner, *Alone of All Her Sex,* p. 58, sounds a bit less universally accusatory.

41. Daly, *Beyond God the Father,* p. 45.

42. Stone, *When God Was a Woman.*

43. John Anthony Phillips, *Eve: The History of an Idea* (San Francisco: Harper & Row, 1984), p. 41.

44. Ibid., p. 171. See also Phyllis Trible, "Depatriarchalizing in Biblical Interpretation," in *The Jewish Woman: New Perspectives,* ed. Elizabeth Koltun (New York: Schocken Books, 1976).

45. Stone, *When God Was a Woman,* pp. 199, 211.

46. Harding, *Woman's Mysteries,* p. 53.

47. Genesis 3:15, quoted in Stone, *When God Was a Woman,* p. 221.

48. Nina Auerbach, *Woman and the Demon: The Life of a Victorian Myth* (Cambridge, Mass.: Harvard University Press, 1982), pp. 8–9.

49. Daly, *Pure Lust,* p. 390.

50. Phillips, *Eve,* pp. 42, 44.

51. Stone, *When God Was a Woman,* p. 220.

52. See Daly, *Beyond God the Father;* Stone, *When God Was a Woman,* chap. 11.

53. Eva Cantarella, *Pandora's Daughters,* trans. Maureen B. Fant (Baltimore and London: Johns Hopkins University Press, 1987), p. 34. She quotes the story from Hesiod, *Works and Days.*

54. See Fatima Mernissi, *Beyond the Veil* (Bloomington and Indianapolis: Indiana University Press, 1987).

CHAPTER THREE

1. See Coventry Patmore's poetic tribute to married love, *The Angel in the House* (New York: E. P. Dutton, 1876).

2. Virginia Woolf, "Professions for Women," in *Collected Essays* (London: Hogarth Press, 1966), 2:285.

3. See Paulo Freire, *Pedagogy of the Oppressed,* trans. Myra Bergman Ramos (New York: Herder & Herder, 1970).

4. Plato, *Republic* 5.

5. Shulamith Firestone, *The Dialectic of Sex: The Case for Feminine Revolution* (New York: William Morrow, 1970), p. 206; italics in original. Quoted in Alison M. Jaggar, *Feminist Politics and Human Nature* (Totowa, N.J.: Rowman & Allanheld, 1983), p. 92.

6. Jane Alpert, "Mother Right: A New Feminist Theory," *Ms.,* August 1973, p. 92; quoted in Jaggar, *Feminist Politics,* p. 97.

7. See Jessie Bernard, *The Future of Motherhood* (New York: Penguin Books, 1975), chap. 18 and passim.

8. In *The Trinity,* book 12, Augustine claims that a woman united to a man is a unit in the "image of God," but alone—as a woman—she is not in God's image. In *Confessions,* book 13, he claims that despite her natural intelligence woman must be subject to the rational mind of man because of her *bodily sex*—a feature that associates her clearly and irrevocably with the despised corporeal.

9. For a full and fascinating discussion of this judgment, see Marina Warner, *Alone of All Her Sex* (New York: Alfred A. Knopf, 1976).

10. See Aristotle, *Generation of Animals.*

11. See Aristotle, *Politics.*

12. See the discussion linking Augustine to Plato and Aquinas to Aristotle in Mary Briody Mahowald, ed., *Philosophy of Woman* (Indianapolis: Hackett, 1983).

13. M. Esther Harding, *Woman's Mysteries* (New York: Harper Colophon Books, 1976), pp. 16–17.

14. Christine Downing, *The Goddess* (New York: Crossroad, 1984), pp. 4–5.

15. Ibid., p. 5.

16. Carol P. Christ, "Why Women Need the Goddess: Phenomenological, Psychological, and Political Reflections," in *The Politics of Women's Spirituality,* ed. Charlene Spretnak (Garden City, N.Y.: Anchor Books, 1982), pp. 73, 80.

17. Edward Burton Tylor, *Primitive Culture* (New York: Henry Holt, 1899), 1:416.

18. Sheila Greeve Davaney, "Problems with Feminist Theory: Historicity

and the Search for Sure Foundations," in *Embodied Love: Sensuality and Relationship as Feminist Values,* ed. Paula M. Cooey, Sharon A. Farmer, and Mary Ellen Ross (San Francisco: Harper & Row, 1987), p. 89.

19. Erich Neumann, *The Great Mother* (Princeton: Princeton University Press, 1955), pp. 27–28, 51.

20. Immanuel Kant, *Observations on the Feeling of the Beautiful and Sublime;* quoted in Hilde Hein, "Woman—A Philosophical Analysis," in *Philosophy of Woman,* ed. Mahowald, p. 344.

21. Estella Lauter and Carol Schreier Rupprecht, eds., *Feminist Archetypal Theory* (Knoxville: University of Tennessee Press, 1985), pp. 5–6.

22. Ann Belford Ulanov, *The Feminine in Jungian Psychology and in Christian Theology* (Evanston, Ill.: Northwestern University Press, 1971), pp. 18, 255. The quotation is from Erich Neumann, *The Psychological Stages of Feminine Development,* trans. and rev. by Hildegard Nagel and Jane Pratt (New York: Analytical Psychology Club, 1959), p. 77.

23. Irene Claremont de Castillejo, *Knowing Woman* (New York: Harper Colophon Books, 1974), pp. 76, 77, 78.

24. On the spirit / earth dichotomy, see, for example, Edward C. Whitmont, "Reassessing Femininity and Masculinity: A Critique of Some Traditional Assumptions," *Quadrant* 13, no. 2 (1980): 109–122. But see also Whitmont's earlier discussion of anima and animus in *The Symbolic Quest* (Princeton: Princeton University Press, 1969). On redefining archetypes, see James Hillman, "An Inquiry into Image," *Spring: An Annual of Archetypal Psychology and Jungian Thought* 83 (1977). For more on the "valuing" of archetypal processes, see Hillman's *Re-Visioning Psychology* (New York: Harper & Row, 1975); see also the commentary in Lauter and Rupprecht, *Feminist Archetypal Theory.*

25. Neumann, *Great Mother,* p. 39.

26. Adrienne Rich, "Prepatriarchal Female / Goddess Images," in *Politics of Women's Spirituality,* ed. Spretnak, p. 36 (reprinted from *Of Woman Born: Motherhood as Experience and Institution*).

27. Mary Daly makes this point repeatedly in *Pure Lust* (Boston: Beacon Press, 1984).

28. Harding, *Woman's Mysteries,* pp. 32–33.

29. See Downing, *Goddess;* and Jean Shinoda Bolen, *Goddesses in Everywoman* (San Francisco: Harper & Row, 1984).

30. John Welch, *Spiritual Pilgrims: Carl Jung and Teresa of Avila* (New York: Paulist Press, 1982), p. 73. For fuller descriptions of archetypes, see Carl G. Jung, *The Archetypes and the Collective Unconscious,* part 1 of vol. 9, *Collected Works* (Princeton: Princeton University Press, Bollingen Series, 1959); Jolande Jacobi, *Complex / Archetype / Symbol,* trans. Ralph Mannheim (Princeton: Princeton University Press, Bollingen Series, 1959).

31. Neumann, *Great Mother,* p. 4.

32. Alasdair MacIntyre, "Carl Gustav Jung," in *The Encyclopedia of Philosophy,* ed. Paul Edwards (New York and London: Macmillan, 1972), 4:296.

33. See Hillman, *Re-Visioning Psychology.*

34. Carl G. Jung, *Answer to Job,* trans. R. F. C. Hull (Princeton: Princeton University Press, Bollingen Series, 1973), p. 102.

35. Hillman, *Re-Visioning Psychology,* p. 148.

36. Neumann, *Great Mother,* p. 19.

37. Problems in this area are fascinating. See, for example, the conflicting descriptions of *mother* in Ulanov, *The Feminine* (where Ulanov adapts conceptions from Toni Wolff); and in Estella Lauter, "Visual Images by Women," in *Feminist Archetypal Theory,* ed. Lauter and Rupprecht, pp. 46–92.

38. Lauter, "Visual Images by Women," pp. 49–50. But compare a view that recognizes what such a shift means for Jung's theology: Naomi Goldenberg, *Changing of the Gods* (Boston: Beacon Press, 1979).

39. See Nina Auerbach, *Woman and the Demon: The Life of a Victorian Myth* (Cambridge, Mass.: Harvard University Press, 1982).

40. Neumann, *Great Mother,* p. 75.

41. Mary Daly, *Beyond God the Father* (Boston: Beacon Press, 1974), p. 62.

42. Walter E. Houghton, *The Victorian Frame of Mind, 1830–1870* (New Haven: Yale University Press, 1957), p. 355; quoted in Bernard, *Future of Motherhood,* p. 4.

43. Junius Moreland Martin, *Mother: Heart Songs in Prose and Verse* (Salem, Iowa: Junius Moreland Martin, 1932), p. 21; quoted in Bernard, *Future of Motherhood,* p. 6.

44. On the Protestant contribution, see Jane Dempsey Douglass, "Women and the Continental Reformation," in *Religion and Sexism,* ed. Rosemary Radford Ruether (New York: Simon & Schuster, 1974), pp. 292–318. On the Catholic, see Warner, *Alone of All Her Sex.*

45. Bernard, *Future of Motherhood,* p. 7.

46. For a powerful description of what is at stake here, see Sara Ruddick, "Maternal Thinking," *Feminist Studies* 6, no. 2 (1980): 342–367.

47. For examples of the renewed interest in virtues, see Alasdair MacIntyre, *After Virtue* (Notre Dame: University of Notre Dame Press, 1981); Lawrence R. Blum, *Friendship, Altruism, and Morality* (London: Routledge & Kegan Paul, 1980). For a recent example of literature on the values and virtues of mothering, see Kim Chernin, *In My Mother's House* (New York: Harper Colophon Books, 1984); for an older one, see Pearl S. Buck, *The Exile* (New York: Triangle Books, 1936).

48. Auerbach, *Woman and the Demon,* p. 17.

49. Virginia Woolf, *To the Lighthouse* (New York: Harcourt, 1927), pp. 14, 161.

50. Auerbach, *Woman and the Demon,* p. 185.

51. Page Smith, *Daughters of the Promised Land* (Boston and Toronto: Little, Brown, 1970), p. 125. See also Erna Olafson Hellerstein, Leslie Parker Hume, and Karen M. Offen, *Victorian Women* (Stanford: Stanford University Press, 1988).

52. See James J. Preston, "Conclusion: New Perspectives on Mother Worship," in *Mother Worship,* ed. Preston (Chapel Hill: University of North Carolina Press, 1982), pp. 325–343.

53. See Merlin Stone, *When God Was a Woman* (New York: Dial Press, 1976).

54. See the accounts in ibid., p. 23, and in Neumann, *Great Mother.*

55. Neumann, *Great Mother,* p. 133.

56. Ibid., p. 295.

57. From a painting by Nardon Penicaud, reproduced in Warner, *Alone of All Her Sex,* facing p. 101.

58. See Paul Hershman, "Virgin and Mother," in *Symbols and Sentiments,* ed. I. M. Lewis (London: Academic Press, 1977), pp. 269–292.

59. Preston, "Conclusion," p. 335.

60. Susan Brownmiller, *Femininity* (New York: Simon & Schuster, Linden Press, 1984), p. 224.

61. Ibid., pp. 15–16.

62. Quoted in Daly, *Pure Lust,* p. 212.

63. Simone de Beauvoir, "The Second Sex," in *Philosophy of Woman,* ed. Mahowald, p. 83.

64. Germaine Greer, "The Stereotype," in *Philosophy of Woman,* ed. Mahowald, p. 12.

65. Midge Decter, "The Liberated Woman," in *Philosophy of Woman,* ed. Mahowald, p. 41.

CHAPTER FOUR

1. Paul Ricoeur, *The Symbolism of Evil,* trans. Emerson Buchanan (Boston: Beacon Press, 1969), p. 19.

2. Doris Lessing, *The Diaries of Jane Somers* (New York: Vintage Books, 1984), p. 232.

3. Ibid., pp. 223, 232.

4. Ibid., p. 214.

5. Ibid., pp. 230, 224.

6. See Paul Tillich, *The Courage to Be* (New Haven: Yale University Press, 1952); Jean-Paul Sartre, *Being and Nothingness,* trans. Hazel E. Barnes (New York: Washington Square Press, 1956). But see also Sartre's discussion of the limitations on freedom and thus on the feeling of anguish as well in *Search for a Method,* trans. Hazel E. Barnes (New York: Vintage Books, 1968).

7. Gerda Lerner, *The Creation of Patriarchy* (New York and Oxford: Oxford University Press, 1986), p. 228.

8. Lessing, *Diaries of Jane Somers,* p. 239.

9. See Jean Watson, *Nursing: The Philosophy and Science of Caring* (Boulder: Colorado Associated University Press, 1985); and Watson, *Nursing: Human Science and Human Care* (Norwalk, Conn.: Appleton-Century-Crofts, 1985).

10. See Carol Gilligan, *In a Different Voice* (Cambridge, Mass.: Harvard University Press, 1982).

11. Pearl S. Buck, *The Exile* (New York: Triangle Books, 1936), p. 310.

12. Pearl S. Buck, *Fighting Angel* (New York: John Day, 1936), pp. 298–299.

13. Ibid., p. 11.

14. Mary Gordon, *The Company of Women* (New York: Ballantine Books, 1980), p. 280.

15. Ibid., pp. 287, 289.

16. See Nel Noddings, *Caring: A Feminine Approach to Ethics and Moral Education* (Berkeley and Los Angeles: University of California Press, 1984), pp. 37–40.

17. Pearl S. Buck, *The Good Earth* (New York: Books, 1945), p. 194.

18. Jean-Paul Sartre, *What Is Literature?* trans. Bernard Frechtman (New York: Philosophical Library, 1949), p. 275.

19. Gordon, *Company of Women*, p. 288.

20. Ibid., p. 274.

21. But see Benjamin G. Foster, "'Facing the Gods': Archetypal Images of Father and Son in *The Odyssey*," *Independent School* 3, no. 44 (1985), Symposium, pp. 8–20.

22. Claude Lévi-Strauss, *The Elementary Structures of Kinship* (Boston: Beacon Press, 1969), p. 481. See also Lerner, *Creation of Patriarchy*, p. 24.

23. Lerner, *Creation of Patriarchy*, p. 18.

24. Ken Follett, *The Man from St. Petersburg* (New York: Signet Books, 1982), p. 114.

25. See the description of Emmeline Pankhurst's work in this area in ibid. and also in Marilyn French, *Beyond Power* (New York: Summit Books, 1985), pp. 214–215.

26. Ellen Condliffe Lagemann, ed., *Jane Addams on Education* (New York: Teachers College Press, 1985), p. 7. Lagemann cites James Weber Linn, *Jane Addams: A Biography* (New York: D. Appleton-Century, 1935), pp. 22–23.

27. Addams spoke of this allegiance to the ideal in her address to the class of 1881 at the Junior Exhibition, Rockford Seminary. See the account in Lagemann, *Jane Addams on Education*, p. 13.

28. See the accounts in Page Smith, *Daughters of the Promised Land* (Boston and Toronto: Little, Brown, 1970), pp. 244–251; and in Alison M. Jaggar, *Feminist Politics and Human Nature* (Totowa, N.J.: Rowman & Allanheld, 1983), pp. 51–82, 207–248.

29. Jane Roland Martin, *Reclaiming a Conversation* (New Haven: Yale University Press, 1985), pp. 6, 197.

30. See Sheila Rowbotham, *Woman's Consciousness, Man's World* (Harmondsworth, Eng.: Penguin Books, 1973).

31. Charlotte Perkins Gilman, *Women and Economics*, ed. Carl Degler (New York: Harper & Row, 1966).

32. Smith, *Daughters of the Promised Land*, pp. 248, x.

33. Louise Andrews Kent, *The Vermont Year Round Cookbook* (Boston: Houghton Mifflin; Cambridge, Mass.: Riverside Press, 1965), p. 44.

34. Jean Anderson, *The Grass Roots Cookbook* (New York: Times Books, 1977), p. 44.

35. Kent, *Vermont Year Round Cookbook*, p. 91.

36. Sylvia Plath, *The Bell Jar* (New York: Bantam Books, 1972), p. 68.

37. Charlotte Perkins Gilman, *Woman and Economics*, ed. Carl N. Degler (New York: Harper & Row, 1966).

38. Plath, *Bell Jar*, pp. 18, 19.

39. See Shulamith Firestone, *The Dialectic of Sex: The Case for Feminine Revolution* (New York: William Morrow, 1970).

40. See Elizabeth Cady Stanton, Susan B. Anthony, and Matilda Joslyn Gage, eds., *History of Woman Suffrage* (Rochester, N.Y.: Charles Mann, 1889), vol. 1.

41. Sara Ruddick, "Maternal Thinking," *Feminist Studies* 6, no. 2 (1980): 342–367.

42. See Jean Grimshaw, *Philosophy and Feminist Thinking* (Minneapolis: University of Minnesota Press, 1986); Jean Bethke Elshtain, *Women and War* (New York: Basic Books, 1987).

43. Buck, *Exile*, p. 65.

44. Alice Walker, *In Search of Our Mothers' Gardens* (San Diego: Harcourt Brace Jovanovich, 1983), pp. 16, 21.

45. See Augustine, *City of God.*

46. Judith Stacey, "The New Conservative Feminism," *Feminist Studies* 9, no. 3 (1983): 559–583.

47. See Mary Daly, *Pure Lust* (Boston: Beacon Press, 1984).

CHAPTER FIVE

1. There are, of course, numerous exceptions. See Jean Bethke Elshtain, *Women and War* (New York: Basic Books, 1987); see also Angela Browne, *When Battered Women Kill* (New York: Free Press, 1987).

2. Ernest Becker, *Escape from Evil* (New York: Free Press, 1975), p. 1.

3. William James, *The Varieties of Religious Experience* (New York: Mentor Books, 1958), p. 138.

4. Doris Lessing, *The Diaries of Jane Somers* (New York: Vintage Books, 1984), pp. 226, 242.

5. Ibid., p. 243.

6. Paula M. Cooey, "The Word Become Flesh: Woman's Body, Language, and Value," in *Embodied Love: Sensuality and Relationship as Feminist Values,* ed. Paula M. Cooey, Sharon A. Farmer, and Mary Ellen Ross (San Francisco: Harper & Row, 1987), p. 31.

7. Daniel Maguire, "The Feminization of God and Ethics," *Christianity and Crisis,* March 15, 1982, p. 61.

8. Ken Kesey, *One Flew over the Cuckoo's Nest* (New York: Viking Press, 1962).

9. Carole Anderson, *All the Troubles and All That They're Worth: Accounts of Physically Disabled Persons Attempting the Ordinary Life* (Ph.D. diss., University of Colorado, 1977), p. 116.

10. Kari Waerness, "The Rationality of Caring," *Economic and Industrial Democracy* 5, no. 2 (1984): 188.

11. Jean Watson, *Nursing: Human Science and Human Care* (Norwalk, Conn.: Appleton-Century-Crofts, 1985), pp. 37, 59.

12. Frederick R. Abrams, "Medical Ethical Perspectives on Human Suffering" (Paper presented at the conference Perspectives on Human Suffering, University of Colorado, Boulder and Denver, November 1985).

13. See Rasa Gustaitis and Ernle W. D. Young, *A Time to Be Born, a Time to Die* (Reading, Mass.: Addison-Wesley, 1986).

14. James Rachels, "Active and Passive Euthanasia," in *Moral Issues,* ed. Jan Narveson (Toronto: Oxford University Press, 1983), p. 2.

15. See Cicely Saunders, "The Moment of Truth: Care of the Dying Person," in *Death and Dying: Current Issues in the Treatment of the Dying Person,* ed. Leonard Pearson (Cleveland: Case Western Reserve University Press, 1969); Elizabeth Kübler-Ross, *On Death and Dying* (London: Macmillan, 1970).

16. See, for example, Cooey, Farmer, and Ross, *Embodied Love;* Sharon D. Welch, *Communities of Resistance and Solidarity* (Maryknoll, N.Y.: Orbis Books, 1985); Elisabeth Schussler Fiorenza, *In Memory of Her: A Feminist Theological Reconstruction of Christian Origins* (New York: Crossroad, 1983); Catherine Keller, *From a Broken Web* (Boston: Beacon Press, 1986).

17. See Philippa Foot, "Euthanasia," in Foot, *Virtues and Vices* (Berkeley and Los Angeles: University of California Press, 1978), pp. 33–61.

18. Daniel C. Maguire, *Death by Choice* (Garden City, N.Y.: Image Books, 1984), p. 154. He also recommends that such groups make decisions on euthanasia. Prototypes, such as the Committee of the Person constituted to act for an incompetent, are already in place, but they are not empowered to choose euthanasia.

19. Jonathan Glover, *Causing Death and Saving Lives* (Harmondsworth, Eng.: Penguin Books, 1977).

20. Foot, "Euthanasia," p. 43.

21. Ibid., p. 58.

22. Ibid., p. 55.

23. Maguire, *Death by Choice,* p. 29.

24. See Tish Sommers and Laurie Shields, *Women Take Care* (Gainesville, Fla.: Triad, 1988).

25. See Gustaitis and Young, *Time to Be Born,* and the physician's statement in Rachels, "Active and Passive Euthanasia," p. 2.

26. Foot, "Euthanasia," p. 58.

27. See Ann Hallum, *The Impact on Parents of Caring for an Adult-Age Severely Disabled Child* (Ph.D. diss., Stanford University, 1989); Rosalyn B. Darling, *Families Against Society* (Beverly Hills: Sage, 1979); Rosalyn B. Darling, *Children Who Are Different* (St. Louis: Mosby, 1982); Helen Featherstone, *A Difference in the Family: Life with a Disabled Child* (New York: Basic Books, 1980); Judy Garber and Martin E. P. Seligman, eds., *Human Helplessness: Theory and Applications* (New York: Academic Press, 1980).

28. See L. Wayne Sumner, "Abortion: A Third Way," in *Moral Issues,* ed. Narveson, pp. 194–214.

29. Michael Tooley, "In Defense of Abortion," in *Moral Issues,* ed. Narveson, pp. 215–233.

30. Ibid., p. 231.

31. Alison Jaggar, "Abortion and a Woman's Right to Decide," *Philosophical Forum* 5 (Fall–Winter 1973–1974): 350, 359.

32. Beverly Wildung Harrison, *Our Right to Choose* (Boston: Beacon Press, 1983), pp. 255–256.

33. See Kristin Luker, *Abortion and the Politics of Motherhood* (Berkeley and Los Angeles: University of California Press, 1984).

34. Robert D. Goldstein, *Mother-Love and Abortion* (Berkeley and Los Angeles: University of California Press, 1988), pp. 91–92.

35. See A. I. Melden, *Rights and Persons* (Oxford: Oxford University Press, 1977).

36. Sumner, "Abortion," p. 199.

37. See Henry Sidgwick, *The Method of Ethics* (London: Macmillan, 1907; Indianapolis: Hackett, 1981).

38. The Roman Catholic theologian Richard McCormick takes this position in "To Save or Let Die," *Journal of the American Medical Association* 131 (1974): 169–173.

39. See, for example, Steven L. Ross, "Abortion and the Death of the Fetus," in *Moral Issues,* ed. Narveson, pp. 239–249.

40. See Judith Jarvis Thomson, "A Defense of Abortion," in *Women and Values,* ed. Marilyn Pearsall (Belmont, Calif.: Wadsworth, 1986), pp. 268–

279; in the same volume, see Mary Anne Warren, "On the Moral and Legal Status of Abortion," pp. 279–291.

41. See Ross, "Death of the Fetus."

42. For a discussion of the ethic of care and abortion, see Carol Gilligan, *In a Different Voice* (Cambridge, Mass.: Harvard University Press, 1982); for a discussion of caring as a relation, see Nel Noddings, *Caring: A Feminine Approach to Ethics and Moral Education* (Berkeley and Los Angeles: University of California Press, 1984).

CHAPTER SIX

1. Doris Lessing, *The Diaries of Jane Somers* (New York: Vintage Books, 1984), pp. 47, 50.

2. Ken Follett, *The Man from St. Petersburg* (New York: Signet Books, 1982), pp. 118–119.

3. Ibid., p. 161. See also the account in Marilyn French, *Beyond Power* (New York: Summit Books, 1985), pp. 214–216.

4. French, *Beyond Power*, p. 215.

5. See the account in Barbara M. Brenzel, *Daughters of the State* (Cambridge, Mass.: MIT Press, 1983).

6. Quoted in ibid., p. 23.

7. Paulo Freire, *Pedagogy of the Oppressed*, trans. Myra Bergman Ramos (New York: Herder & Herder, 1970), p. 28.

8. Ibid., p. 29.

9. Ibid., pp. 34–35.

10. Sharon D. Welch, *Communities of Resistance and Solidarity* (Maryknoll, N.Y.: Orbis Books, 1985), p. 27.

11. Ibid., p. 28.

12. Ibid., p. 45; quoted from Dorothee Soelle, *Beyond Mere Dialogue: On Being Christian and Socialist* (Detroit: American Christians Toward Socialism, 1978), p. 34.

13. Welch, *Communities of Resistance and Solidarity*, p. 46.

14. Ibid., p. 89.

15. Ivan Illich, *Deschooling Society* (New York: Harper & Row, 1971), pp. 3, 1.

16. Ibid., pp. 102–103.

17. Ibid., pp. ix–x, 100–101.

18. Ibid., p. 114.

19. Freire, *Pedagogy of the Oppressed*, p. 40.

20. Nicholas Gage, *Eleni* (New York: Random House, 1983), p. 151.

21. Ibid., p. 336.

22. See Diane Koos Gentry, *Enduring Women* (College Station: Texas A & M University Press, 1988), pp. 150–175; the quotation is from pp. 155–156.

23. See Carol Gilligan, *In a Different Voice* (Cambridge, Mass.: Harvard University Press, 1982).

24. On this important point see Nel Noddings, *Caring: A Feminine Approach to Ethics and Moral Education* (Berkeley and Los Angeles: University of California Press, 1984), pp. 65–74.

25. Quoted in Robert N. Bellah, Richard Madsen, William M. Sullivan,

Ann Swidler, and Steven M. Tipton, *Habits of the Heart* (Berkeley and Los Angeles: University of California Press, 1985), p. 86; from Alexis de Tocqueville, *Democracy in America,* trans. George Lawrence, ed. J. P. Mayer (New York: Doubleday, Anchor Books, 1969), p. 603.

26. Tish Sommers and Laurie Shields, *Women Take Care* (Gainesville, Fla.: Triad, 1987), pp. 15, 21, 181; italics in original.

27. Ibid., p. 181.

28. Ibid., p. 120.

29. Ibid., p. 123.

CHAPTER SEVEN

1. Seth L. Schein, *The Mortal Hero* (Berkeley and Los Angeles: University of California Press, 1984), p. 16.

2. See the introduction to Richard A. Wasserstrom, ed., *War and Morality* (Belmont, Calif.: Wadsworth, 1970).

3. Dewey, quoted by Herbert W. Schneider, *Dialogue on John Dewey,* ed. Corliss Lamont (New York: Horizon Press, 1959), p. 90. See also Jane Addams, *Peace and Bread,* with an introduction by John Dewey (New York: Columbia University Press, 1945).

4. On the balance of power, see the discussion in Hans J. Morgenthau, *Politics Among Nations* (New York: Alfred A. Knopf, 1973); see also Ernst Haas, "The Balance of Power: Prescription, Concept or Propaganda?" in *Power, Action and Interaction,* ed. George H. Quester (Boston: Little, Brown, 1971). On deterrence, see Frank C. Zagare, *The Dynamics of Deterrence* (Chicago: University of Chicago Press, 1987). On GRIT, see Charles E. Osgood, *An Alternative to War or Surrender* (Urbana: University of Illinois Press, 1965). On tit for tat, see Robert Axelrod, *The Evolution of Cooperation* (New York: Basic Books, 1984).

5. William James, *The Varieties of Religious Experience* (New York: Mentor Books, 1958), p. 284.

6. William James, "The Moral Equivalent of War," in *War and Morality,* ed. Wasserstrom, p. 5. For other powerful accounts of the cruelty and bellicosity of the Athenians, see Schein's commentary on the *Iliad* in *Mortal Hero;* see also Eva Cantarella, *Pandora's Daughters,* trans. Maureen B. Fant (Baltimore and London: Johns Hopkins University Press, 1987).

7. Some authors argue that Greek method (Aristotle's in particular), especially in ethics, is basically right even though its content may reflect errors traceable to the social context. See Alasdair MacIntyre, *After Virtue,* 2d ed. (Notre Dame: University of Notre Dame Press, 1984).

8. James, "Moral Equivalent of War," p. 7.

9. Jane Roland Martin discusses this point in "Martial Virtues or Capital Vices? William James' 'Moral Equivalent of War Revisited,'" *Journal of Thought* 22, no. 3 (1987): 32–44.

10. See James, *Varieties of Religious Experience,* pp. 282–285.

11. Ibid., p. 284.

12. Ibid., pp. 282, 285.

13. Schein, *Mortal Hero,* p. 80.

14. Quoted in John C. Ford, S. J., "The Morality of Obliteration Bombing," in *War and Morality,* ed. Wasserstrom, p. 30.

15. Daniel C. Maguire, *The Moral Choice* (Garden City, N.Y.: Doubleday, 1978), p. 63.

16. See Nel Noddings, *Caring: A Feminine Approach to Ethics and Moral Education* (Berkeley and Los Angeles: University of California Press, 1984).

17. See Carol Gilligan, *In a Different Voice* (Cambridge, Mass.: Harvard University Press, 1982); see also Nona Plesser Lyons, "Two Perspectives: On Self, Relationships, and Morality," *Harvard Educational Review* 53 (1983): 125–145.

18. The notion of engrossment resembles Iris Murdoch's notion of "attention," which she credits to Simone Weil. See Murdoch, *The Sovereignty of Good* (London: Routledge & Kegan Paul, 1970).

19. Noddings, *Caring*, p. 80. The problem of summonability has been a stumbling block for philosophers who want to base ethics on affect. How do we summon tender and compassionate feelings when we need them to guide ethical action? See the discussion in Lawrence R. Blum, *Friendship, Altruism, and Morality* (London: Routledge & Kegan Paul, 1980), pp. 20–23, 194–203. See also Philip Mercer, *Sympathy and Ethics* (Oxford: Clarendon Press, 1972). For an earlier treatment, see Henry Sidgwick, *The Methods of Ethics* (London: Macmillan, 1907; Indianapolis: Hackett, 1981).

20. See Richard Rorty, "Postmodernist Bourgeois Liberalism," in *Hermeneutics and Praxis,* ed. Robert Hollinger (Notre Dame: University of Notre Dame Press, 1985), pp. 214–221.

21. Joan Tronto makes this point well in "Beyond Gender Difference to a Theory of Care," *Signs* 12, no. 4 (1987): 644–663.

22. See Jean Watson, *Nursing: Human Science and Human Care* (Norwalk, Conn.: Appleton-Century-Crofts, 1985).

23. John Knowles, *A Separate Peace* (New York: Bantam Books, 1975), p. 46.

24. See Robert Slavin, *Cooperative Learning* (New York: Longman, 1983); but see also the discussion of intergroup competition in David W. Johnson, "Cooperative Learning," in *Character Policy: An Emerging Issue,* ed. Edward A. Wynne (Washington, D.C.: University Press of America, 1982), pp. 147–148.

25. Paul Tillich, *The Courage to Be* (New Haven: Yale University Press, 1952).

26. James, *Varieties of Religious Experience*, p. 284.

27. Knowles, *Separate Peace*, p. 193.

28. See Ernest L. Boyer, *High School: A Report on Secondary Education in America* (New York: Harper & Row, 1983); Noddings, *Caring*, pp. 187–193.

29. Jean-Paul Sartre, *What Is Literature?* trans. Bernard Frechtman (New York: Philosophical Library, 1949), p. 275; Paulo Freire, *Pedagogy of the Oppressed* (New York: Herder & Herder, 1970), p. 60; Martin Buber, in "Dialogue Between Martin Buber and Carl Rogers," in *The Worlds of Existentialism,* ed. Maurice Friedman (Chicago: University of Chicago Press, 1964), p. 487.

30. On inclusion, see Martin Buber, "Education," in Buber, *Between Man and Man* (New York: Macmillan, 1965), pp. 83–105.

31. See the account in Michael Walzer, *Just and Unjust Wars* (New York: Basic Books, 1977), p. 261.

32. Ibid.
33. Ibid., p. 256.
34. Ibid., p. 324.
35. Ibid.
36. See Sissela Bok, *Lying: Moral Choice in Public and Private Life* (New York: Vintage Books, 1979), pp. 141–153.
37. Knowles, *Separate Peace*, p. 196.
38. Keith L. Nelson and Spencer C. Olin, Jr., *Why War?* (Berkeley and Los Angeles: University of California Press, 1979), pp. 17–18.
39. Hugh Dalziel Duncan, *Communication and Social Order* (New York: Bedminster, 1962), p. 132.
40. See Nancy Chodorow, *The Reproduction of Mothering* (Berkeley and Los Angeles: University of California Press, 1978).
41. John Fowles, *The Magus* (Boston and Toronto: Little, Brown, 1978), p. 413.
42. See Sara Ruddick's argument in "Maternal Thinking," *Feminist Studies* 6, no. 2 (1980): 342–367.
43. Jean Bethke Elshtain, *Women and War* (New York: Basic Books, 1987), p. 93.

CHAPTER EIGHT

1. See D. J. C. Carmichael, "Of Beasts, Gods, and Civilized Men," *Terrorism* 6 (1982): 1–26.
2. Hugh Dalziel Duncan, *Symbols in Society* (New York: Oxford University Press, 1968), pp. 115, 116.
3. See Stanley Milgram, "Behavioral Study of Obedience," *Journal of Abnormal and Social Psychology* 67 (1963): 371–378. See also Milgram's *Obedience to Authority: An Experimental View* (New York: Harper & Row, 1974).
4. Milgram, "Behavioral Study of Obedience," pp. 375–377; the excerpts are from Arthur G. Miller, *The Obedience Experiments: A Case Study of Controversy in Social Science* (New York: Praeger, 1986), p. 11.
5. See Miller, *Obedience Experiments.*
6. Ibid., pp. 184–185.
7. From the cover of Simon Wiesenthal's *The Sunflower* (New York: Schocken Books, 1976).
8. Roger Ikor, in Wiesenthal, *Sunflower*, p. 141.
9. Edward H. Flannery, in ibid., p. 113.
10. Friedrich Torberg, in ibid., p. 208.
11. Wiesenthal, ibid., p. 99.
12. Catherine Keller, *From a Broken Web* (Boston: Beacon Press, 1986), p. 2.
13. Christopher Hibbert, *Tower of London* (New York: Newsweek, 1971), p. 87.
14. Quoted in ibid., pp. 90–91.
15. Jean Rousset, *La Littérature à l'âge baroque en France* (Paris: José Corti, 1954), p. 88; quoted in Philippe Ariès, *The Hour of Our Death* (New York: Alfred A. Knopf, 1981), p. 371. For a description of nineteenth-century

sadism and misogyny, see Bram Dijkstra, *Idols of Perversity* (New York and Oxford: Oxford University Press, 1986).

16. Kenneth Surin, *Theology and the Problem of Evil* (Oxford: Basil Blackwell, 1968), p. 9; Alasdair MacIntyre and Paul Ricoeur, *The Religious Significance of Atheism* (New York: Columbia University Press, 1969), p. 74.

17. Marquis de Sade, *Juliette* (Paris: Pauvert, 1954), 4:21; quoted in Ariès, *Hour of Our Death*, p. 368.

18. Swinburne, quoted in Georges Bataille, *Literature and Evil*, trans. Alastair Hamilton (New York and London: Marion Boyars, 1985), p. 105.

19. Bataille, *Literature and Evil*, pp. 121–122.

20. Ibid., p. 121.

21. See, for example, D. Goleman, "The Torturer's Mind: A Complex View Emerges," *International Herald Tribune*, May 18–19, 1985, p. 16.

22. See Jean-Paul Sartre, *Saint Genet*, trans. Bernard Frechtman (New York: W. H. Allen, 1963). Sartre's comment appears to contradict his earlier statement in *What Is Literature?* that evil is real and cannot be redeemed. The contradiction may only be apparent. We can reconcile the two statements by noting that people commit real evil in the name of all sorts of goods (duty, knowledge, equality, and so on), not in the name of evil itself. Good persons desist when it is clear that their acts are evil. The mark of evil persons is precisely that they persist but continue to rationalize their evil as good. Sartre would say that their evil is increased by their unwillingness to choose it authentically. I thank Hazel Barnes for pointing out the need for this note.

23. See Albert Bandura, "Mechanisms of Moral Disengagement," in *The Psychology of Terrorism: Behaviors, World-Views, States of Minds*, ed. W. Reich (New York: Cambridge University Press, 1988).

24. Miguel de Unamuno, *Tragic Sense of Life*, trans. J. E. Crawford Flitch (New York: Dover, 1954), pp. 12–13.

25. See Paula M. Cooey, Sharon A. Farmer, and Mary Ellen Ross, eds., *Embodied Love: Sensuality and Relationship as Feminist Values* (San Francisco: Harper & Row, 1987); Charlene Spretnak, ed., *The Politics of Women's Spirituality* (Garden City, N.Y.: Anchor Books, 1982); Sharon D. Welch, *Communities of Resistance and Solidarity* (Maryknoll, N.Y.: Orbis Books, 1985); Dorothee Soelle, *Beyond Mere Dialogue: On Being Christian and Socialist* (Detroit: American Christians Toward Socialism, 1978); Daniel C. Maguire, *The Moral Choice* (Garden City, N.Y.: Doubleday, 1978).

26. Simone de Beauvoir, *The Second Sex*, trans. and ed. H. M. Parshley (New York: Bantam Books, 1961).

27. Hazel E. Barnes, "Simone de Beauvoir and Later Feminism," *Simone de Beauvoir Studies* 4 (1987): 10.

28. Ibid., p. 11.

29. See, for example, E. O. Wilson, *Sociobiology: The New Synthesis* (Cambridge, Mass: Harvard University Press, 1975).

30. Sherwood L. Washburn and C. S. Lancaster, "The Evolution of Hunting," in *Man the Hunter*, ed. Richard Lee and Irven DeVore (Chicago: Aldine, 1968), p. 299.

31. M. Scott Peck, *People of the Lie* (New York: Simon & Schuster, 1983).

32. Ibid., p. 12.

33. Ibid.

CHAPTER NINE

1. Hannah Arendt takes this position both in *Eichmann in Jerusalem* (New York: Penguin Books, 1965) and in *The Life of the Mind: Thinking* (New York: Harcourt Brace Jovanovich, 1977).

2. Homer, *The Odyssey of Homer,* trans. S. H. Butcher and A. Lang (New York: Modern Library, n.d.), 22:352.

3. Jane Roland Martin, *Reclaiming a Conversation* (New Haven: Yale University Press, 1985), p. 198.

4. Ibid., p. 197.

5. Catherine A. MacKinnon, *Feminism Unmodified* (Cambridge, Mass.: Harvard University Press, 1987).

6. Madeleine R. Grumet, "Conception, Contradiction and Curriculum," *Journal of Curriculum Theorizing* 3, no. 1 (1981): 287–298, 293; see also Grumet, *Bitter Milk* (Amherst: University of Massachusetts Press, 1988).

7. Among many examples, see Samuel Bowles and Herbert Gintis, *Schooling in Capitalist America* (London: Routledge & Kegan Paul, 1977); Michael W. Apple, *Ideology and Curriculum* (Boston: Routledge & Kegan Paul, 1979); Apple, *Education and Power* (Boston: Routledge & Kegan Paul, 1982); Daniel Liston, "Faith and Evidence: Examining Marxist Explanations of Schools," *American Journal of Education* 96, no. 3 (1988): 323–350.

8. See Ivan Illich, *Deschooling Society* (New York: Harper & Row, 1971).

9. Maxine Greene, "In Search of a Critical Pedagogy," in *Teachers, Teaching, and Teacher Education,* ed. Margo Okazawa-Rey, James Anderson, and Rob Traver (Cambridge, Mass.: Harvard Educational Review, 1987), p. 248.

10. See Antonio Gramsci, *Selections from the Prison Notebooks,* ed. and trans. Quinton Hoare and Geoffrey Newell Smith (New York: International Press, 1978).

11. James Terry White, *Character Lessons in American Biography* (New York: Character Development League, 1909), table of contents.

12. Harper Lee, *To Kill a Mockingbird* (Philadelphia: J. B. Lippincott, 1960).

13. Paul Ricoeur, *The Symbolism of Evil,* trans. Emerson Buchanan (Boston: Beacon Press, 1969), p. 30.

Selected Bibliography

Anderson, Carole. *All the Troubles and All That They're Worth: Accounts of Physically Disabled Persons Attempting the Ordinary Life.* Ph.D. diss., University of Colorado, 1977.

Anderson, Jean. *The Grass Roots Cookbook.* New York: Times Books, 1977.

Andolsen, Barbara Hilkert, Christine E. Gudorf, and Mary D. Pellauer, eds. *Women's Consciousness, Women's Conscience.* Minneapolis: Winston Press, 1985.

Apple, Michael W. *Education and Power.* Boston: Routledge & Kegan Paul, 1982.

———. *Ideology and Curriculum.* Boston: Routledge & Kegan Paul, 1979.

Arendt, Hannah. *Eichmann in Jerusalem.* New York: Penguin Books, 1965.

———. *The Life of the Mind: Thinking.* New York: Harcourt Brace Jovanovich, 1977.

Ariès, Philippe. *The Hour of Our Death.* New York: Alfred A. Knopf, 1981.

Auerbach, Nina. *Woman and the Demon: The Life of a Victorian Myth.* Cambridge, Mass.: Harvard University Press, 1982.

Augustine. *The City of God.* Translated by Marcus Dods. New York: Modern Library, 1950.

———. *The Confessions of St. Augustine.* Translated by Rex Warner. New York and Scarborough, Ontario: Mentor Books, 1963.

———. *On Free Will.* Translated by John H. S. Burleigh. In *Augustine: Earlier Writings,* ed. John H. S. Burleigh. London: S. C. M. Press; Philadelphia: Westminster Press, 1953.

———. *The Trinity.* Translation of the Nicene and Post-Nicene Library. Vol. 2. Grand Rapids: Eerdmans, 1977.

Axelrod, Robert. *The Evolution of Cooperation.* New York: Basic Books, 1984.

Barnes, Hazel E. "Simone de Beauvoir and Later Feminism." *Simone de Beauvoir Studies* 4 (1987): 5–34.

Barrett, William. *Irrational Man.* Garden City, N.Y.: Doubleday Anchor, 1962.

Bataille, Georges. *Literature and Evil.* Translated by Alastair Hamilton. New York and London: Marion Boyars, 1985.

Beauvoir, Simone de. *The Second Sex.* Translated and edited by H. M. Parshley. New York: Bantam Books, 1961.

Becker, Ernest. *Escape from Evil*. New York: Free Press, 1975.

———. *The Structure of Evil*. New York: George Braziller, 1968.

Bellah, Robert N., Richard Madsen, William M. Sullivan, Ann Swidler, and Steven M. Tipton. *Habits of the Heart*. Berkeley and Los Angeles: University of California Press, 1985.

Bernard, Jessie. *The Future of Motherhood*. New York: Penguin Books, 1975.

Blum, Larry, Marcia Homiak, Judy Housman, and Naomi Scheman. "Altruism and Women's Oppression." *Philosophical Forum* 5 (1975): 222–247.

Blum, Lawrence R. *Friendship, Altruism, and Morality*. London: Routledge & Kegan Paul, 1980.

Bok, Sissela. *Lying: Moral Choice in Public and Private Life*. New York: Vintage Books, 1979.

Bolen, Jean Shinoda. *Goddesses in Everywoman*. San Francisco: Harper & Row, 1984.

Bowles, Samuel, and Herbert Gintis. *Schooling in Capitalist America*. London: Routledge & Kegan Paul, 1977.

Brenzel, Barbara M. *Daughters of the State*. Cambridge, Mass.: MIT Press, 1983.

Browne, Angela. *When Battered Women Kill*. New York: Free Press, 1987.

Brownmiller, Susan. *Femininity*. New York: Simon & Schuster, Linden Press, 1984.

Buber, Martin. *Between Man and Man*. New York: Macmillan, 1965.

Buck, Pearl S. *The Exile*. New York: Triangle Books, 1936.

———. *Fighting Angel*. New York: John Day, 1936.

———. *The Good Earth*. New York: Books, 1945.

Cantarella, Eva. *Pandora's Daughters*. Translated by Maureen B. Fant. Baltimore and London: Johns Hopkins University Press, 1987.

Carmichael, D. J. C. "Of Beasts, Gods, and Civilized Men." *Terrorism* 6 (1982): 1–26.

Castillejo, Irene Claremont de. *Knowing Woman*. New York: Harper Colophon Books, 1974.

Chernin, Kim. *In My Mother's House*. New York: Harper Colophon Books, 1984.

Chodorow, Nancy. *The Reproduction of Mothering*. Berkeley and Los Angeles: University of California Press, 1978.

Collins, Margery L., and Christine Pierce. "Holes and Slime: Sexism in Sartre's Psychoanalysis." *Philosophical Forum* 5 (1975): 112–127.

Cooey, Paula M., Sharon A. Farmer, and Mary Ellen Ross, eds. *Embodied Love: Sensuality and Relationship as Feminist Values*. San Francisco: Harper & Row, 1987.

Daly, Mary. *Beyond God the Father*. Boston: Beacon Press, 1974.

———. *Pure Lust*. Boston: Beacon Press, 1984.

Darling, Rosalyn B. *Children Who Are Different*. St. Louis: Mosby, 1982.

———. *Families Against Society*. Beverly Hills: Sage, 1979.

Dijkstra, Bram. *Idols of Perversity*. New York and Oxford: Oxford University Press, 1986.

Downing, Christine. *The Goddess*. New York: Crossroad, 1984.

Duncan, Hugh Dalziel. *Communication and Social Order*. New York: Bedminster, 1962.

———. *Symbols in Society*. New York: Oxford University Press, 1968.

Ehrenreich, Barbara, and Deirdre English. *Witches, Midwives and Nurses*. Old Westbury, N.Y.: Feminist Press, 1973.

Elshtain, Jean Bethke. *Women and War*. New York: Basic Books, 1987.

Featherstone, Helen. *A Difference in the Family: Life with a Disabled Child*. New York: Basic Books, 1980.

Fiorenza, Elisabeth Schüssler. *In Memory of Her: A Feminist Theological Reconstruction of Christian Origins*. New York: Crossroad, 1983.

Firestone, Shulamith. *The Dialectic of Sex: The Case for Feminine Revolution*. New York: William Morrow, 1970.

Follett, Ken. *The Man from St. Petersburg*. New York: Signet Books, 1982.

Foot, Phillippa. *Virtues and Vices*. Berkeley and Los Angeles: University of California Press, 1978.

Fowles, John. *The Magus*. Boston and Toronto: Little, Brown, 1978.

Freire, Paulo. *Pedagogy of the Oppressed*. Translated by Myra Bergman Ramos. New York: Herder & Herder, 1970.

French, Marilyn. *Beyond Power*. New York: Summit Books, 1985.

Friedman, Maurice, ed. *The Worlds of Existentialism*. Chicago: University of Chicago Press, 1964.

Gage, Nicholas. *Eleni*. New York: Random House, 1983.

Garber, Judy, and Martin E. P. Seligman, eds. *Human Helplessness: Theory and Applications*. New York: Academic Press, 1980.

Gardner, Martin. *The Whys of a Philosophical Scrivener*. New York: Quill, 1983.

Gentry, Diane Koos. *Enduring Women*. College Station: Texas A & M University Press, 1988.

Gilligan, Carol. *In a Different Voice*. Cambridge, Mass.: Harvard University Press, 1982.

Gilman, Charlotte Perkins. *Women and Economics*. Edited by Carl Degler. New York: Harper & Row, 1966.

Glover, Jonathan. *Causing Death and Saving Lives*. Harmondsworth, Eng.: Penguin Books, 1977.

Goldenberg, Naomi. *Changing of the Gods*. Boston: Beacon Press, 1979.

Goldstein, Robert D. *Mother-Love and Abortion*. Berkeley and Los Angeles: University of California Press, 1988.

Gordon, Mary. *The Company of Women*. New York: Ballantine Books, 1980.

Greene, Maxine. "In Search of a Critical Pedagogy." In *Teachers, Teaching, and Teacher Education*, ed. Margo Okazawa-Rey, James Anderson, and Rob Traver. Cambridge, Mass.: Harvard Educational Review, 1987.

Grimshaw, Jean. *Philosophy and Feminist Thinking*. Minneapolis: University of Minnesota Press, 1986.

Grumet, Madeleine R. *Bitter Milk*. Amherst: University of Massachusetts Press, 1988.

Gustaitis, Rasa, and Ernle W. D. Young. *A Time to Be Born, a Time to Die.* Reading, Mass.: Addison-Wesley, 1986.

Hallum, Ann. *The Impact on Parents of Caring for an Adult-Age Severely Disabled Child.* Ph.D. diss., Stanford University, 1989.

Harding, M. Esther. *Woman's Mysteries.* New York: Harper Colophon Books, 1976.

Harding, Sandra. *The Science Question in Feminism.* Ithaca and London: Cornell University Press, 1986.

Harrison, Beverly Wildung. *Our Right to Choose.* Boston: Beacon Press, 1983.

Hartshorne, Charles. *The Logic of Perfection.* La Salle, Ill.: Open Court, 1962.

Hellerstein, Erna Olafson, Leslie Parker Hume, and Karen M. Offen. *Victorian Women.* Stanford: Stanford University Press, 1988.

Hibbert, Christopher. *Tower of London.* New York: Newsweek, 1971.

Hick, John. *Evil and the God of Love.* London: Macmillan, 1966.

Hillman, James. *Re-Visioning Psychology.* New York: Harper & Row, 1975.

Hollinger, Robert, ed. *Hermeneutics and Praxis.* Notre Dame: University of Notre Dame Press, 1985.

Homer. *The Odyssey of Homer.* Translated by S. H. Butcher and A. Lang. New York: Modern Library, n.d.

Illich, Ivan. *Deschooling Society.* New York: Harper & Row, 1971.

Jacobi, Jolande. *Complex / Archetype / Symbol,* trans. Ralph Mannheim. Princeton: Princeton University Press, Bollingen Series, 1959.

Jaggar, Alison M. "Abortion and a Woman's Right to Decide." *Philosophical Forum* 5 (Fall–Winter 1973–1974): 347–360.

———. *Feminist Politics and Human Nature.* Totowa, N.J.: Rowman & Allanheld, 1983.

James, William. *The Varieties of Religious Experience.* New York: Mentor Books, 1958.

Jung, Carl G. *Answer to Job.* Translated by R. F. C. Hull. Princeton: Princeton University Press, Bollingen Series, 1973.

———. *Collected Works.* Princeton: Princeton University Press, Bollingen Series, 1959.

Kant, Immanuel. *The Metaphysics of Morals.* Translated by Mary J. Gregor. New York: Harper & Row, 1964.

———. *Religion Within the Limits of Reason Alone.* Translated by Theodore M. Greene and Hoyt H. Hudson. New York: Harper Torchbooks, 1960.

Keller, Catherine. *From a Broken Web.* Boston: Beacon Press, 1986.

Kent, Louise Andrews. *The Vermont Year Round Cookbook.* Boston: Houghton Mifflin; Cambridge, Mass.: Riverside Press, 1965.

Kesey, Ken. *One Flew Over the Cuckoo's Nest.* New York: Viking Press, 1962.

Klaits, Joseph. *Servants of Satan.* Bloomington: Indiana University Press, 1985.

Knowles, John. *A Separate Peace.* New York: Bantam Books, 1975.

Koltun, Elizabeth, ed. *The Jewish Woman: New Perspectives*. New York: Schocken Books, 1976.

Kübler-Ross, Elizabeth. *On Death and Dying*. London: Macmillan, 1970.

Lagemann, Ellen Condliffe, ed. *Jane Addams on Education*. New York: Teachers College Press, 1985.

Lauter, Estella, and Carol Schreier Rupprecht, eds. *Feminist Archetypal Theory*. Knoxville: University of Tennessee Press, 1985.

Lee, Harper. *To Kill a Mockingbird*. Philadelphia: J. B. Lippincott, 1960.

Lee, Richard, and Irven DeVore, eds. *Man the Hunter*. Chicago: Aldine, 1968.

Lerner, Gerda. *The Creation of Patriarchy*. New York and Oxford: Oxford University Press, 1986.

Lessing, Doris. *The Diaries of Jane Somers*. New York: Vintage Books, 1984.

Lévi-Strauss, Claude. *The Elementary Structures of Kinship*. Boston: Beacon Press, 1969.

Lewis, C. S. *A Grief Observed*. Toronto: Bantam Books, 1976.

———. *The Problem of Pain*. New York: Macmillan, 1962.

Lewis, I. M., ed. *Symbols and Sentiments*. London: Academic Press, 1977.

Lindsey, Hal. *Satan Is Alive and Well on Planet Earth*. Grand Rapids, Mich.: Zondervan, 1972.

Liston, Daniel. "Faith and Evidence: Examining Marxist Explanations of Schools." *American Journal of Education* 96, no. 3 (1988): 323–350.

Luker, Kristin. *Abortion and the Politics of Motherhood*. Berkeley and Los Angeles: University of California Press, 1984.

Lyons, Nona Plesser. "Two Perspectives: On Self, Relationships, and Morality." *Harvard Educational Review* 53 (1983): 125–145.

MacIntyre, Alasdair. *After Virtue*. 2d ed. Notre Dame: University of Notre Dame Press, 1981.

MacIntyre, Alasdair, and Paul Ricoeur. *The Religious Significance of Atheism*. New York: Columbia University Press, 1969.

MacKinnon, Catherine A. *Feminism Unmodified*. Cambridge, Mass.: Harvard University Press, 1987.

Maguire, Daniel C. *Death by Choice*. Garden City, N.Y.: Image Books, 1984.

———. "The Feminization of God and Ethics." *Christianity and Crisis*, March 15, 1982.

———. *The Moral Choice*. Garden City, N.Y.: Doubleday, 1978.

Mahowald, Mary Briody, ed. *Philosophy of Woman*. Indianapolis: Hackett, 1983.

Martin, Jane Roland. *Reclaiming a Conversation*. New Haven: Yale University Press, 1985.

Melden, A. I. *Rights and Persons*. Oxford: Oxford University Press, 1977.

Mercer, Philip. *Sympathy and Ethics*. Oxford: Clarendon Press, 1972.

Mernissi, Fatima. *Beyond the Veil*. Bloomington and Indianapolis: Indiana University Press, 1987.

Midgley, Mary. *Wickedness*. London: Routledge & Kegan Paul, 1984.

Milgram, Stanley. "Behavioral Study of Obedience." *Journal of Abnormal and Social Psychology* 67 (1963): 371–378.

———. *Obedience to Authority: An Experimental View.* New York: Harper & Row, 1974.

Miller, Arthur G. *The Obedience Experiments: A Case Study of Controversy in Social Science.* New York: Praeger, 1986.

Morgenthau, Hans J. *Politics Among Nations.* New York: Alfred A. Knopf, 1973.

Murdoch, Iris. *The Sovereignty of Good.* London: Routledge & Kegan Paul, 1970.

Murray, Margaret. *The Witch Cult in Western Europe.* Oxford: Clarendon Press, 1921.

Narveson, Jan, ed. *Moral Issues.* Toronto: Oxford University Press, 1983.

Nelson, Keith L., and Spencer C. Olin, Jr. *Why War?* Berkeley and Los Angeles: University of California Press, 1979.

Neumann, Erich. *The Great Mother.* Princeton: Princeton University Press, 1955.

Nietzsche, Friedrich. *Beyond Good and Evil.* Translated by R. J. Hollingdale. Harmondsworth, Eng.: Penguin Books, 1973.

Noddings, Nel. *Caring: A Feminine Approach to Ethics and Moral Education.* Berkeley and Los Angeles: University of California Press, 1984.

Nussbaum, Martha C. *The Fragility of Goodness.* Cambridge: Cambridge University Press, 1986.

Osgood, Charles E. *An Alternative to War or Surrender.* Urbana: University of Illinois Press, 1965.

Pearsall, Marilyn, ed. *Women and Values.* Belmont, Calif.: Wadsworth, 1986.

Pearson, Leonard, ed. *Death and Dying: Current Issues in the Treatment of the Dying Person.* Cleveland: Case Western Reserve University Press, 1969.

Peck, M. Scott. *People of the Lie.* New York: Simon & Schuster, 1983.

Phillips, John Anthony. *Eve: The History of an Idea.* San Francisco: Harper & Row, 1984.

Plath, Sylvia. *The Bell Jar.* New York: Bantam Books, 1972.

Preston, James J., ed. *Mother Worship.* Chapel Hill: University of North Carolina Press, 1982.

Quester, George H., ed. *Power, Action and Interaction.* Boston: Little, Brown, 1971.

Reich, W., ed. *The Psychology of Terrorism: Behaviors, World-Views, States of Mind.* New York: Cambridge University Press, 1988.

Ricoeur, Paul. *The Symbolism of Evil.* Translated by Emerson Buchanan. Boston: Beacon Press, 1969.

Rowbotham, Sheila. *Woman's Consciousness, Man's World.* Harmondsworth, Eng.: Penguin Books, 1973.

Ruddick, Sara. "Maternal Thinking." *Feminist Studies* 6, no. 2 (1980): 342–367.

Ruether, Rosemary Radford. *Sexism and God-Talk.* Boston: Beacon Press, 1983.

———, ed. *Religion and Sexism.* New York: Simon & Schuster, 1974.

Russell, Jeffrey Burton. *Lucifer: The Devil in the Middle Ages.* Ithaca and London: Cornell University Press, 1984.

———. *Satan: The Early Christian Tradition.* Ithaca and London: Cornell University Press, 1981.

Sagan, Eli. *Freud, Women, and Morality.* New York: Basic Books, 1988.

Sartre, Jean-Paul. *Being and Nothingness.* Translated by Hazel E. Barnes. New York: Washington Square Press, 1956.

———. *Saint Genet.* Translated by Bernard Frechtman. New York: W. H. Allen, 1963.

———. *Search for a Method.* Translated by Hazel E. Barnes. New York: Vintage Books, 1968.

———. *What Is Literature?* Translated by Bernard Frechtman. New York: Philosophical Library, 1949.

Schein, Seth L. *The Mortal Hero.* Berkeley and Los Angeles: University of California Press, 1984.

Schopenhauer, Arthur. *Studies in Pessimism.* Selected and translated by T. Bailey Saunders. London: Swan Sonnenschein, 1893.

Schüssler Fiorenza, Elisabeth. *See* Fiorenza, Elisabeth Schüssler.

Sidgwick, Henry. *The Methods of Ethics.* London: Macmillan, 1907; Indianapolis: Hackett, 1981.

Slavin, Robert. *Cooperative Learning.* New York: Longman, 1983.

Smith, Page. *Daughters of the Promised Land.* Boston and Toronto: Little, Brown, 1970.

Soelle, Dorothee. *Beyond Mere Dialogue: On Being Christian and Socialist.* Detroit: American Christians Toward Socialism, 1978.

Sommers, Tish, and Laurie Shields. *Women Take Care.* Gainesville, Fla.: Triad, 1987.

Sontag, Frederick. *The God of Evil.* New York: Harper & Row, 1970.

Sprenger, Jakob, and Heinrich Kramer. *Malleus Maleficarum.* Translated by Montague Summers. London: Pushkin Press, 1928.

Spretnak, Charlene, ed. *The Politics of Women's Spirituality.* Garden City, N.Y.: Anchor Books, 1982.

Stacey, Judith. "The New Conservative Feminism." *Feminist Studies* 9, no. 3 (1983): 559–583.

Stone, Merlin. *When God Was a Woman.* New York: Dial Press, 1976.

Surin, Kenneth. *Theology and the Problem of Evil.* Oxford: Basil Blackwell, 1968.

Tillich, Paul. *The Courage to Be.* New Haven: Yale University Press, 1952.

Tronto, Joan. "Beyond Gender Difference to a Theory of Care." *Signs* 12, no. 4 (1987): 644–663.

Tylor, Edward Burton. *Primitive Culture.* New York: Henry Holt, 1899.

Ulanov, Ann Belford. *The Feminine in Jungian Psychology and in Christian Theology.* Evanston, Ill.: Northwestern University Press, 1971.

Unamuno, Miguel de. *Tragic Sense of Life.* Translated by J. E. Crawford Flitch. New York: Dover, 1954.

von Franz, Marie-Louise, *Shadow and Evil in Fairy Tales*. Dallas: Spring, 1983.

Waerness, Kari. "The Rationality of Caring." *Economic and Industrial Democracy* 5, no. 2 (1984): 185–211.

Walker, Alice. *In Search of Our Mothers' Gardens*. San Diego: Harcourt Brace Jovanovich, 1983.

Walzer, Michael. *Just and Unjust Wars*. New York: Basic Books, 1977.

Warner, Marina. *Alone of All Her Sex*. New York: Alfred A. Knopf, 1976.

Wasserstrom, Richard A., ed. *War and Morality*. Belmont, Calif.: Wadsworth, 1970.

Watson, Jean. *Nursing: Human Science and Human Care*. Norwalk, Conn.: Appleton-Century-Crofts, 1985.

———. *Nursing: The Philosophy and Science of Caring*. Boulder: Colorado Associated University Press, 1985.

Weil, Simone. *Gravity and Grace*. Translated by Arthur Wills. New York: G. P. Putnam's Sons, 1952.

Welch, John. *Spiritual Pilgrims: Carl Jung and Teresa of Avila*. New York: Paulist Press, 1982.

Welch, Sharon D. *Communities of Resistance and Solidarity*. Maryknoll, N.Y.: Orbis Books, 1985.

White, James Terry. *Character Lessons in American Biography*. New York: Character Development League, 1909.

Whitehead, Alfred North. *Process and Reality*. Cambridge: Cambridge University Press, 1929.

Whitmont, Edward C. "Reassessing Femininity and Masculinity: A Critique of Some Traditional Assumptions." *Quadrant* 13, no. 2 (1980): 109–122.

———. *The Symbolic Quest*. Princeton: Princeton University Press, 1969.

Wiesenthal, Simon. *The Sunflower*. New York: Schocken Books, 1976.

Wilson, E. O. *Sociobiology: The New Synthesis*. Cambridge, Mass.: Harvard University Press, 1975.

Woolf, Virginia. *Collected Essays*. London: Hogarth Press, 1966.

———. *To the Lighthouse*. New York: Harcourt, 1927.

Zagare, Frank C. *The Dynamics of Deterrence*. Chicago: University of Chicago Press, 1987.

Index

Compositor:	Graphic Composition
Text:	10/13 Sabon
Display:	Sabon
Printer:	Braun-Brumfield, Inc.
Binder:	Braun-Brumfield, Inc.